# An American

# Spectator in Paris

# ALSO BY JOSEPH HARRISS

*The Tallest Tower: Eiffel and the Belle Epoque*

"Harriss succeeds admirably... This is a well-organized, exceptionally readable book; highly recommended."
—*Library Journal*

"An interesting story interestingly told, and as such it is welcome."
—*The New York Times*

"A comprehensive account... The book is written with wit and charm."
—*Los Angeles Times*

*About France*

"Joseph Harriss is a reporter of the old—and best—school, whose sharp insights illuminate whatever subject to which he turns his considerable talents."
—Carey Winfrey, Editor, *Smithsonian* Magazine

# An American Spectator in Paris

J OSEPH  H ARRISS

**Unlimited Publishing LLC**
http://www.unlimitedpublishing.com

First Edition

ISBN-13:

978-1-58832-229-6

Unlimited Publishing LLC is a proud member of the Independent Book Publishers Association (IBPA-online.org), a nonprofit institution serving thousands of publishers across North America and around the world since 1983.

*For Claudie and Christopher*

# WHERE TO FIND THIS BOOK

Author 'Blog:
http://spectator.org/people/joseph-a-harriss

General Trade Editions (US, UK, EU):
http://www.unlimitedpublishing.com/harriss

Special Edition to Benefit the American Spectator
Foundation:
http://www.unlimitedpublishing.com/amspec

Coming Soon:
Affordable e-Book editions for Kindle, Kindle-for-iPad, Mac,
PC and Smartphones:
http://www.unlimitedpublishing.com/harriss

# TABLE OF CONTENTS

# FOREWORD

IN THE CONTEMPORARY WORLD in which we dwell
one can nip over to Paris for a few days or a few weeks. It is not
such a vast undertaking as in days gone by. It does put a dent in
one's wallet, but that aside it is not a strenuous voyage thanks to
the jetliner and to the credit card and the ATM. Whereas earlier
travelers such as *The American Spectator*'s forebears, George Jean
Nathan and H. L. Mencken, would journey to Paris only a few
times in their lives, I can now travel there a few times in a
decade, and always enjoy myself with the food, the wine, the
museums, the theater, and the sparkle of the Parisian way of
life—at least for a week or ten days. Then I am glad to get home.

There are also the French. That has often presented a
problem, though not as great as one might think. There were in
my early years intellectuals who were pro-American, such as the
formidable Raymond Aron and Jean-François Revel. There was
the wonderful editor and musicologist, Georges Liebert, who is
still with us. And there were the interesting, if slightly more
skeptical writers, such as Olivier Todd. The French, for me, are
problematic, but there has been relief with friends like these.

Now I mostly spend my time with the head of our Paris
Bureau, Joseph Harriss. He is utterly civilized as you are about to
discover, and he is totally American. In fact he is *An American
Spectator in Paris*. What a find he was! He had lived in Paris for

decades, owing, I suspect, to the pull of his splendid wife, the French beauty Claudie. He had been with the Paris bureau of *Time* for a number of years, and served as a Paris-based roving correspondent covering Europe for the *Reader's Digest* for several more years. There is a closely held secret about the *Digest* I shall reveal to you here for the first time. The old *Reader's Digest*, though distinctly middle brow, always had among the most sophisticated journalists in any city where it maintained a bureau. Certainly that has been true of Washington, D.C., and it was always true of Paris, Exhibit A, Joe Harriss.

Certain writers have a talent for bringing the reader with them into a scene. Joe does it, putting me in mind of a less caustic but still insightful Malcolm Muggeridge. As you read these columns see if you do not find yourself joining the sport of girl watching on the boulevards or at the cafés of Paris ("Here's Looking at You, Kid"). Then see his pieces about the outsized role women have always played in France ("*Cherchez la Femme*"), or when to *tutoyer* a Frenchman. He also takes you behind closed doors with the pols, as in "Celebrating Seven Decades of French Socialism," or "Requiem for a Failed President."

What is more, Joe conveys a feel for the history and culture and politics of the country, reminding me of Luigi Barzini. In the pieces that follow he takes us through the lives, the triumphs, and the pratfalls—withal the vicissitudes of politicians, bureaucrats, and hangers-on. He introduces us to the problems of statism, questions the continued relevance to American security of the NATO alliance, probes the failure of a perverted UNESCO, and more.

Some are problems we are experiencing here, for instance, deficits for as far as the eye can see. Some we have yet to experience, for instance, violent demonstrations in the street ("Riots? What Riots?") ignited by unassimilated immigration or the dreaded austerity programs. He introduces us to rogues like Frédéric Mitterrand—"Monsieur Sleaze"—and the invaluable Dominique Strauss-Kahn or DSK—invaluable for his exemplary fall from grace into a lonely jail cell, if only briefly. Those French gents do know how to live.

Joe has dressed up these columns with an added "Context" for an introduction and a concluding "Update" for contemporaneity. I cannot think of any writer who ever created such useful editorial aids. A column written for *The American Spectator* some years ago is made timely by these two devices. See for yourself if I am not right.

Joe has been one of the star writers for the *Spectator* for years. He will be so for years to come, and one thing more. There is a special edition of this book for *AmSpec* readers, with a percentage of the proceeds going to the Foundation that supports the magazine. Now, how is that for a nice little *cadeau*?

R. Emmett Tyrrell, Jr.
Editor-in-Chief
*The American Spectator*

# PROLOGUE

FRANCE is probably not the country you think it is. The French are quite possibly not the people you think they are.

Nearly everyone, Francophile or not, has an image of the country and its inhabitants formed by reading history and literature, going to museums, occasional visits, and, of course, the ubiquitous media. I know that certainly was my case when I disembarked at Cherbourg long ago on my way to study French at the Sorbonne. It took me years of living in the country and observing it as a Paris-based journalist to get rid of some persistent preconceptions. So it is not to insult the reader's intelligence or his personal experience as a visitor to France to point out a few common ones.

There is, for example, the idea that the French are nonconformist individualists with a revolutionary bent. Storming the Bastille, barricades in the streets, frequent strikes, and all that. The fact is that, while they love to *rouspéter,* or protest, they are more conservative, hidebound, and resistant to real, fundamental change than any people in Europe. Reform-minded leaders like Nicolas Sarkozy, who was elected president in 2007 on his promise of a clean break with the past, lament this but inevitably are unable to overcome it. Seemingly paralyzed by a mistrust of the new, inculcated during centuries of cunning peasant life rooted in the land, the French advance reluctantly toward the future with their eyes fixed on the past. This holds true, paradoxically, even though France has changed more in the last half-century in terms of modernization of its infrastructure— it had a long way to go—than the protean, neophiliac United States.

As for being nonconformist, they obey strict unwritten codes. (Where, exactly, do you seat guests at a dinner party, considering their age, gender, profession, family relationships and other intangibles? When and how do you decide to use the familiar form of address with someone?) An individual, French or foreign, flouts these at the risk of being labeled uncivilized, not quite *comme il faut*, or, heaven forbid, *peu fréquentable*. In everyday social and professional life there are certain immutable ways of doing things that instantly reveal an individual's origins—and exclude most foreigners from ever being fully accepted, no matter how long they reside there. That may help explain the result of a recent poll of international travelers that found the French the world's rudest people. Proof that you can be formally polite, which the French usually are (those codes again), without being courteous (a question of empathy and consideration), which they seldom are.

Another illusion, a result of the widespread study of French literature and the popularity of Impressionist painting, is that French education is largely literary and artistic, as exemplified by the Sorbonne and the École des Beaux Arts in Paris's Latin Quarter. It's true that men of letters and artists are more honored in France than in America or just about any other country, as the names of many streets attest. But the primary goal of the educational system is not to encourage individual creativity, it is to put all into the same rigid mold. The top universities, those that confer the most prestige, are the likes of Polytechnique, École Nationale d'Administration, École Centrale, and so on. They are dedicated either to engineering based on the most rarified mathematics, or to turning out—molding—good and faithful civil servants, with little imagination or initiative, who serve an abstract entity called The State. A survey of the ambitions of French young people showed where their hearts lie: fully 75 percent hoped to become functionaries in government jobs until retirement. Nonconformist, literary? Not if they can help it.

What about France as a Catholic country, the eldest daughter of the Church, source of missionaries who brought the Christian religion to the New World and founded schools like my alma mater, the University of Notre Dame? Home, after all, of magnificent medieval cathedrals? It hasn't been that for well over two centuries. The Enlightenment *philosophes* of the vaunted *Siécle des Lumières,* from Voltaire to Diderot and Rousseau, actually provided the intellectual underpinning for the vicious anti-religion, anti-God destruction of the French Catholic Church during the Revolution.

Today barely 5 percent of the French practice Catholicism. Those who do often show up at Mass for social and political reasons more than religious. (More codes: Catholicism is synonymous with conservative attitudes and politics.) Except for a handful of diehard faithful, church attendance is limited to Christmas and Easter, along with marriages and funerals. The great cathedrals, still bearing signs of the Revolution's crazed hacking at their sacred statuary, stand neglected and empty, echoing to the footsteps of American and Asian tourists. Many churches are being razed to the ground—of some 100,000 still standing, only 15,000 are protected as historical monuments, and 200 are currently scheduled for what is euphemistically called "deconstruction." Others are transformed into mosques for France's fastest-rising religion, the Islam of its newly arrived immigrants.

Other widely-held ideas include France as a leader in Western culture. Despite the best promotional efforts of organizations like the Alliance Française and the Ministry of Culture, that is France's past, not its present. In truth, its artistic creativity has been much reduced since the days of Impressionist painting. A hundred years after what was known naively as the Great War—there was a greater one yet to come—it is easy to forget that France was bled white by the slaughter of trench warfare. A nation cannot lose virtually an entire generation of its young men and still retain its creative vitality. The humiliating capitulation to and collaboration with the Nazis from 1940 to 1945 further sapped its spirit and self-confidence.

Most great artists and writers associated with France during the 20th century—Picasso, Chagall, Miro, Ionesco, Beckett, to name a few, not to mention the American writers who flocked to Paris starting in the 1920s—were foreigners. Except for the small production of the heavily subsidized film industry, the French today import their popular culture from the U.S. American serials dominate French TV screens, pop music is mostly made in U.S.A. The biggest stage hits in Paris lately have been *The Lion King, West Side Story,* and *Mamma Mia!* You can, after all, stand only so many versions of *Carmen* or *Cyrano de Bergerac.*

Then there is the beautiful French language which many of us love. So elegant, so precise (except when it refers to *les Anglo-Saxons,* a meaningless concept). It's a pity that more of the French themselves don't feel that way. French as it is spoken today is a barbarous mélange of French and English known as *franglais.* This is due to an incessant adoption by the French of American expressions, often transformed almost beyond recognition. Years ago the government tried to do something about it. It set up the High Commission for the Defense and Expansion of the French Language. The commission's president said the threats to French were "a relaxing of syntax, a bastardizing of vocabulary, less intellectual rigor, a decadence of taste, and an insensibility to ridicule." Its labors have been to no avail: a recent lexicon has fully 620 pages of English expressions now current in French, from "American Dream" (*espoir de devenir un jour très riche*) to "brain trust" (*groupe d'economistes et d'intellectuels*), "time is money" (*le temps, c'est de l'argent*) to "vamp" (*femme fatale*).

The above might give the impression that I am overly critical of France. But this is not an exercise in France-bashing. I have lived in Paris for several decades partly due to professional reasons—as we say in the trade, you can't be a foreign correspondent in your own country—and partly to personal circumstances, my wife and son being French and Franco-

American, respectively. Then there is the simple fact that I like the country and am generally fond of its people. I enjoy France's physical beauty from the Alps to the Atlantic, the Channel to the Mediterranean. I appreciate the average French person's vivacity, sense of history and feel for aesthetics.

I do not, however take France quite as seriously as the French, with a unique lack of detached self-awareness, do. Being self-critical, believing there is something they might learn from other nations, other cultures, is virtually unknown to them. Self-deprecating, *moi? Jamais!* I must admit to a fondness for the astute observation of the 19th century Swiss philosopher, Henri-Frédéric Amiel, who noted in 1871, "The French cannot break the hard shell of their personalities, and they do not understand a single nation apart from themselves." I find that such insular self-regard is best treated with all due irreverence. Despite my affection for the country, as an American observer I find it hard to resist the temptation to take a pin to the balloon of preening pretention that often surfaces in France.

The aim of this collection, written from 2004 to 2012, is to help dispel some myths like those mentioned above, and to shine light on many aspects of the reality of France today. The subjects range from politics during the Nicolas Sarkozy era—a time dominated by gathering storm clouds and ending with his defeat at the polls—to wrenching social and economic change, with due attention to frivolities. We get into some of the glories and foibles of French culture, taken in the large sense of both high culture and the informal culture that shapes daily life. And because my journalistic mandate also covers the international scene as observed from Paris, there are pieces on that bogus exercise in smoke and mirrors known as the European Union, and the throes of its artificial currency, the euro. International organizations like UNESCO and NATO also come under scrutiny.

All these articles were originally published in *The American Spectator*. I like writing for it as its Paris correspondent because of its contempt for hypocrisy, its steadfast fidelity to its ideals, and, not least, its respect for writers. Its editors have been indulgent toward my idiosyncratic interests and accepting of my personal voice. That has made working with this magazine a special pleasure.

# PART ONE: *LA POLITIQUE*

CONTRARY to much of the received wisdom, France's favorite pastime is neither eating and drinking, nor vacationing, nor even bedroom sports. Politics wins hands down. This is politics with a vengeance, the poisonous ideological kind that has been infecting much of American politics and making official Washington an exercise in futility. In France's case, Marxism fell on fertile soil, lending itself to endless intellectualizing. That produced the socialism that has turned France into a nation drained of its dynamic creativity, its people in a state of dependency on the state.

Most of the political period covered by these articles corresponded to the era of Nicolas Sarkozy. This energetic son of a Hungarian immigrant came into office in 2007 full of resolution to make a break with France's stifling past. However, he soon was derailed by problems in his personal life, flaws in his style, and impulsive management. This was evident early on in some of his cabinet appointments. They included an unprecedented number of women who turned out to be capricious, quarrelsome, and embarrassingly ineffective. It did not take long for the French to decide they did not like President Sarkozy, whatever he did. That led to his defeat in the 2012 election, making him a one-term president.

To be fair, Sarkozy faced some big unexpected problems. Biggest was the financial crisis that began with the subprime disaster in the U.S. and then threatened to engulf the European Union. Here, his hyperactive, pushy style served him well as he took the lead in prodding European leaders to come to grips with the threat. He was less effective, however, in dealing with France's growing problems of crime and violence. He had campaigned on the promise of cleaning that up. But spreading unrest among its Muslim community led to riots and worse, while organized crime from Russia and Eastern Europe took advantage of France's porous borders to do largely as it pleased.

Rising populism produced new political leaders like Marine Le Pen of the right-wing National Front. She benefited from French voters' disgust with traditional business-as-usual politics, sensing that something more was needed to cope with the country's unprecedented problems. Le Pen set herself the goal of destroying Sarkozy's chance of re-election and then demolishing his UMP party. His defeat put her on the road to achieving both, with incalculable consequences for French politics that will become clear only in coming years.

# CELEBRATING SEVEN DECADES OF FRENCH SOCIALISM

How the French became afraid of freedom.

**Context:** *The French used to be a self-confident, swashbuckling, even domineering people. For centuries they rode roughshod over Europe. After Napoleon's* Grande Armée *was finally stopped at Waterloo, they then undertook to colonize much of Africa and Southeast Asia. I praise neither war mongering nor colonialism, but at least they testified to a people's hardy quest for something other than economic security and physical comfort. Likewise, they were hard-working and proud of it. French craftsmanship was a byword for quality and taste. Today all that has been sapped by their reliance on the government to take care of them.*

IT IS HARD to argue with Nicolas Baverez when he calls France "the sick man of Europe." You can feel malaise in the atmosphere of anxiety and defeatism that hangs over the country like a shroud. You can hear it when chattering class commentators talk of "collective despair." You can see it in the frequent, angry street demonstrations. You can read it in the statistics: GDP growth of less than 1 percent; exploding national debt in the trillions; unemployment of nearly 10 percent, with double that among young people.

Baverez, a top corporate lawyer and economist and author of the best-selling *France in Decline,* is one of a growing number of French analysts who warn that their country is heading for the wall. Another is Christophe Lambert, who keeps his finger on the French pulse as president of a big advertising agency. His book, *The Fearful Society*, maintains that for decades the French have felt that their chances for a better life are shrinking and their future is threatening, leaving them depressed and frightened. Baverez best pinpoints the root cause of France's sickness. Contrasting French decline with the democratic vitality and technological advance of the U.S., he declares that "France is the only developed country that strains to keep the obsolete, 1960s model of a closed and dirigiste economy. It's an aberration to think that the solution to every problem is to spend public monies and hire more civil servants."

Such symptoms speak for themselves: France has a bad case of chronic socialism. This wasting malady drains an energetic, creative people of their self-reliance, paralyzes them with fear of risk, and reduces them to a state of infantile dependency on the state.

France came down with the socialism virus in 1936, with the election of the Socialist-Communist Popular Front government of Premier Léon Blum. Even with energetic communist support, Blum's government lasted barely a year. Still, it managed to push through entitlement and nationalization programs that put France on the road to lasting socialism. With it came the attitude that the government can and should handle most of life's problems, and the concomitant lack of individual responsibility and personal initiative.

Today Blum is revered by the Left as one of its patron saints. In 2006 the Socialist Party commemorated the 70th anniversary of his government with all due rhetorical pomp. The Communist Party nostalgically vowed it would finish what Blum started, "if, happily, the Left became the majority again," as CP Secretary General Marie-George Buffet wistfully put it. "We would never let social progress stop. We would have a great struggle by the citizens, full mobilization of the population." Some dreams die hard.

The Left's other icon, François Mitterrand, set out to make France the most socialist country in Western Europe. After his election in 1981 he joyfully embarked on a two-year rampage of ideologically-based nationalizations in industry and finance that came close to ruining the economy before market reality took over. His 14 years of preaching inalienable entitlements, his demonization of capitalism, his scornful references to investors as "people who get rich while they sleep" further locked France into a socialist mindset. Today polls show the French fondly consider the cynical, duplicitous Mitterrand— not Charles De Gaulle, nor Georges Pompidou, nor Valéry Giscard d'Estaing, certainly not Jacques Chirac—the best president in postwar history.

With Eastern Europe and China shedding their collectivist past as fast as they can, France is one of the last places where people still believe government knows best. But Marxism has always fallen on fertile ground here. Some French economists actually twist themselves into calling the country's "social model," with its high unemployment and low growth rate, "a Soviet model that works."

As far as the shrugging Gaul in the street is concerned, socialism seems to offer great perks. With work a four-letter word, a necessary evil at best—the French work some 300 hours less a year than Americans; a recent bestseller tells how to do the least possible on the job—the mandated 35-hour work week allows for some serious vacationing. Even the French hardly know what to do with a three-day weekend every other week, besides six weeks or more of vacation. But if that isn't enough, they can resort to abundant sick leave, on doctor's orders of course. The average French physician orders his patients 2,882 days of sick leave per year. Studies show that about 15 percent of those are fraudulent.

If they have to work, the French today want to be civil servants if possible, the top career goal of three-quarters of the young. If not, being jobless is next best. With the unemployment compensation system handing out over $30 billion a year and little effort made at enforcing the rules, defrauding it is a cottage industry. The temptation is great to pocket generous severance when fired, go on the jobless rolls, then work on the black market for double income. The more imaginative create shell companies that then fire them. In creating a fraud-based society, French socialism is indeed "a Soviet model."

The French pay dearly to make Léon Blum's dream a reality. Welfare eats up nearly 30 percent of France's GDP; direct paycheck deductions amount to a similar percentage.

Some find ways not to pay. Wealthy Frenchmen are leaving the country in droves for neighboring Belgium and Switzerland— one estimate puts it at one millionaire a day over the last decade, including members of 13 of France's 25 wealthiest families—to escape punitive taxes on success, particularly the wealth tax.

But French socialism's worst price is in the tragic waste of human potential, in frustrated dreams and spiritual discouragement. Labor legislation running to 2,631 pages designed to protect jobs actually does the opposite. Because it's so fiendishly difficult to fire, companies hire as little as possible. Thus highly-qualified young people shunt, with dying hope for their futures, from one low-paying internship or temporary contract to another for years. The more adventurous simply leave: nearly 1 million French men and women under 35 have headed for countries like the U.S. and Britain—over 400,000 now live in the U.K.—where they find more flexibility, opportunity, and appreciation of their talents. Others decide to live on the dole or opt out entirely: France boasts the sad distinction of having Europe's highest suicide rate among the young.

To their credit, conservative French governments occasionally ram through parliament new laws to try to free up the labor market. But true to France's socialist traditions, they inevitably try to square the circle by promising job security. They are, after all, up against 60 million timorous, change-resistant Frenchmen, each digging in his heels to keep his entitlements. Short of a virtual revolution, that rules out a truly free labor market and the invigorating sense of opportunity that goes with it. Seven decades of socialism does that to a country.

Update: *For the last half-century, French socialism has dovetailed neatly with the efforts of the European Union bureaucracy to create a Europe-wide social democratic welfare state. This self-reinforcing synergy has produced the crisis that both France and the EU have been going through since the euro zone began to implode in 2011. The progressives have succeeded not only in making France the sick man of Europe, but in making Europe the sick man of the world.*

# RIOTS? WHAT RIOTS?

France's dangerous social blockage.

**Context:** *France's socio-economic gridlock leads to rage and destruction as it struggles to become an immigrant country. Visceral rejection of ethnic diversity makes it fertile ground for Islamic jihadists.*

AS LONG AGO as the Paris mayhem of May 1968, France's great conservative thinker, Raymond Aron, pointed to extreme blockage as the country's enduring, intractable problem. "There is no evolution in France," lamented Aron, one of the few intellectuals in postwar Paris to stand up to the Marxist pandering of Jean-Paul ("Hell is other people") Sartre. "So once in a while we have to have a revolution."

Though that chaos was no revolution, it amounted to some of France's worst homegrown violence of the 20th century and nearly brought down the proud government of Charles de Gaulle. But the college kids throwing up cobblestone barricades in the Latin Quarter and the labor union strikes were an undergraduate panty raid compared with the burning, destruction and defiance of public authority in early 2006. The danger is that French officialdom, locked into its autistic self-satisfaction, has not understood, as the late Aron surely would have, the country's violent paradigm shift.

In the 1968 tumult, which I covered as a young *Time* correspondent, the students spent most of their days yelling slogans in the Sorbonne, while workers took time off. They didn't burn some 10,000 automobiles and trash 255 schools, 233 public buildings and 51 post offices in some 300 cities and towns all over France. Or viciously attack police and riot troops to cries of Allah Akhbar, using everything from Molotov cocktails to pickaxes, dropping steel *pétanque* balls and manhole covers on them from apartment balconies. Or coordinate their attacks commando-style via web pages, cell phones and instant messaging. Or cause anything like $300 million of destruction, provoking the country's first three-month, nationwide state of emergency in living memory. James Baldwin would have loved the scene: it's the fire *this* time.

In the process, the insurgents—the word seems as appropriate here as in Iraq—have shot down in flames France's vaunted "social model," which it has long held up for worldwide admiration. Based on lavish welfare payments, locked-in job security and lots of cushy civil service jobs, it seemed to work for about 30 years after WW II, thanks to rising prosperity. There was no ethnic tension, making it easy for France to feel morally superior to an America experiencing race problems. First-generation North African immigrants were content to work hard and dream that their children would be full-fledged French citizens.

Besides, they lived beyond the pale. Large, often polygamous families were crammed into ugly public housing projects in the *banlieues*, or suburbs—known coyly today as "sensitive urban zones." In a sort of geographic apartheid, the immigrants rarely came in contact with those who considered themselves the real French, the ones whose primary education began with rote learning of the phrase, "Our ancestors the Gauls." Unemployment ran 20 percent on average, twice that for men under 25. But they were expected to buy into the idea of France's grandeur.

For a while they did. Until they eventually ran up against the country's innate, visceral xenophobia. They learned that ethnic epithets and sotto voce muttering about Jews and other minorities are the stuff of everyday French conversation. (Ariel Sharon actually urged French Jews to flee to Israel to escape anti-Semitism.) And they concluded that anyone who can't talk about how his grandmother made tripe sausage or breaded pig's feet, can't possibly be French.

E Pluribus Unum? Try it in *Amérique, mon ami*, not in our back yard. As my journalistic colleague in Paris, John Vinocur, sums up superbly in the *International Herald Tribune*, "An Arab kid in Clichy-sous-Bois may not articulate it, but what rage it must create to hear he lives in the greatest, smartest, most fair country in the world, revered as Islam's best-friend-in-the west from Algeria to Oman, and then have to deal with a French reality of racist scorn and rejection."

That rage has been building for decades, while France looked the other way and went on vacation. Descendents of North African immigrants staged their first peaceful Paris demonstrations in 1982. In the mid-1990s a French film entitled *La Haine* (Hatred) vividly described suburban youths' seething resentment. Boom boxes and car stereos began throbbing with French gangsta rap with lyrics like "France is a bitch / You have to [expletive] her to exhaustion / You have to treat her like a whore, man!"

Automobiles in flames became a common sight several years ago in the *banlieues*: in recent years, upwards of 40,000 cars have burned nationwide annually. At international soccer matches in Paris, individuals of Arab and African descent loudly jeer the *Marseillaise*.

So why the blow-up now? The official line, supported by a docile police report, is that it is simply a "spontaneous popular revolt." In other words, just a bunch of poor kids reacting to poverty and racism. The ever tanned Prime Minister Dominique-Marie-François-René Galouzeau de Villepin looked a CNN interviewer in the eye and said, "There have been no riots in France, only some social unrest." Whatever it is, government and media studiously avoid any suggestion that Islamic jihadists may have a hand in it. Maybe not, but there are disturbing coincidences.

In late September, for example, the radical Salafist Group for Preaching and Combat (GSPC from its French initials) issued a statement by its leader, Abdelmalek Droukdal, a.k.a. Abu Mossab Abdelwadoud, calling France "enemy number one." "The only way to teach France to behave is jihad and the Islamic martyr," he declared. Islamist websites picked up the message, calling on French Muslims to join the fight against France. It was a "land of infidels," where cops were "crusader police forces." Their prayer: "Allah, grant us victory." Days before the *banlieues* erupted, Algerian police arrested a top GSPC operative. He confirmed that the group, which had already bombed the Paris Metro in 1995, killing seven, planned to hit high-value French targets again.

Shortly after the worst rioting was over—with burned cars down to a "normal" level of less than 100 per night—the biggest police sweep in years netted over two dozen Islamic radicals, several with links to Al Qaeda. Also discovered in Clichy-sous-Bois, one of the main riot sites near Paris, were caches of AK-47 assault rifles, ammunition, plastic explosives, bulletproof vests, and stolen riot squad uniforms. Stashed spontaneously, of course.

Meanwhile, the government struggles to get a handle on the volatile, explosive situation. Lame duck President Jacques Chirac was the invisible man during the riots; not for him a shirt-sleeved visit to witness the *banlieue* bonfires. Neither he nor Villepin has a convincing course of action beyond hand-wringing rhetoric about the country's "profound malaise" and "identity crisis," and promised efforts at integration.

Here again the blockage that worried Raymond Aron comes into play, preventing affirmative action or accepting the reality of ethnic diversity. With impeccable Gallic logic, France officially has no minorities—everyone is by definition equal. The law prohibits statistics based on race or religion. There's no yardstick even to measure the problem.

The French, as you might expect, have a word for it: they call it dancing on a volcano.

**Update:** *Despite token efforts at including non-French ethnics in movies and on television programs, the country still has a long, probably violent, way to go before coming to terms with its social reality, as other articles will make clear.*

# FRANCE'S ISLAMIST POWDER KEG

How not to deal with jihadists.

**Context:** *From the first intelligence surveillance to the final shootout, France's clumsy handling of its spate of Islamic terrorism in March 2012 was a case study in how not to deal with a jihadist. With the largest Muslim community in Europe—nearly 10 percent of the population—and thousands of young Frenchmen going to Pakistan, Afghanistan, Egypt and Yemen on the pretext of studying the Koran, it does not bode well for the country's domestic tranquility.*

FRENCH OFFICIALDOM has long been in denial about the jihadist threat to the country, minimizing it for fear of alarming the public and antagonizing its increasingly restive ethnic-Arab minority. Thus tranquillized, the French public shrugs and says *pas de problème*: a recent poll shows only 53 percent think the terrorist threat is dangerous, the lowest level of concern since 2001.

Mohamed Merah, the 23-year-old Frenchman of Algerian descent who shot three French soldiers point blank in the South of France in late March, then slaughtered a teacher, his two young sons and an 8-year-old girl at a Jewish school in Toulouse, said loud and clear that he was acting for al-Qaeda. His coolly professional assassinations intended to "bring France to its knees"—President Nicolas Sarkozy compared them to the 9/11 attacks in the U.S.—bore the jihadist imprint right down to filming them and ensuring he died a martyr's death seen on the world's television screens. His signed his social network account "Mohamed Merah-Forsane Alizza," meaning "Knights of Pride," an outlawed France-based jihadist outfit.

Yet the government energetically pooh-poohed the idea that France was seriously threatened by Islamic fundamentalists. "These crimes were the work of a fanatic and a monster," Nicolas Sarkozy insisted. "To look for an explanation ... would be a moral fault." He instructed the French not to blame the attacks on "our Muslim compatriots [who] had nothing to do with the crazy motivation of a terrorist." Most of the obedient French media went along with the politically correct whitewash.

Despite his claims to the contrary, Merah was officially described as a loner with no assistance from any al-Qaeda affiliate. Indeed, the favorite theory of the chattering class was that he must be a right-wing neo-Nazi. Or failing that, just your typical underprivileged, disaffected guy who had had a miserable childhood in the slums. The left-leaning *Le Monde* reported that he had "an angelic face, a fascinating beauty." His 15 arrests and doing time for everything from stoning busses to violent theft and fighting with rivals? Liberals outdid themselves to show he was the psychologically disturbed victim of an unjust society. "A pathetic young man... the victim of a social order that had already doomed him, and millions of others like him, to a marginal existence, and to the non-recognition of his status as a citizen equal in rights and opportunities," explained the Muslim apologist Tariq Ramadan, who was denied a U.S. visa for providing material support to a terrorist organization before the ACLU persuaded Hillary Clinton to lift the ban.

The failure of the French domestic intelligence agency, the DCRI, to spot Merah as a serious threat, and its subsequent efforts at self-justification, would have been comic were we not dealing with tragedy. Its chief called him a self-radicalized young man with a split personality, a lone wolf who operated alone and below the radar. Besides, he pleaded, Merah had not followed the usual path taken by Islamist extremists. He wasn't visibly part of any network. He even went to nightclubs instead of mosques, for heaven's sake, so how could we know he was a jihadist? "We had absolutely no reason to believe he was commissioned by al-Qaeda to carry out these attacks." No doubt it would have helped to have a copy of his marching orders on an al-Qaeda letterhead.

He and other officials tried to make light of a 2010 trip Merah made to Afghanistan's Kandahar province, spiritual home of the Taliban. But as information leaked out, it became clear that this poor kid, who lived on welfare payments of about $600 a month, had left tracks all over the Middle East, with somebody else obviously paying the bills. Besides Afghanistan, he later visited Egypt, Turkey, Syria, Lebanon, Jordan and Israel in the space of two years. Strangely, he was reportedly arrested by Afghan police on his first trip and handed over to American forces there, who returned him to France. The FBI's counterterrorism department put him on the no-fly list, barring entry to the U.S. The French ignored this, either through sheer sloppiness, to avoid any appearance of profiling, or for some more murky reason involving counterespionage.

They did, however, put him under loose surveillance. Nearly a year after his first trip to Afghanistan, a DCRI agent in Toulouse finally called his cell number to ask him to come in for a talk. He didn't bat an eye when Mohamed answered and said sorry, he couldn't—he was busy in Pakistan at the time. When he finally did drop in months later, these Keystone Kops approvingly looked over the photos he brought along as proof he was there as a tourist, said something like *très bien, mon ami,* and let him go. (This casual relationship and other aspects of the case led to speculation that Merah was perhaps a double agent, an informer for the DCRI who was turned by al-Qaeda; a lawyer hired by his father claims to have video proof that he was "manipulated" and "liquidated" by the police.)

The official French version that Merah was a lone wolf inspired by his solitary reading of the Koran looked even more foolish when it became known that he had trained for two months in North Waziristan on the Af-Pak border, likely with the Tehrik e Taliban Pakistan (TTP), an umbrella group of Pakistani factions. He would have been anything but alone: Pakistani intelligence officials told the Associated Press that dozens of French Muslim militants, many with dual French-North African nationality, are training there as the Jihad e Islami group. They learn to use explosives and other weapons at camps near the town of Miran Shah and in the Datta Khel area. They are led by a French commander who goes by the name Abu

Tarek. When they return to France, all it will take to waken these sleeping agents will be a call from Kandahar.

Merah certainly learned about firearms. Somehow, right under the noses of French surveillance and with financial assistance from guess who, he amassed a stash of guns including several Colt .45 automatics with extra magazines, an automatic Sten pistol, a Colt Python revolver, a pump-action shotgun and an Uzi submachine gun, along with ingredients for Molotov cocktails. With this arsenal he was able to intimidate and toy with a 15-man French SWAT team for all of 32 hours, wounding five and repeatedly forcing them to retreat when they tried to enter his small, three-room apartment in Toulouse.

Taking Merah down was as amateurish as the earlier intelligence failures. When the SWAT team finally did succeed in blowing off the door and entering, they riddled him with bullets instead of taking him alive for interrogation. Much of France wondered along with Christian Prouteau, the retired chief the gendarmerie's elite GIGN commando unit (the SWAT team were police, not better-trained paramilitary gendarmes), who asked, "How can a top police unit botch the capture of a lone gunman? If they had pumped his apartment with tear gas, he wouldn't have lasted five minutes." Some Israeli security experts were even harsher. Alec Ron, a former head of the Israel police commando unit, told Israeli public radio the operation was marked by "utter confusion and unprofessionalism… It was an absolute disgrace."

One reason for this foul-up was that Sarkozy ordered the merger of two domestic intel agencies in 2008, a fusion that has yet to gel. Another might have been political interference, in an election year, with police work. But the main problem is that France is ill equipped, psychologically and politically, to deal with a huge, unassimilated Muslim population increasingly tempted by radicalism. France poses as a beacon of human rights and *égalité,* which to the Gallic mind rules out affirmative action (that would be unequal) or even accepting the reality of ethnic diversity. With impeccable logic, it officially has no minorities—everyone is by definition French and therefore equal.

This in turn has meant that the government, ever so careful about treading on anybody's ethnic or religious toes, tries to avoid any appearance of cracking down on Muslim activism that could lead to radical Islamicism. If, as Mao wrote, the guerrilla must swim in the people as a fish swims in the sea, jihadist guerrillas can find good swimming in French Muslim waters. It might get even easier for them to disappear from police view if Socialist François Hollande becomes president. He has made the ultimate politically correct campaign promise: if elected he would ask parliament to remove the word "race" from the constitution. Nobody here but us Gauls.

Whatever the outcome of the 2012 presidential election, the slaughter of the innocents in Toulouse is a wake-up call that France ignores at its considerable peril. As an adviser to Sarkozy said, sotto voce, "This is going to raise questions about our system of integration, our approach to fundamentalism, and our tolerance of certain practices here." For sure. Meanwhile, no one knows when or where the French Islamist powder keg will blow next.

**Update:** *Shortly after this incident (and days before the presidential election), French police began rounding up various Islamists, including members of the Forsane Alizza jihadist group, in Paris, Toulouse, and half-a-dozen other cities. The raids netted numerous firearms and uncovered plans to kidnap a judge in Lyon. The Forsane Alizza group carried out commando training in forests in the Paris region. Their leader said, "If Allah wills it, we will become true warriors. Anyone who doesn't understand that our revolt is going to include action is completely stupid."*

# MONSIEUR SLEAZE

Sex tourism is okay if you're cultured.

Context: *The two words you never hear in connection with French politics are "character" and "morality." The French pride themselves on being indifferent to politicians' private lives, however deviant from conventional morality. Ask them whether a bad man can be a good public official, and you get a look of incomprehension. "But he's so intelligent," will come the answer, as if mental prowess trumped all. But the case of Frédéric Mitterrand might indicate that that attitude is now changing.*

FLUSTERED FRENCH PARENTS hurriedly shooed their children away from the TV in October 2009 as a bland discussion program suddenly turned into a torrid description of cruising for gay sex in Asian brothels. "I got into the habit of paying for boys," one of the participants read from a text. "All these rituals of a fair for the sale of Adonises, of a slave market, excite me enormously.... The profusion of very attractive and immediately available boys puts me into a state of desire which I no longer need to restrain or conceal.... Western morality, guilt and shame shatter to pieces. And the rest of the world can go to hell."

The reading was from an autobiography baldly entitled *La Mauvaise Vie* ("The Bad Life") by Frédéric Mitterrand, the French government's minister of culture. It was being read by

Marine Le Pen, leader of the right-wing National Front party, who was attacking Mitterrand for his passionate defense of Roman Polanski.

When Swiss police arrested Polanski in Zurich in September 2009 at the request of U.S. authorities on charges of raping a 13-year-old girl in Los Angeles in 1977, one of the first to fly to the film director's defense was France's minister of culture. He was "horrified" by the way a French citizen and a major artist was being treated, "thrown to the lions because of ancient history… a frightening America has just shown its face." It was an astonishing statement by a high official of a government theoretically friendly to the U.S.

Many in France were uncomfortable with Mitterrand's emotional justification of an avowed pedophile rapist. But Le Pen was one of the few to show up his brazen hypocrisy. "Does belonging to the showbiz caste exonerate its members from respecting laws and authorize them to escape prosecution for 30 years?" she asked. Then she began quoting from Mitterrand's lurid account of his experiences as a sex tourist buying young men in Thailand and Indonesia, enjoying smiling kids trying to escape poverty by sweet-talking a middle-aged Frenchman who liked to hear them say in broken English, "I want you happy." She concluded with a call for his resignation as being unfit to serve in a government that actively campaigns against sex tourism. *Touché!*

But Le Pen had done more than denounce France's twisted position on Polanski. She had called attention to Mitterrand's sordid past, shocking those who had not seen fit to read his 2005 autobiography, meaning most of France, including members of the government and your correspondent. Until now Mitterrand has been known, if he was known at all, as a lightweight radio and television personality who also happened to be the nephew of the late socialist president François Mitterrand.

After his election in 2007, Nicolas Sarkozy picked him to head the French Academy in Rome, a sinecure with artistic pretensions. Though Mitterrand had no visible qualifications for the post, the move was part of Sarkozy's policy of *ouverture*, including leftists in his administration as a way of defanging the opposition. Mitterrand had never been active in politics, but his name was synonymous in the public's mind with 14 years of socialist government.

When Sarkozy discussed the new job with Mitterrand during a cabinet reshuffle, Mitterrand says he asked the president whether the autobiography might be a problem. He now claims Sarkozy replied, "No, I found it courageous and talented." That seems an unlikely comment from a man not known for his love of literature. A more likely explanation for the choice, many here believe, is the influence of Sarkozy's wife, Carla Bruni, who has been coaching him in the finer things. A card-carrying member of the showbiz/arty set, she is credited with considerable influence over the president. She counts Mitterrand among her friends.

It didn't take long for the socialists to seize on the issue that their virulent adversaries, the National Front, had raised, seconding Le Pen in calling for Mitterrand's head. "We can't have a minister who represents France encouraging the violation of our international engagements to fight sexual tourism," said one socialist leader calling for his portfolio to be revoked.

France does indeed consider itself in the forefront of the fight against sex tourism, but Sarkozy's team danced around this in trying to defend Mitterrand. "He hasn't said anything against France's position on that," declared an obviously embarrassed Henri Guaino, the president's special counselor, completely begging the question of his fitness for the job. The justice minister, Michele Alliot-Marie, philosophized that "There are difficult periods and shadows in everyone's life." The one word that no one uttered, either government members or media commentators, was that great taboo in sophisticated, post-Christian France: morality.

Mitterrand may have felt he could hide behind that, as well as the reluctance of the French media to report on politicians' private lives. His uncle the president, after all, had maintained a secret second family, with mistress and illegitimate daughter kept in a Paris apartment at public expense, about which the complaisant press reported nothing. But possible sexual abuse by a minister was pushing even French tolerance too far.

Sensing that he was losing the battle for public opinion, Sarkozy—who has made no public statement on the affair as of this writing—huddled with his advisers early Wednesday morning and decided Mitterrand should go on TV to explain himself. His appearance is not his trump card: with his fleshy, pendulous lower lip, hang-dog eyes, and soft, purring, insinuating voice, Mitterrand, 62, is perfectly cast as a sex tourist on the prowl through the boy brothels of Bangkok. Not the sort you would like to see scoutmaster of your son's troop.

In an interview on a prime time nightly news program, he bobbed and weaved, trying to deflect questions about his ethics and making fine distinctions between his homosexuality and pedophilia. Visibly upset, he admitted to sex tourism but denied buying sex from minors, while saying, "Yes, I had relations with boys." Asked to clear that up, he explained that, in his personal vocabulary of perversion, he habitually refers to the male prostitutes he has frequented as *garçons* or boys, and sometimes as *gosses*, or kids. In fact, he maintained, the prostitutes were about his age.

He condemned sex tourism belatedly, some might find, and pedophilia, "in which I have never participated." Polls show only about one-quarter of viewers found him convincing. As of now, Mitterrand still has not said exactly what he did in those Thai and Indonesian brothels, or how he knew that the "slaves" he abused were actually adult. And the basic question in all this remains unanswered: How can a man of his past and proclivities—a former sex tourist—be the official personification of French culture?

Besides the stain on the face of French culture, the other loser in *l'affaire Mitterrand* is Nicolas Sarkozy's presidency. When the socialist opposition is exhibiting more moral clarity than the supposedly conservative government, you know something is rotten in the state of France. Sarkozy came into office two years ago promising to repair the moral damage done by the 1968 student revolt and resulting relativism of values. Now his relations with the traditionalist and conservative voters who brought him to power are seriously compromised.

If the letters columns of newspapers and the comments on their websites are any indication, a great many French citizens feel disgusted with their government over this. Some are taking to the streets: when Mitterrand inaugurated an art exhibit in Bordeaux, he was jeered by protesters pushing baby carriages and carrying posters saying, "Don't touch our children. Mitterrand resign!"

Update: *Frédéric Mitterrand was never prosecuted for violating France's laws on sex tourism and kept his job as culture minister. At times he seems particularly well suited to that position, as when overseeing exhibits at the National Library of the original manuscript of Casanova's steamy memoirs, or its secret archive of erotic art, including more than 350 sexually explicit lithographs, photos, film clips, and, of course, cardboard pop-ups.*

# "I LIKE WOMEN"

## Strauss-Kahn's Libidinous Fall from Grace

Context*: Unfortunately there is no getting around the fact that the arrest of the director of the International Monetary Fund on charges of sexual assault was one of the most important news stories of 2011. I know, it's sordid stuff worthy of a gossip magazine. But besides being the head of the IMF, this man was a sure bet (as sure as anything can be in politics) to be the next president of France. His sudden downfall, caused by a deep, compulsive character flaw, had all the ingredients of Greek tragedy.*

IRONICALLY, his luck began to change imperceptibly that happy spring day in 2011 when Dominique Strauss-Kahn took the wheel of a $135,000, V-8, 500-horsepower Porsche Panamera sedan on a Paris street. Before he could even test its acceleration (0 to 60 in 4.2 seconds), a guy with a cell phone snapped a photo of him. And as people do these days, he sold it to a Paris newspaper. No matter that the car actually belonged to a friend of his. When you're a prominent member of the French Socialist Party, indeed, the front-runner in pre-election polls and its strongest bet in years to beat Nicolas Sarkozy for the presidency in 2012, you're supposed to be helping the laboring masses, not tooling around in luxury automobiles with a smug smile on your face. The distant rumbling of an uproar could be heard in the chattering class.

The rumble grew and the luck curve continued down a few days later. Published stories reported that 62-year-old DSK, as he is known, wore decidedly non-working class clothing: $35,000 (sic) suits from a fancy tailor in Washington, where as managing director of the International Monetary Fund he plays Master of the Universe bailing out nations in financial trouble. Not so, he countered furiously, but few believed him, it was so in character.

Some began toting up the signs of his un-Socialist lifestyle: two apartments in fashionable Paris neighborhoods, a vacation home in Marrakech, and, since he joined the IMF in 2007, a red brick mansion in Georgetown with a BMW SUV in the driveway. His tax-free salary at the IMF is reportedly $420,930, plus an annual "scale of living" allowance of $75,350. His wife Anne Sinclair, an American-born French TV journalist, inherited paintings by Picasso, Matisse and Degas from her art merchant father. How bad could it be?

Well, how about a 48-hour descent into the netherworld of New York City's criminal justice system? Complete with police lineup, forensic medical exam, complete body-cavity search, and perp walk in handcuffs under popping flash bulbs and leering TV cameras?

Strauss-Kahn's personal Götterdämmerung on a Saturday came with stunning swiftness. The day before, he had checked into the upscale Sofitel in the Times Square area, staying in a $3,000 a night suite with foyer, conference room, living room, marble bathroom and bedroom. It was a lavish layout for a personal trip whose purpose was unclear; an embarrassed IMF stated firmly that he was not on official business.

He was due in Berlin on Sunday to meet Chancellor Angela Merkel, followed by two days of meetings in Brussels to work on Europe's sovereign debt crisis. He could easily have taken a flight from Washington's Dulles airport without going through New York. Oddly, when police pulled him off an Air France flight Saturday afternoon just minutes before it left the gate, the plane was headed not to Berlin, but to Paris.

The police arrested DSK in response to allegations by a hotel housekeeper that he had violently sexually assaulted her around noon after trying to lock her in the room. They booked him on charges of a criminal sex act, attempted rape and unlawful imprisonment (or as the official complaint nicely puts it, "oral sexual conduct and anal sexual conduct with another person by forcible compulsion"). At his arraignment the judge agreed with the Manhattan district attorney's argument that Strauss-Kahn was a flight risk and ordered him held without bail—Sinclair wired $1 million to him overnight, just in case, pending his appearance before a grand jury. He was sent to an 11 by 13-foot cell along with several thousand other inmates at the tough Rikers Island prison complex. If found guilty on all four felony counts and three misdemeanor counts, he won't board another flight to Paris for 25 years.

French media and politicians can't decide whether DSK's spectacular downfall is an earthquake or soap opera. "Shock. Political Bomb. Thunderclap," headlined one newspaper. "KO," ran another, next to a full-page photo of a dazed, unshaven Strauss-Kahn. "It's an episode from the TV serial *Dallas*, and DSK is JR," said a lawmaker in Nicolas Sarkozy's UMP party. "Totally hallucinating," said another. (Sarkozy himself, hitting new lows every week in the polls, has carefully said nothing, though he must be all smiles behind Elysée Palace doors.) Conspiracy theories are rife, but several politicos recognized it was humiliating for France. As one put it frankly, "Now everyone will point at us and say, 'Look how the French act.'" For sure.

Strauss-Kahn secured top legal talent with the sure touch and speed of someone who would seem to have been through something like this before. In a matter of hours he hired the celebrity New York attorney Benjamin Brafman, whose past criminal cases include the likes of Michael Jackson and the rapper Jay-Z. DSK also quickly retained the services of William Taylor, a top Washington lawyer who reportedly advised him in 2008 in the case of his scandalous affair with an IMF staff member. He was immediately visited in his cell by the French consul general in New York, who assured him that "The French embassy and consulate are mobilized," whatever that means.

The fact is, DSK *has* been through something like this before, only without the grave legal consequences that he may now face. His extramarital affairs have long been the stuff of Paris gossip and newsroom banter, where he was dubbed "the great seducer." In broad-minded France where politicians' private lives are off-limits to reporters (think François Mitterrand's love child hidden for years in broad daylight and financed with public monies), a dash of expected promiscuity only adds to a public figure's luster. This after all is the country where the medieval tradition of *cuissage* gave nobles the inalienable right to sleep with a peasant's bride on her wedding night. Thus few eyebrows were raised when DSK gave an interview to a Paris paper two weeks ago in which he addressed his womanizing. "Yes, I like women," he declared with superb aplomb. "So what?"

Sometimes he went too far. Like three years ago, early in his stint as IMF chief, when a furious Argentine economist publicly blamed DSK for seducing his Hungarian wife, who was then an IMF staff member, at the Davos international business forum. Both admitted the affair (she has since left for another job). The IMF glossed over the case, contenting itself with noting that he had not actually used his hierarchical position to abuse an underling. Strauss-Kahn issued an apology, saying "I accept that this incident represents a serious error of judgment. I am committed, going forward, to uphold the high standards expected of an IMF managing director." Case closed. But it is clear now that the IMF was seriously remiss in not dismissing him at the time, however embarrassing that would have been.

As France goes through a period of soul-searching in the light of DSK's arrest, other skeletons may well emerge. Assistant District Attorney John A. McConnell told the judge Monday that New York crime officials are investigating at least one other case of "conduct similar to the conduct alleged" in the present case. He did not elaborate.

In Paris, a young journalist named Tristane Banon spoke up to say she had been sexually assaulted by Strauss-Kahn in

2002 when she interviewed him. "He was like a chimpanzee in heat," she says, describing how he wrestled her to the floor, undoing her bra and trying to pull her blue jeans off before she managed to flee. Her mother dissuaded her from filing suit at the time, because there had not been an actual rape and public opinion would have sided with the great man. But her lawyer says she is likely to sue now because "she knows she will be heard and be taken seriously."

A few French opinion leaders are beginning to speak out publicly. One of the first was the National Front's president, Marine Le Pen. "The truth, and everyone knows it, is that Paris has buzzed for months if not years in political and journalistic circles about the pathological relationship Monsieur Strauss-Kahn has with women," she said. "This week's news is not exactly surprising."

Another was the lawmaker Bernard Debré, a well-known member of Sarkozy's UMP party and son of one of the authors of the Constitution of the Fifth Republic. He told a news magazine that DSK had engaged in this sort of behavior several times at the Sofitel in New York, where he has stayed five times over the last year, and that hotel employees knew about it. "Enough is enough, you have humiliated France," he said. "You have ridiculed and soiled your country. Your best hope now is to seek the help available for sexual delinquents."

To be sure, every man is innocent until proven guilty. No one can be certain what may come to light as this murky *affaire* goes forward. But at least one fortunate consequence is now clear: contrary to predictions of just a week ago, Dominique

Strauss-Kahn will not be the next president of France. As a French friend told me the other day with heartfelt gratitude, "This makes twice that you Americans have saved us. First when you liberated us from the Nazis in 1945, and now from Strauss-Kahn as president."

Update: *A careful District Attorney Cyrus Vance, Jr., finally decided that he might not be able to convince a New York jury of the charges of sexual assault against Strauss-Kahn. The DSK saga went on and on after he returned to Paris. Diallo's dogged lawyers continued to prepare her civil case. Tristine Banon's case was finally dismissed because the statute of limitations for sexual assault, as opposed to actual rape, was only three years. Then the "Carlton Affair" broke. Vice squad police investigating organized prostitution centering on the luxury Carlton hotel in Lille, north of Paris, came across Strauss Kahn's name in the organizers' text messages. It was alleged that they delivered French and Belgian prostitutes to him not only in Lille, but also in Washington and New York. He denied charges of participating in organized prostitution, claiming he didn't know the girls were prostitutes because—get this—"they weren't dressed at the time." Poor man, the law even shuttered his favorite Paris wife-swapping club.*

# ROYAL MISTRESS

A *femme* plays gender politics with a vengeance.

**Context:** *The big news in France's 2007 presidential election was that, for the first time in the country's history, there was a woman candidate. In a Latin land where only 12 percent of the National Assembly is female, this alone was enough to make her attractive to an electorate hungry for change.*

NO NEED to play *cherchez la femme* in France's perfervid election season, with its 40-odd—many very odd indeed— candidates vying for president of all Gaul. She has dominated political discourse here for months on the sole strength of her gender.

At first Paris salons buzzed with the question whether Mademoiselle Ségolène Royal, mistress to the Socialist Party first secretary François Hollande, could get the party's nomination as its candidate in the April 2007 vote. When she did, chatter turned to whether she could actually win in a macho Latin country. After all, France had not had a woman leader since Joan of Arc—an unpromising precedent since a French court had her burned at the stake. But enough of politics. The real question for many was whether she might be still another illegitimate daughter (one was outed shortly after his death) of her roving political idol, President François Mitterrand.

With all this tickling the body politic, virtually every magazine in the country's corner kiosks has had the titillating lady on its glossy cover. No sooner has one dubbed Ségolène, or Ségo as she is familiarly known, the Madonna of the Polls, than another tops that by naming her no less than the "political revelation of the year." And—look ma, no hands!—she has done it with very little in the way of a program or vision for France's future.

No matter. Polls show that the Frenchman in the street who intends to vote for Ségolène will do so not because he believes in her politics. No, that is mostly hidden somewhere in a cloud of smiling Delphic utterances. The basic, fundamental, underlying reason is that she is, well—how you say in Eengleesh?—a woman. You know, a frou-frou female of the opposite sex. *Une femme, quoi!*

How did politics in the land of Descartes, Diderot and Danton, not to mention the Enlightenment, the society with a political class of intellectuals who can split the hairs on Karl Marx's beard four different ways, come to this?

It all began modestly enough in the 1980s when the comely young woman rode Mitterrand's coattails into the National Assembly. Along the way, she became the live-in mistress of Hollande, a Socialist Party apparatchik now, conveniently, the party's leader. This all made them Paris's political fun couple of the left. Principled Socialists, they begat four children while religiously shunning bourgeois marriage.

Clearly one of Mitterrand's favorites (thus the rumor, unlikely but never convincingly denied, about her paternity), Mademoiselle Royal held three junior ministerial portfolios during his 14-year reign. Her most memorable contribution to the quality of French family life was making the morning-after pill available to teenage girls as minister of family affairs. Later she burnished her political credentials by getting elected president of the Poitou-Charentes region in southwestern France, a largely ceremonial post but one that kept her in the political swim.

As Jacques Chirac's feckless second term approached its end, Royal flummoxed the Socialist Party hierarchy by quietly starting a grass-roots campaign. Party heavyweights like Laurent Fabius, a former prime minister, and Dominique Strauss-Kahn, a former finance minister, expected to make back-room deals on the nomination as usual. But she was out stumping the country, smiling her surgically improved smile eight days a week and addressing party faithful with vague, reassuring talks in small gatherings.

The media loved it. In a country where women got the vote only in 1946 and only 12 percent of the National Assembly are women, here was a *femme* making political waves. Too, in a land beset with rigid doctrines and ideologies, where suits with elitist trappings mouthed eloquent speeches full of past-tense subjunctives but did little about things like high unemployment, an antiquated educational system, and burgeoning race and crime problems, she artfully projected feeling the pain of real people in the hinterland. She even asked for their views and complaints, in what she calls participatory democracy. This was news! And it was being made by—did I say this before?—a woman!

In her trademark white jacket—symbol of purity and the opposite of dark suits—the Socialist leader's 52-year-old concubine cultivates an air of maternal concern on the hustings. Although she is not above showing a generous expanse of thigh when the wind catches one of her flouncy skirts, her style is dishwater drab. On the podium her voice drones in a minor key, making her sound more like a Mater Dolorosa than a Madonna. But voters hungry for a clean break with the past, frustrated with same-old, same-old of French society, go for it. As one pollster puts it, "The French want to turn the page on the past. Not just to change governments, but to change eras."

Voting *une présidente* into the Élysée Palace—which has seen many foolish things in its long history, including a president who died enjoying fellatio in his office, but never a presidential *concubinage*—instead of *un président* would certainly be a change. Still, Mademoiselle Royal is no solid Angela Merkel of Germany or Vaira Vike Freiberga, the steely president of Latvia, or even less a strong-willed Margaret Thatcher who knew exactly where she wanted to lead Britain. She even makes Hillary Clinton look statesmanlike. (Royal wanted a leftist-ladies-together photo-op with Clinton, but Hillary's handlers took one look at her and nixed it.) "The main thing about her," says *Le Figaro* ironically, "is being a woman. This at least is one promise of change that voters can be sure she will stick to."

Her vacuous speeches are laced here and there with the party's 19th-century Marxism. She promises to "scare the capitalists" with their "financial anarchy that destroys the planet's environment and crushes social rights... Free markets mean disorder." Hostility to America is a given. It is a "hyperpower" that is "tempted to use force" and must be curtailed by a stronger European Union. From there it is only a short step to tarring her conservative rival, Nicolas Sarkozy, as pro-American, especially since he had the nerve to visit Washington and shake George Bush's hand. He is, she says, merely "a sort of French franchise of Bush and Co., an American neo-conservative with a French passport."

The energetic, pugnacious, pragmatic Sarkozy has indeed been making the right noises about freeing up France's rigid, job-killing labor market and shrinking the bloated state machinery that tries to micro-manage the economy. As twice minister of the interior and thus the country's top cop, he is also tough on law and order issues, which appeals to voters alarmed by growing gratuitous violence—tens of thousands of cars were burned by rampaging youths in France last year. Given the urgency of France's needs in those areas, a nonentity like Royal would have little chance in a rational political situation. But no one familiar with the history of France since 1789 would accuse the French of being politically rational. And two jokers in the game could also upset predictions.

One is Jean-Marie Le Pen, the far-right National Front leader who could divide the conservative vote. The other, perversely, is Jacques Chirac. Though of the same UMP party, Chirac hates Sarkozy and has maneuvered against him. It sounds like politics fiction, but many here speculate that Chirac would rather be succeeded by France's first woman president, even if a Socialist, rather than give way to a male rival of the right.

So all bets are off. As a Paris banker friend told me with visible apprehension, "The French are so starved for some kind of change, any kind, that they could just vote for Ségolène because she's different. Anything can happen here." And did I mention that the Socialist Party candidate for president of France is a *woman?*

Update: *Ségolène didn't beat Sarkozy, but thanks to her gender play she gave him a run for his money. The Socialist Party was embarrassed when, the day after the vote, she and Hollande revealed they were splitting up after nearly 30 years together. She hoped to be a presidential candidate again in 2012, but—oh irony of fate—the party chose her former partner Hollande to face Sarkozy.*

# STYLE IS THE MAN

Alas, the French don't like Sarkozy's.

Context: *Despite his decidedly unFrench name and uncouth background, Nicolas Sarkozy, the abrasive, brazenly ambitious son of a Hungarian immigrant, won the 2007 presidential election thanks to two things: the weak, unconvincing campaign of his socialist rival Ségolène Royal, and his promise to bring what he called* rupture, *real change, to French politics. The French soon found that they got more change than they bargained for.*

WHAT A DIFFERENCE a year makes. It seems only yesterday that Nicolas Sarkozy was handily elected president of France on a wave of popular enthusiasm. With his sound conservative program, nervous energy, and raw pugnacity, the hope was that he would lead, prod, and cajole a torpid France out of its slough of politco-socio-economic despond. Polls ranked him the most popular president since Charles de Gaulle 40 years ago. "The French people have chosen change," he declared on his victory night in May 2007. He would "break with the ideas, the habits and the behavior of the past."

He got off to a promising start. He faced down, as no previous president had, public sector workers who went on strike over his reform of their unduly generous retirement benefits. He made some initial moves toward ending the country's debilitating 35-hour workweek. It became moderately easier to hire and fire employees. In foreign policy he ended France's knee-jerk anti-Americanism, and brokered a treaty to replace the misbegotten European Union Constitution.

Unfortunately, in the process he has managed to—in no particular order—tarnish the image of the august French presidency, alienate most of those who swept him into office, revive the prospects of the languishing Socialist party, dent the Franco-German special relationship, and incidentally become an international laughing-stock due to his harum-scarum love life. Mirabile dictu, he has even made Jacques Chirac look good in retrospect to many who a year ago were sick of him.

His popularity plunged within months from a record high 67 percent to a record low 37 percent. And whereas hostility to this most conservative president in recent memory was expected in leftist enclaves, now it festers in bourgeois living rooms from Paris to Perpignan, Brest to Bordeaux. So unpopular is he that in the recent municipal elections, many candidates in his own UMP party actually asked him to stay away from their campaigns and deleted the party logo from their leaflets. They lost 38 of France's largest towns and cities to the Socialist Party anyway, in what was clearly a rebuke to Sarkozy.

What happened? It's the style, stupid. We might indulge a doughnut-gobbling, DNA-splashing Bill Clinton in the White House, but in the land of the phrase, *le style c'est l'homme,* the wrong manner can be disastrous. Sarkozy's erratic, tone-deaf style has been not only wrong, it's been obliviously self-destructive. The cocky son of a Hungarian immigrant, so obsessed with his quest for the presidency that he admitted he thought of it every morning while shaving, flubbed the transition to life in the Élysée Palace. Thus it is that for the first time in the 50-year existence of the Fifth Republic, indeed in the country's multi-millennial history, the leader of this paragon of taste has—*quelle horreur*—no class.

I know, France's usual remote, condescending, monarchical governing style has no place in the 21$^{st}$ century (had none in the 19$^{th}$ or 20$^{th}$, for that matter) and good riddance. But replacing that with the non-stop Sarko Show of luxury vacations, millionaires' yachts and private jets, jogging shorts and worn jeans, fancy sunglasses and fancier wristwatches, a sudden divorce followed by a quick, furtive marriage on the rebound to a trophy wife of disconcerting background—it's all enough to give the French a bad case of political indigestion. Add to that a soap opera mix of offspring from three marriages, on-again, off-again romances, and catty comments by former wives, and the Sarkozy presidency looks like something out of Baywatch.

We should have known that someone as physically jittery—the constantly shifting shoulders, the compressed lips, the need for perpetual motion—would be emotionally unsteady. As for presidential demeanor, the evening of his election triumph Sarkozy shunned the usual simple celebration with political cronies and spent the night at a luxurious Champs-Élysées restaurant with a collection of celebrities from rock stars to the *fine fleur* of France's new-money billionaires. The next day he and his wife Cécilia took off in a businessman's executive jet for the Mediterranean, where they spent a few sybaritic days on the friend's luxury yacht—and appearances of a newly elected president accepting expensive favors be damned.

Soon we were being treated to photos in the celebrity press of Sarkozy in shirt sleeves, feet on desk, amid the gilded trappings of his palace office; Sarkozy's bedroom with its immaculate linen; Sarkozy's pet Chihuahua (ever so cutely named Big); Sarkozy lighting a huge stogy. As one curmudgeonly British observer put it, "Sarkozy seems to be rapidly evolving into the P. Diddy of the political world." It didn't help that one of his first moves in office was to double his salary, to $360,000, as the French grappled with a slumping economy and soaring inflation.

In permanent photo-op mode, this jack-in-the-box president pops up everywhere, with media crews just happening to be on hand. No sparrow falls but he leaps to take charge: quickly on the scene of every disaster, praising the gendarme wounded in the line of duty, commiserating with the fireman injured while retrieving granny's cat from a tree, comforting the upset granny herself, stroking the errant cat. A group of citizens suffering from Sarko fatigue vainly petitioned for a Non-Sarkozy Day on which no story about him would be published.

His official trips abroad leave eyes rolling at home. His flashy style, the hugging/back slapping/cheek kissing inflicted on foreign leaders makes them cringe (Germany's severe chancellor Angela Merkel let it be known she didn't want to be touched) and traditional French elites writhe in exasperation. Visiting the Vatican, he was 18 minutes late for an audience with Pope

Benedict and surreptitiously consulted text messages on his cell phone while in the Holy Presence. He did the same during a meeting with the Chinese premier in Beijing, horrifying the diplomatic corps. "It's embarrassing and extremely discourteous," later commented a French diplomat *sotto voce*. "You simply cannot do that sort of thing."

True, all this may say as much about the hidebound French as about Sarkozy. But every democratic citizenry in the world knows "presidential" class when it sees it, and many French no longer see it in him. "Can he incarnate France with dignity and legitimacy?" wonders Dominique Moisi, a senior advisor at the French Institute for International Relations. "Has he already lost touch with reality, surrounded as he is by a court of media courtesans?" The newsmagazine *L'Express* has a simple solution: "He needs to put a little more De Gaulle and a bit less Tom Cruise into his cocktail of presidential modernity."

Try to imagine De Gaulle gallivanting with a Folies Bergère can-can dancer and you get an idea of how Sarkozy's ostentatious love life has gone over. Private presidential hanky panky is fine with the French, but flaunting it as he has done with Carla Bruni offends their well-developed sense of hypocrisy. They could have felt sympathy after the departure of his second wife Cécilia, which by all accounts left him distraught. But taking up so soon with a supermodel and luxury rock chick, flamboyant former mistress of a string of conquests with names like Trump and Jagger, self-styled man-eater on record as preferring polygamy and polyandry? That pushed Gallic tolerance to the breaking point.

Also troubling was Sarkozy's bizarre courtship manner. Reversing the usual order of things, he deliberately exhibited his pre-marital trysts, which most people in our latitudes, especially politicians, tend to keep quiet, only to marry clandestinely in a quickie ceremony at the Élysée Palace. With a bad case of divorce-rebound, he took Bruni to the same places where he had courted Cécilia, such as the pyramids in Egypt and the pink ruins of Petra in Jordan. There she sported the same heart-shaped diamond ring he had bought Cécilia, from the same shop.

It hardly mattered whether the report was true that days before wedding Carla he had texted Cécilia, "Come back and I'll call it all off." The important thing was that the French were so ready to believe it, accustomed as they are to his unpredictable antics ("Cherie, guess what he's done now!"). Fully 4 (sic) percent of the French said the marriage improved his image.

Concern about Sarkozy's stability has also built due to his hair-trigger temper. He storms out of an interview with CBS after a question he doesn't like. Berates his staff as cretins, imbeciles, and worse. Threatens a fisherman during a demonstration over rising fuel costs. Lashes out "Get lost, you poor jerk," at a man who refuses to shake his hand—a filmed incident that immediately circled the Internet world. As a member of the far-right, politically incorrect National Front party put it, "Is there any way we can take the nuclear button away from him? This impulsiveness is getting worrying."

At stake is much more than the dignity of the French presidency, for the country direly needs his reform agenda. Aides say he is now making "adjustments" to the behavior that has squandered so much of the political goodwill needed to push that through. With four years to go on his term, there is still time for him to change style and grow into the job. But can he?

**Update:** *Sarkozy was quickly dubbed "President bling-bling" because of his lifestyle. The moniker, and the distaste his countrymen felt for his flashy manner, stuck. He attempted to change his image, dropping the aviator sunglasses, chunky watches, and parties on friends' yachts, but couldn't resist the appeal of a luxurious new presidential plane, apparently modeled on Air Force One, known to wags as Air Sarko. Personal dislike of him and his style was a major reason for his failure in his re-election bid in 2012.*

# GIRL TROUBLE

Sarkozy's feminist ploy backfires.

**Context:** *True to the French stereotype, Nicolas Sarkozy has an urgent need of feminine companionship. He also has had disastrous trouble managing that need. This became abundantly clear when he took over as president in 2007. Besides going through a very public divorce and remarriage only months into his term, he immediately appointed more women to cabinet posts than any previous French leader. Both developments were to cost him dearly in popularity and effectiveness.*

FIRST OF ALL, let's get one thing straight: I am *not* the father of Rachida Dati's new baby. Admittedly that disclaimer might be superfluous, because of all the many names mentioned since the birth of Zohra, mine is not yet among them. Still, it's best to get this on the record for reasons that will become clear.

Miss Dati is one of the several women whom President Nicolas Sarkozy, to please feminists and bring a whiff of modernity to hidebound French government, picked for his cabinet after his 2007 election. With women newly holding cabinet positions from the interior to finance to justice, and on through housing, health, culture, and education, Sarkozy has prided himself on bringing more women into high government office than any previous French leader. The political correctness squad gave him double points for two new faces in particular: Rama Yade, the Senegal-born state secretary for human rights, and Rachida Dati, of North African immigrant origin, as minister of justice.

But Sarkozy, for all his nervous energy and laudable attempts to instill a new governing style, is very much in the traditional French mold when it comes to women: he dotes and depends on them. Like French leaders from 15th-century Charles VII on down to François Mitterrand, he gladly submits to their influence. (He was especially dependent on his second wife, Cécilia, for moral support and counsel, avowing publicly, "She is part of me.") And like many of his predecessors, Sarkozy now is paying the political price of a spot of girl trouble.

When Cécilia abruptly left him only months after his election, he speedily courted and married Carla Bruni, model and pop singer. Whether it's an excess of testosterone, as one biographer argues, or outsized emotional need, he likes to have plenty of the opposite sex around. The little harem Sarkozy formed in his cabinet immediately became known to irreverent observers as the Sarko Babes. But he didn't reckon with the inconvenience, in the serious business of government, of those delightful feminine qualities so celebrated in French boulevard farce: caprice, vanity, and jealousy.

Rama Yade, a duskily attractive 32-year-old, is the youngest of the Babes and the only black cabinet member. Initially touted by Sarkozy as France's Condoleeza Rice, Yade became his poster child for ethnic diversity. But her inexperience, lack of tact, and newly discovered political ambition soon made her a political liability. When the Libyan weirdo Muammar Qaddafi made a state visit to Paris, she embarrassed Sarkozy by trumpeting that France should not be a doormat where Qaddafi could "wipe the blood of his crimes from his feet." And when Barack Obama was elected she regretted publicly that, unlike the U.S., France's political parties were prejudiced against its ethnic minorities. True perhaps, but as the French wisely say, not all truths are good to be spoken—especially if you're a cabinet minister.

The last straw for Sarkozy came when he asked her recently to run for the insignificant European Parliament in next June's elections as part of his UMP party. "*Non,*" came her blunt reply. That would be "like a forced marriage," when what she really wanted was an important political career in France. Sarkozy was vocally disappointed by what he considered his young protégée's betrayal.

Her planned promotion to minister of European affairs is now dropped, despite her sending him a box of heart-shaped chocolates as proof of her affection. "There are so many proofs of love that you can find, and I assure you that I am working on them," she told an interviewer. Sarkozy appears unmoved by what—this being France—resembles a lovers' tiff more than government business. "I've zapped Rama," he reportedly told other cabinet members. "She's totally finished." Today the French government's token black is in political limbo and Sarkozy's judgment has taken a hit.

Yade had already been snubbed by a carom shot from another Sarko Babe. When Sarkozy made his official visit to China in November 2007, she expected to go along to treat the vexed question of human rights with Chinese officials, a subject on which France claims to hold strong views. But she was pointedly excluded from the delegation after being nixed by her pushy sister in government—and rival for Sarkozy's attention—Rachida Dati.

Dati's relationship with Sarkozy has had French tongues wagging for years, and not only because he appointed her to head his justice department despite lacking any visible qualifications. One of 12 children of poor Moroccan-Algerian parents, she had a hardscrabble childhood in tough public-housing projects. After managing to attend magistrates' school and a brief stint as a junior magistrate, she began bombarding Sarkozy with letters when he was interior minister under Jacques Chirac. When he finally agreed to meet, he liked her well enough to give her a minor job in the ministry. During his presidential campaign he made her a press attaché. When Sarkozy and Cécilia vacationed in Vermont in the summer of 2007, Dati, for reasons no one but they understood, went along.

Cécilia left Sarkozy but Dati stayed. A striking, headstrong, 43-year-old brunette with a thousand-watt smile, she was on his arm during a White House dinner, accompanied him to a World Cup rugby match, was his partner at a state banquet in Morocco. He affectionately called her "*ma beurette*," friendly slang for "my little North African girl." Thanks to her looks and nouveau riche taste for ostentatious luxury—designer pantsuits at the office, glossy magazine covers in expensive dresses, fishnet stockings and spike-heeled boots, spectacular gems on loan from top Paris jewelers in the evening—the celebrity press couldn't get enough of her. For a while this single-minded arriviste was the brightest star in the French political firmament, and it went to her head. On November 5 she imperiously ordered Sarkozy's minions to give her Obama's cell phone number, as if she were on a presidential level.

They refused because Sarkozy had changed his game and sidelined her. After months of backlash against his flashy ways, he dropped the ostentatious lifestyle that had so alienated public opinion. Dati's fondness for the likes of Dior, Prada and Vuitton clashed with the sober new tone at the Elysée Palace. A friendly newspaper tried to help by airbrushing off her finger an imposing Chaumet ring worth an estimated $20,000; that backfired when the ruse became known. Moreover, Carla was not Dati's friend. She let it be known that while showing Dati around the official residence, they paused at the presidential bed. "You would have liked to be in there, wouldn't you?" Carla teased, not altogether affectionately.

On cue, Government sources began leaking exasperation over her using plush executive jets for her frequent trips abroad—and insisting that the French ambassador be on hand to welcome her at all hours. Justice ministry insiders criticized her for needlessly alienating the judicial establishment by forcing through reforms without the customary dialogue, and swearing at assistants during temper tantrums. (In her first 18 months as minister, over 20 top aides left in protest.) Trying to downplay his embarrassingly glam minister, Sarkozy told his press service to "de-celebritize" Dati. But she had one third-act feminine ploy left: pregnancy.

After she announced proudly last year that she was expecting, but would not name the father because her private life was "complicated," every salon and dinner table in Paris echoed with the question, *qui est le père?* The celebrity press had a new angle as photographers chronicled her swelling form. She did nothing to conceal it, teasing reporters with lines like "the papa travels a lot," and "I've invited him to dinner." Even as little Zohra was born January 2, names flew: was her daddy a well-known top executive at Gucci? A high official in the government of Qatar, where she travels frequently? A certain former Spanish prime minister (denied as "totally and completely false")? François Sarkozy, the president's taller, younger brother who visited her in the maternity clinic ("I'm the wrong horse")? Or had she resorted to anonymous artificial insemination?

*Hélas*, we may never know, the only certitude being, trust me, that it is not your faithful correspondent. But Sarkozy, finally fed up with the Dati Show, called her on the carpet in late January. She could either leave the government empty-handed, he told his tearful minister, or leave for the European Parliament, and this time he wouldn't take *non* for an answer.

By no coincidence two journalists with good contacts in Sarkozy's circle then published a scathing attack on her, quoting government insiders saying she was totally inept and clueless as a minister. But as she prepared to head reluctantly to that graveyard of political ambitions that is the phony parliament in

Strasburg, she let it be known she had other political plans, including a possible run for Paris City Hall. She also had a sort of last word: in a recent poll the smitten French public voted her the best symbol of Gallic womanhood today for her style, looks and independence.

Sarkozy, presumably sadder and wiser after the very public failure of his diversity gadget, can at least rely on the ultimate Sarko Babe, Carla, to help wipe the egg off his face. It must be some comfort that his much younger wife vows she has given up her man-eating ways that reportedly included a string of boyfriends from Mick Jagger to Donald Trump. "I no longer seduce because I love my husband," she purred to a magazine recently. "We don't say much, we kiss."

To help keep those home fires burning, Sarkozy has a new feminine recruit named Julie. This 26-year-old personal trainer specializes in shaping up the pelvic floor, i.e., the perineum. Besides helping him lose weight and overcome his chocolate addiction, the technique is claimed to improve other important aspects of her client's life. "Sexual relations are better if the male perineum is in good shape," explains the knowing Julie. One can only speculate what beneficial effect this may have on France's steroidal president, and wish him many happy returns.

Update: *The Sarko Babes turned out to be so many feminine loose cannons. As he began his campaign for re-election in early 2012, Sarkozy ruefully admitted that he had given too much power too soon to Rachida Dati and Rama Yade. A year earlier he had had to dismiss*

*Michèle Alliot-Marie, after only a few unsuccessful months as foreign minister; she had embarrassed him by appearing to offer France's know-how in riot control to Tunisia's corrupt President Zine El Abidine Ben Ali as the Arab Spring began to spread across North Africa and the Middle East.*

# IS SARKOZY DEAD?

If he can make a comeback in the 2012 election, call him Lazarus.

**Context:** *Nicolas Sarkozy has many qualities, but as a politician he is tone deaf. He seldom appears to realize the impact on public opinion of his actions and statements. Why else would he say, for instance, that he was finished if France lost its top credit rating, when S&P already had signaled that it was likely? That came on top of his failure to fulfill many of the promises he made to get elected. Small wonder that the 2012 election was a struggle for him.*

THE FRENCH, who do things differently, believe that Friday the 13th is a lucky day. Key rings and other amulets often sport a 13, sales of lottery tickets soar on that day—newspapers have already published the happy information that there will be no less than four of them this year. But Friday, January 13, 2012, brought a nasty omen for President Nicolas Sarkozy. France, to his considerable consternation, saw its credit rating downgraded from AAA to AA+ by Standard & Poor's.

No matter that the U.S. showed last year there is life after a ratings downgrade. Few Americans noticed, the Cardinals won the World Series, and the holiday season rolled merrily on. Not in France. The triple A was, Sarkozy's minions had declared repeatedly, a "national treasure" to be preserved at all costs. That was the stated reason for two back-to-back austerity programs—including raising the retirement age and paying higher value added taxes on basic consumer items like food and beverages—to reduce France's budget deficit and cut its unsustainable national debt. Those hurt, but it was the price the French had to pay to keep that iconic rating, their president explained.

For Sarkozy personally, it was a badge of honor, gilt-edged proof that he could successfully steer the good ship *France* through Europe's economic storm and deal as an equal with Germany's Chancellor Angela Merkel. In terms of sheer politics, a downgrade risked being seen by voters in the April presidential election as a verdict on his whole five-year term. So much was at stake, he told his cabinet, that "if we lose our triple A, I'm dead."

He lost it, and only 100 days before the ballot. Thus the visible consternation at the Elysée Palace, with scrambling cabinet ministers and advisors going into full damage control mode. Some vented their anger at this intrusive American ratings agency that was obviously playing anti-French politics. After all, another agency, Fitch, had assured French authorities that it wouldn't touch the triple A in 2012. (It's surely just a coincidence that Fitch belongs to a French owner, Marc Ladreit de Lacharrière.) "We should have hit them hard them over their mistakes during the subprime crisis two years ago," clamored one. Sarkozy himself appeared in denial, insisting at a press conference that "it changes nothing." Asked whether the downgrade was a sign of failure that might reduce his influence in Europe, he lost his cool and replied testily that he did not understand the question. "Ask me a question I can understand," he snarled at the reporter.

Sarkozy's opponents jumped on the downgrade as a godsend and painted it as an unmitigated disaster. "It's Sarkozy's policies that have been downgraded, not France itself," said Socialist Party candidate François Hollande. "It's the first time since rating agencies exist that France has been rated lower than Germany. We don't play in the first division anymore." The right-wing National Front candidate Marine Le Pen called it "the end of the myth of the president who protects us," adding, "France is now on the same down staircase as Italy and Greece."

What no politician had the courage to say was that the French are witnessing, in slow motion, the end of their welfare state, known locally as The French Social Model. For the last 30 years it has been sustained through political sleight of hand and financed on credit. The French were assured they were entitled to work only 35 hours a week, take five weeks of vacation, have single-payer health care, pocket generous unemployment benefits, and enjoy a cornucopia of handout programs. As a result, they work on average six fewer weeks a year than the Germans, fewer hours even than the laidback Greeks. Let the good times roll was the implicit program of politicians both left and right. Now the inevitable bill is coming due right at election time. There's no way Sarkozy can avoid paying the political price.

As this campaign churns on, French voters aren't likely to hear such home truths from either Sarkozy or his main opponent, Hollande. A lifelong Socialist apparatchik, Hollande learned his politics in the 1970s and '80s from that consummate welfare fabulist, François Mitterrand, and headed the Socialist Party from 1997 to 2008. A bland, bespectacled 57-year-old with all the charisma of your local high school principal, he has never held a cabinet post. Segolène Royal, Hollande's former live-in mistress, mother of their four children, and unsuccessful Socialist Party presidential candidate in the 2007 election (they split immediately after the ballots were in), now says with all the contempt of a scorned woman, "Can the French people name a single thing he has achieved in 30 years in politics?" Asked about his rival, Sarkozy mocks, "Do you see this sugar cube? It seems solid enough. Drop it in water and see what's left. That's Hollande."

But with national distaste for the twitchy Sarkozy running high, the Socialist candidate may just be able to turn his image as an ordinary guy—think a quiet, unprepossessing Mr. Normal who rides a scooter to the office vs. an agitated, hyperactive Super Sarko who relishes traveling the world in his new presidential jet—to his advantage. He consistently leads Sarkozy in the polls after a politically savvy makeover, shedding 20 pounds, donning designer eyeglasses, and modeling his body language and intonations on Mitterrand. And he can mock Sarkozy right back. In an off-record parody of Sarkozy's plea to voters, he mimicked, "I'm a president who has failed for five years; I'm a jerk, but re-elect me because in these hard times, I'm the only one who can do it."

Nipping at the heels of both Sarkozy and Hollande, only a couple of points behind, is Marine Le Pen. With contempt for mainstream politicians growing even faster in France than in the U.S., her pungent populist platform calling for ending the euro and returning to the French franc, restricting immigration, and protecting French industries from foreign competition is gaining traction by the day.

One poll showed that 31 percent of voters agreed with her ideas, up from 22 percent a year ago and 11 percent in 1999. "We are witnessing a de-demonizing of the NF," says one pollster, referring to the legitimacy the charismatic Le Pen, 43, has been able to give the party since taking it over from her pugnacious, unelectable father, Jean-Marie. Those figures don't take into account the silent constituency of voters who won't admit they favor the Front. With the NF now successfully challenging the mainstreamers, few analysts would be surprised if she made it into the runoff second round on May 6—and not against Sarkozy, but Hollande. "The game is wide open at this point," says one.

Some of Sarkozy's tone-deaf moves give the impression of a political death wish. One recent trial balloon had him favoring homosexual marriage or some sort of civil union equivalent in his platform. Nothing could be better designed to alienate his conservative core constituency. Then the interest rate on savings accounts, which is set by the government twice a year based on a mathematical formula including inflation, was not raised in early 2012 as everyone expected. With inflation running at its highest level in three years, public disappointment—nearly all French have one of these tax-free accounts, a traditional gift to newborn babies—was sharp. If Sarkozy wanted to drive voters into the arms of a right-wing populist like Le Pen, he couldn't have done better.

Such incomprehensible sallies have made many of his countrymen doubt that he would after all run for a second term. His game of political hide and seek hasn't helped. He was expected to declare his candidacy after he wound up France's G20 presidency in November, 2011, but did not. Then as the list of candidates lengthened into a field of nearly 20 from parties of all stripes, he remained silent. (Within his own UMP party there are eight hopefuls not counting him, showing serious divisions within his ranks and his inability to corral his supporters.) If he did declare only weeks before the ballot, he would have to conduct a lightning campaign.

It would be an uphill slog. Instead of benefitting from the usual advantages of the incumbent, Sarkozy, his numbers languishing in the low 30s, bears the burden of being the most unpopular president since Charles de Gaulle founded the Fifth Republic in 1958. The French simply do not like him as a person. He was elected *faute de mieux* when the Socialists foolishly put up Segolène Royal against him. Then he rubbed them the wrong way the very night of his election when he celebrated tastelessly at a glitzy Champs-Elysées watering hole with an unsavory cohort of business and show biz pals. From then on, whether being ostentatiously dumped by his wife Cécilia, publicly courting the Italian model-turned-pop singer Carla Bruni, or generally acting in ways the French found unpresidential, enmity grew.

Then there is the bad smell of unending corruption scandals that have marred his term, with hardly a month going by without new allegations: that a billionaire heiress illegally financed his political career; that the government carried out illegal spying on a *Le Monde* journalist to plug a leak; that he was involved in the "Karachi affair" of alleged kickbacks from French arms sales to Pakistan in the 1990s; that his wife was implicated in a charity funding scandal with millions of euros funneled to close friends and favored companies. To name a few. They made a mockery of Sarkozy's promise to make France an "irreproachable republic."

Similarly, the French won't forgive his failure to deliver on more bread-and-butter promises. He was going to be "the buying power president," but incomes have stagnated while inflation rose. He was going to effect a "rupture" with the past, modernizing France's state-dominated economy, reforming taxes, getting rid of the debilitating 35-hour workweek, reducing bureaucracy. None of this happened on his watch. Most visibly he promised to clean up the country's increasingly violent crime so individuals could take public transport without being mugged, park their car in the street overnight without having it burned, leave their home with a good chance it wouldn't be burgled. But violent crime has increased 22 percent over the last decade, burglaries were up 16 percent just last year, and tens of thousands of automobiles continue to burn annually in the streets.

Although he is a formidable campaigner and never better than with his back to the wall, this leaves Sarkozy with very little to run on. Not only is he personally disliked and his record disappointing, but now the humiliating S&P downgrade means he cannot even claim to be a safe pair of hands protecting France during Europe's economic crisis. But maybe he still has one ploy in reserve to make a Lazarus-like comeback. So far, he and Carla have refused to allow photographers access to their daughter Giulia, born last October, making Sarkozy the first serving president to become a father. Could some cuddly magazine-cover photos of him *en famille* produce a vote-getting baby bounce? His aides are said to be quietly hoping so.

**Update:** *Sarkozy finally was unable to overcome his compatriots' distaste and disappointment. He ran a vigorous, pugnacious campaign, but became a one-term president. He lost by three points to François Hollande, whom he had underestimated. And no magazine covers were graced by the Sarkozy baby.*

# NONE OF THE ABOVE

Disgusted with politics as usual, the French turn increasingly to populist parties.

Context: *French politicians are in double trouble. As in the United States, the mainstream pols are under fire for being out of touch with their constituents' basic concerns of jobs, eroded purchasing power, poor schooling for their children, and the like. But in France, as in most of Western Europe, the equation is complicated by membership in the European Union. The French increasingly feel that the EU has sapped their national sovereignty—most regulations are made now in Brussels—without their consent. The financial straitjacket of the euro currency, which prevents devaluation to improve competitiveness on world markets, exacerbates their discontent.*

HOWEVER THE FRENCH VOTE April 22 in the first round of their 2012 presidential election, or in the runoff May 6, the long-term winners in terms of real political change will be neither the putative conservative Nicolas Sarkozy of the UMP (*Union pour un Mouvement Populaire)* nor the Socialist Party's François Hollande. They will be the newly puissant populist parties of far right and left. If you combine the expected votes of the right-wing National Front and the new, communist-backed Left Front, they would outnumber those of either Sarkozy or

Hollande. In fact, the National Front already dominates France's youth vote: with 26 percent, more 18-to-24-year-olds plan to vote for it than any other party. This suddenly reverses the traditional pattern of voting left at 20 and right at 30.

Hardly surprising then that a large majority of French voters, disgusted with politics as usual, say flatly they don't want the predictable Hobson's choice runoff between Sarkozy and Hollande. The rejection cuts across class, age, professional and even political lines including former Gaullists and socialists: they no longer trust the established mainstream parties. While the two mainstreamers have bobbed and weaved for months with tired variations on the theme of a chicken in every pot—most appropriate in the land of Henry IV, the first to pledge a *poule au pot* for every mother's son in the realm—the fiery populist speeches of the National Front's Marine Le Pen and the Left Front's Jean-Luc Mélenchon, challenging what they term a corrupt economic and political system, make them the revelations of this campaign.

What they reveal is a hunger for something other than routine rhetoric—hardball, edgy programs that tackle France's grievous socio-economic problems head-on and restore the feeling of distinct national and political identity eroded by uncontrolled immigration and globalization. Even if those proposals, on close examination, sometimes constitute an insult to the intelligence of the Gaul in the street. Or pander with simple solutions to complex problems. Or appeal to racial and class conflict.

What the French apparently don't want in 2012, whatever he promises, is five more years of Nicolas Sarkozy. Some 64 percent disapprove of him, a much worse figure than the 46 percent disapproval rating of Valérie Giscard d'Estaing in 1981, the only Fifth Republic president who failed to win a second term. Sarkozy is expected at least to make it into the runoff. But polls point to a loss to Hollande by up to 16 points then—even former president Jacques Chirac of Sarkozy's own UMP party says he will vote for Hollande. Sarkozy, who exudes nervous energy and never shies from a fight, but has little political flair, has spent his flailing campaign 1) apologizing for the mistakes of his first term and promising to be different if re-elected, 2) casting himself as the only captain with the experience to steer the good ship *France* through the current economic crisis, 3) telling the French they should be more like the Germans (a real vote-getter, that), and 4) seeing that none of this worked, rebranding in seeming panic to an unconvincing hard-right campaign as "the people's candidate" speaking for the "silent majority" against Parisian elites.

This last tactic shows the burgeoning influence of the National Front, expected to garner 17 percent or more of the vote. (Pollsters admit the figure could be much higher, many NF supporters hesitating to say they favor the politically incorrect Marine Le Pen.) Borrowing liberally from its playbook, Sarkozy has jumped from one hot-button issue to another almost daily in a shifting, carpet-bomb campaign.

Depending on which way the wind was blowing that day, he vowed to cut immigration from the current 200,000 a year to half that, pass new security laws to protect against the Islamist threat, keep Muslim halal meat out of public school canteens, turn the screws on welfare abusers, protect French products from foreign competition, tighten border controls even if the European Union objected—all proposed months ago by Marine Le Pen. In his drive to siphon off votes wherever he can, Sarkozy even finds nice things to say about the Trotskyite head of the other populist party, the pugnacious Jean-Luc Mélenchon, who calls for things like a "citizens' revolution" against capitalism and "civic insurrection" against just about everything. "Concerning his ideas on the human level," Sarkozy said coolly if cryptically the other day, "I must say I have no complaints." Another example of his political tone deafness: the Left Front's rabid supporters would rather take their party underground than back a "bourgeois capitalist" like Sarkozy.

Socialist François Hollande, too, winks in the direction of populist voters, mainly of the Left Front. Though personally mild-mannered and moderate, at his political rallies he punches the air as he declares that his main enemy is the world of finance: "I will be the president of a republic much stronger than the markets," he vows, "a France stronger than finance." He promises to "profoundly reform" France to keep it the most generous welfare state in the world, unpleasant economic realities notwithstanding.

Lest the left populists suspect he is merely another capitalist tool, a conservative sheep in liberal wolf's clothing— after all, on a campaign visit to London, Europe's financial center, he assured audiences, "I am not dangerous"—Hollande pledges to implement a confiscatory 75 percent tax rate on personal income over $1.30 million. (Mélenchon, who sees the capitalist U.S. as "the world's primary problem," tops him with his rabble-pleasing plan to confiscate personal income over $470,000.) To signal his independence from a domineering Uncle Sam, he would pull French troops out of Afghanistan by the end of this year, two years ahead of the NATO schedule. That, he hopes, will help persuade Left Front believers to vote for him after Mélenchon, credited with about 14 percent in the first round, fails to make it to the runoff.

The French turn to populism actually comes late compared with the rest of Europe. From the True Finns in Finland to the Northern League in Italy, the British National Party to the Danish People's Party and emerging regional movements across the Continent, voters increasingly have been turning away from traditional parties that they feel are out of touch. Cosy consensus, comfortable right-left alternation with a wink and a nudge are out, fragmentation, rejection and the quest for new answers are in. Angry and often incoherent, the populists represent what Pierre Poujade, a now-forgotten French post-war populist, called "the ripped-off, lied-to little people." The similarities to the Tea Party are obvious. But, being European, these populists typically are also concerned about a loss of national sovereignty and control over their own affairs due to the usurpation of power by the European Union. They are also further along in organization, structure and ideology.

With voters casting their protest ballots for a field of 10 candidates in the first round before getting down to the business of choosing between the two frontrunners in the second, surprises are possible on both ballots. One obvious joker is abstention: results could be skewed by a low turnout. But while France's new populists don't seriously expect Marine Le Pen or Jean-Luc Mélenchon to be president come May, they are gunning for a healthy bloc of seats in the follow-up parliamentary elections in June. That could begin to durably change the face of French politics.

Update: *The National Front and Left Front together polled nearly 30 percent in the first round, more than either of the mainstream parties. Sarkozy tried hard in the runoff to woo Front supporters with platform planks blatantly borrowed from her programs. It didn't work. Mainstream parties will have to find better, more responsive, ways to attract the politically savvy populists, or face the prospect of going out of business.*

# THE POWER OF LE PEN

Two cheers for Marine.

Context: *The president of France's National Front party holds that the nation-state is the only legitimate basis of government. She cordially despises that usurper of national sovereignty, the European Union, and its ersatz currency, the euro. She dares proclaim that France and the rest of Europe are in dire danger of being swamped by illegal immigrants, especially with half of North Africa landing on Europe's Italian doorstep. She says that if Muslims want to live in France, they must make the effort to assimilate and accept France's Christian heritage.*

FACED with positions like this, Paris intellectuals recoil in the righteous horror they reserve for the politically *very* incorrect. The mainstream media, led by flagrantly biased TV interviewers, are in league against her. The established parties, from Nicolas Sarkozy's nominally conservative UMP to the socialists, ecologists, communists, et al., loathe and fear her in equal measure. Instead of responding to her ideas, they resort to ad hominem attacks and try to ostracize her with a political *cordon sanitaire*, charging that her party lacks "republican values."

She must be doing something right.

To be sure, there are reasons to be wary of the Front, on which more later. But there can be no doubt that Marine Le Pen stands at the very center of France's—and to some extent, Europe's—political discourse. All the country's elitist traditional parties, the very ones that, with a wink and a nudge, have so long colluded to do nothing real about France's real problems, now scurry with unseemly haste to position themselves with respect to the Front. While labeling it dangerously extremist, they pay it the sincerest form of flattery by copying many of its stances, especially on illegal immigration.

Thus Claude Guéant, longtime eminence grise of Nicolas Sarkozy as well as his interior minister, declared at one point that "due to unbridled immigration the French sometimes no longer feel at home." How odd that no one in Sarkozy's government, much less Himself, ever said anything of the sort until the NF pulled even with the other parties in 2011 with poll numbers in the 20s. A UMP member pleaded almost comically with the party's leadership, "For four weeks now we've been discussing how to handle the Front. Can't we talk about our own program?"

The NF's sudden new status as the fulcrum of French politics has been a long time coming. It is the result of decades of growing displeasure with globalism and its concomitants, among them porous national borders and undigested immigration, offshoring of industrial production and lost local jobs, the bewildering malaise of lost national identity. Similar painful symptoms exist in the U.S., but the malady is much more acute in the once-proud nation states of Europe that formerly bestrode the planet.

When the European Common Market, created in the late 1950s as a free-trade zone, started transferring national sovereignty to a Brussels-based organization manned by unelected bureaucrats (think letting the U.S. be run by the United Nations), the seeds of resentment were sown. Throw an aggressive Islamism into the mix, with France now home to six million ostentatious Muslims—ten percent of the population—and the situation becomes toxic if not explosive.

Marine's father, Jean-Marie, founded the Front in 1972. The pugnacious son of a hardscrabble Breton fisherman, he lost an eye as a paratrooper fighting France's 1950s colonial war in Algeria—and boasted of using torture against bomb-throwing terrorists there. With an abiding veneration for Joan of Arc and a vision of a white Catholic France in need of moral revival, he molded the Front from several feckless right-wing factions. It was long seen, mostly correctly, as a motley bunch of Vichyites, skinhead hooligans, unreconstructed colonialists, and ultra-traditionalist, Latin-Mass Catholics.

Led by a confrontational firebrand with a trademark black eye patch who reveled in provoking polite opinion with overtly racist remarks (he famously called the Holocaust gas chambers "a point of detail" of WWII), the Front was a political untouchable. Ironically, it was Socialist President François Mitterrand who, hoping to weaken the conservative vote in the 1980s, reverted to the proportional balloting which had been banned by Charles de Gaulle as a way of bringing bipartite order to fragmented French politics. That opened the door to smaller parties. One unintended consequence was the rise of the far-right Front.

Growing support for the Front stayed under the pollsters' radar for years because few citizens would admit to interviewers they were going to vote NF. France therefore was stunned in 2002 when Jean-Marie surprisingly made it to the second round of the presidential election, beating out the popular socialist Lionel Jospin, a former prime minister. He faced incumbent Jacques Chirac, who unsportingly refused the traditional debate with his opponent (many thought Le Pen, a redoubtable, hard-punching debater, could have won). Le Pen lost in an inevitable landslide as the established parties blocked him with a strange bedfellow, conservative-socialist-communist coalition.

That was then. In January 2011 the 82-year-old Jean-Marie could say, "The situation has changed, the world has changed," as he turned the party over to his daughter after she was elected leader. "Reality has met, and sometimes surpassed, our predictions." With the euro zone sinking under its debt crisis, it was hard to argue with the Front position that European monetary union had been an error. Or, as Paris streets were blocked by the overflow of Muslims from their mosques for Friday prayers, with its warnings about the folly of naïve multiculturalism.

Marine, who in early 2011 made Time magazine's list of the world's 100 most influential people, has been key to the Front's recent quick rise. As long as the craggy, volatile Jean-

Marie was its threatening face, it was easy to relegate the party to the jackbooted, proto-fascist fringe, whatever its positions on the issues. She has changed all that. A handsome, 42-year-old blonde with a ready smile, quick wit and raucous laugh, she radiates vitality and charisma as she sweeps into a press conference in heels, tailored jeans, silk blouse and no makeup. When making some of her most incendiary answers to reporters' questions, she smiles sweetly.

Being a pro-choice, twice-divorced mother of three apparently doesn't bother the Front's traditional base of conservative Catholics. (Nor, apparently, does her living with Louis Aliot, FN vice president, also divorced.) No feminist, she deplores confrontational relations between men and women, dislikes affirmative action: "You never know whether you're hired because of your competence or because you're a woman."

Having forcefully denounced the anti-Semitism that long hobbled the NF, she laughs off extremist labels, accepting the term populist. "If it's a choice between extreme right, fascist, Nazi, or just populist, I find that one okay," she says, asking rhetorically, "What's 'extreme right' about our program?" She points out with impeccable logic that when British premier David Cameron recently called for limiting immigration to the U.K. and better assimilation, no one termed him a fascist.

Trained as a lawyer, she comfortably delivers articulate speeches laying out the Front's positions on a stronger state, law and order, nationalistic protectionism, and social welfare, spiced with a dash of flag-waving, crowd-rousing patriotism. At the party convention in Tours last January she gave a well-crafted acceptance speech with surprising echoes of Lincoln (state power should be "of the people, by the people, for the people"), and eclectic references ranging from Jean Jaurès, a major historical figure of the French Left, to the Catholic mystic writer Charles Péguy. In her stem-winding attack on "identity-killing globalization," she called it "an economic horror, a social tsunami, a moral Chernobyl. The globalized utopia is finished."

In speech after speech across France, Marine hammers home the Front's other pet themes: limiting immigration (flouting European Union rules to re-establish border customs and passport controls), pushing back against the increasingly assertive Muslim community (no head-to-toe burqas on women or public funds for new mosques), exiting the EU ("It's a dead star which seems to be there but no longer really exists"), dropping the euro currency ("It's not viable and already collapsing of itself").

The message, though provocative and often unworkable, is getting through. Some three-quarters of the French consider her "courageous," nearly half agree with her on insecurity and crime, a third on slowing immigration, while 42 percent think she is "close to people's concerns." She rapidly increased the Front's poll numbers, some even showing her close to winning the presidency.

Obviously polls are not an election. But they were borne out in real time in the March 2011 local elections, the last big test before the 2012 presidential ballot. The resurgent socialists got 36 percent to the faltering UMP's 19 percent. But the shocker was the Front's 40 percent in the cantons where it put up candidates. In just a few months, it had gone from marginal to mainstream.

In that it is surfing on the same wave of discontent that is lifting populists across Europe. From Scandinavia to Italy, right-wing parties are shaking up the political scene, whether it be the True Finns in Finland, the Danish People's Party, Austria's FPÖ, the Swiss People's Party or Italy's Northern League. As the conservative French commentator Guy Sorman observed recently, "Given a slow economy, a failed welfare state, and uncontrolled immigration—challenges for which no mainstream parties on the right or left have any coherent proposals—the appeal of the far right's soft populism will continue to haunt France and Europe."

Certainly is it haunting Nicolas Sarkozy. The most unpopular president in the 54-year history of the Fifth Republic is running scared. With good reason, for fully three-quarters of French voters of all political persuasions are now convinced he will lose the Elysée Palace and become a one-term president.

On issues like immigration and Islamification of French society, Marine has him stymied so that whatever he does is wrong. If he fails to take a strong line, the Front wins. If he tries to steal its thunder with copycat proposals, he only makes the Front's program more appealing: why vote for an imitation when you can have the real thing? Fully aware of that, some officers of his own UMP party are calling for political cooperation with the Front, while many of its foot soldiers are already moving toward voting for it.

Short of an earthshaking upset, Marine won't win the presidency. Yet it's just possible that she will succeed in demolishing the decrepit Gaullist party that has dominated French politics for half a century. But a word of caution: if her NF comes to dominate or heavily influence French policies, it could be seriously destabilizing.

Policies like dropping the euro and returning to the franc, fighting a pitched battle with the EU, and preferring a dirigiste economy to free-market capitalism would not be without big costs to France and the West. So too with Marine's position on Franco-American relations. Implementing a prickly nationalism à la Charles de Gaulle, she would withdraw France from NATO, develop a closer relationship with Russia—making Germany nervous—and generally be a difficult partner in any areas, economic, military or diplomatic, where France could possibly appear "servile" to the U.S.

So two cheers for Marine Le Pen for taking on France's political establishment and showing up its elitist hypocrisy and incoherence. But not three. Because if this lady ever became president, all bets are off.

**Update:** *Marine Le Pen predictably did not win the 2012 election. Still, her surprising score of 18 percent in the first round—a new record for the Front—topped analysts' expectations and put the fear of God in Sarkozy's second-round campaign. He courted NF voters hard but couldn't convince enough to join him. (Many, like Le Pen herself, cast blank ballots rather than vote for either mainstream party.) Paradoxically, a Socialist administration will likely* strengthen the NF as a credible conservative opposition in the National Assembly. "We have exploded the monopoly of the two parties," she boasted. "Nothing will ever be the same again."

# WHERE'S JEHANNE WHEN WE NEED HER?

In an election year, the French remember a 600-year-old national heroine.

Context: *Joan of Arc continues to inspire many a cause, as well as writers, artists, and film makers. She is a universal symbol of courage, determination, and resistance to the powers that be. French politicians found that useful in the 2012 ballot.*

EYEBROS UP in feigned sincerity, shoulders hunched against the damp cold, Nicolas Sarkozy glanced at a mutilated statuette of a medieval girl warrior missing one arm and ducked through the door of a rundown little house in the remote village of Domrémy-la-Pucelle, population 155. After a quick look around the dwelling said to be Joan of Arc's birthplace in 1412 (no matter that it was actually built much later) the French president unveiled a commemorative plaque, met a handful of local dignitaries, and greeted a sparse crowd of shivering citizens. It was the first time a sitting president had visited the village since 1920, when the Catholic Church canonized Jehanne d'Arc (the medieval version of her name) and she became France's patron saint.

If Sarkozy was on the hustings in this remote, little-visited corner of Lorraine some 200 miles east of Paris, it was because he was running for his political life in 2012 as the first round of France's presidential election loomed in April. Lagging in the polls for months as the most unpopular president since the founding of the Fifth Republic in 1958, he was beating the bushes all over the country and working every angle. In Domrémy he was exploiting Joan of Arc to work the patriotism angle, a ploy to help counter the growing appeal of the populist National Front's Marine Le Pen. (Le Pen early on identified with the Maid of Orléans by symbolically naming one of her daughters Jehanne.)

He also hoped to recuperate the right wing of his own UMP party, many of whose disappointed members were absconding to the Front. "There was a feeling in the last election in 2007 that Sarkozy was a new Bonaparte, a De Gaulle or even Joan of Arc, who would save France from its problems," said Jean Garrigues, a historian at the University of Orleans. "That's why the disappointment among his followers is so great."

Thus Sarkozy's hurried January pilgrimage to launch the official commemoration of the 600th anniversary of the mystical peasant girl who symbolizes French nationalism and resistance to foreign interference—oblivious to the fact that this is the very opposite of the soulless European Union that he defended so ardently until recently. In a frigid local gymnasium he pointedly invoked France's Christian roots, calling her the symbol of its unity and insisting that "Joan belongs to no party, to no faction, to no clan." She was, he said, "the incarnation of patriotism, which is the love of one's country without the hatred of others." It was a nice try by Sarkozy at tarring the Front with xenophobia and putting Joan on his side. But as a political symbol she was already taken by the National Front.

She's been its icon since the 1980s, when it began celebrating her every May Day as an antidote to the Left's Labor Day braying. A life-size statue of Joan in full body armor stands guard at the entrance to the Front's headquarters in suburban Paris. Its May Day rally is invariably at the foot of the superb gilded equestrian statue of Joan near the Louvre—my favorite in this city of monuments—with her right arm thrusting high her banner and her frowning young face the picture of fierce resolve. And it was there the next day that the Front's founder and Marine's father, Jean-Marie, shot back at Sarkozy that Joan certainly did not belong to politicians that only spoke of her at election time, or "parties that gave over France to globalization, that want to dissolve it in a federal Europe, or that have permitted massive foreign immigration." *Touché!*

It was hardly surprising that Joan of Arc was a touchstone in a French election marked by voters' disoriented malaise due to unemployment, deindustrialization, undigested immigration, rising criminal violence, and a pervasive, confounding sense of lost identity. It's still another measure of the power of Joan's universal symbolism of gutsy valor and moral certitude. She has long been recruited for all manner of causes, and not only in France. At one time or another, seemingly everybody has wanted a piece of her for their own reasons.

After the French themselves neglected her for nearly half a millennium—the naughty Voltaire mocked her as an "unfortunate idiot"—19th century monarchist Catholics resuscitated Joan as a bulwark against godless republicanism. As her image gained momentum, the U.S. put Joan, garishly painted, on a WW I fund-raising poster. In the 1920s flappers adopted her bobbed hair as an early symbol of women's liberation. Later feminists in the U.S. and Canada—not France—claimed her, ignoring that historians note she had a girly side, requesting cloth for dresses in towns she liberated from the English. During France's World War II occupation both the collaborationist Vichy regime and the anti-Nazi resistance co-opted her. Post-war, Latin American revolutionaries idolized Joan as one of the first to resist the powers that be, a sort of female, medieval Che.

Writers and film makers latched on to her and retold her story endlessly. Her unyielding dignity in standing up to her malicious inquisitors inspired writers from George Bernard Shaw to Bertolt Brecht and Jean Anouilh. Mark Twain thought his *Personal Recollections of Joan of Arc* was his best work, Huckleberry Finn notwithstanding. Jean Seberg and Ingrid Berman tried to incarnate her, with varying success, but of the 15 films about her, Carl Dreyer's silent1928 movie, *The Passion of Joan of Arc* is still the gold standard at capturing her mysticism. Today anyone can try his hand at being Joan; the *Jeanne d'Arc* PlayStation game has her fending off both attacking demons and the English army.

Could summoning the indomitable spirit of the illiterate girl who changed the course of the Hundred Years War suffice to win Nicolas Sarkozy a second term? His record was actually not all that bad, even if not comparable to lifting the siege of

Orleans or booting the Goddons (Joan's charming pronunciation of the common English oath) out of France. He did launch major reforms of pensions and higher education. He reacted energetically to the financial crisis that nearly destroyed the euro. He managed to look valorous in supporting the Libyan uprising with military force. If voters were policy wonks, he could squeak through.

Especially since his chief rival and frontrunner in the polls, the Socialist Party's François Hollande, could never be confused with Joan of Arc. A bland party apparatchik, he has never run a company, held a national government post, or done anything else anyone can remember. Billing himself as Monsieur Normal in contrast to the twitchy, impetuous, unpredictable Sarkozy, Hollande looks and sounds on the podium like a facsimile François Mitterrand, whose intonations and mannerisms he imitates. His Marxist-style declaration that the world of finance is his "main foe," and his promise to raise the tax rate to 75 percent on incomes over $1.3 million a year has many wealthy French—and most of the country's overpaid professional soccer players—ready to pack their bags and join others already in Switzerland and Belgium.

Sarkozy's problem was that most don't vote on policy, but gut feeling. And the French found him pushy, transparently ambitious and calculating, and, worst in this style-conscious land, vulgar. This was compounded by a hyper-active, media-grabbing manner that left him over-exposed, a complaint known as Sarko fatigue. "A majority of the French simply cannot stand the idea of having him on their TV screens for another five years," observed Dominique Moisi, a senior advisor at the French Institute for International Relations. "It will be extremely difficult for him to prevent the upcoming election from becoming an emotional and negative referendum on his persona."

To be sure, a minority favored Marine Le Pen. But she could not overcome the third-party handicap of limited resources and the two mutually supportive mainline parties that colluded to crowd her out. Once again, a flawed political system produced flawed, unappealing candidates. As this petty, unsatisfying election campaign ground to a close, many French, longing for a charismatic leader they could believe in, likely felt the best candidate would be a spunky peasant girl speaking to them with resolute conviction.

Update: *America seems even more attracted to Jehanne than the French. There's many a Saint Joan of Arc Catholic parish church throughout the land, often associated with a parochial school. Other examples, at random: Both Philadelphia and Portland, Oregon, have Jeanne d'Arc statues that are reproductions of the one in Paris. Students at Cullman High School in Alabama produced and acted in a 45-minute feature film called* Joan: Maiden, Martyr, Warrior, Witch, *telling her story from four points of view. And note that the oldest trademarked brand of French Brie cheese in the U.S. is called— what else?—Joan of Arc.*

# REQUIEM FOR A FAILED PRESIDENT

No matter what his politics or programs, the French simply
didn't like Nicolas Sarkozy.

Context: *The hectic era of President Nicolas Sarkozy ended abruptly
on Sunday, May 6, 2012, when he conceded victory to the Socialist
François Hollande. Sarkozy was an anomaly in French politics, the
son of an immigrant who didn't go to the Establishment schools and
who flouted most of the conventions of the French presidency. He had
the right ideas about reforming the country, but was unable to
implement them due to an unstable, impulsive personality.*

NOTHING in his presidency became it like the leaving it. "I
take full responsibility for this defeat," Nicolas Sarkozy declared
May 6, 2012, as results from second-round ballot showed that
Socialist François Hollande would be France's new chief of state.
"I did everything I could to defend our party's ideals. Now the
French people have made their choice, there is a new president,
and he is to be respected." The tone was statesmanlike, a
dignified class act. After five hectic, erratic, politically self-
destructive years in the Elysée Palace, when he seemed
indifferent to the impact of his words and actions on public
opinion, Sarkozy had finally learned to be presidential.

His term was a case study in how to disorient and finally alienate those who believed in him and voted him into office. His defeat, making him only the second one-term president in the history of the Fifth Republic—the first was Valéry Giscard d'Estaing, beaten by another Socialist, François Mitterrand, in 1981—was an astonishing fall from grace. This pugnacious, dynamic, brazenly ambitious son of a Hungarian immigrant came into office with a sound conservative program. He promised to bring real change to French politics. He was determined to lead, push, and coax a stagnant France out of its state-dependent slough of politco-socio-economic despond.

Early polls ranked him the most popular president since Charles de Gaulle 40 years ago. "The French people have chosen change," he declared on his victory night in May 2007. He pledged to "break with the ideas, the habits, and the behavior of the past." He praised "those who get up early to go to work," vowed to encourage entrepreneurship. With his free-market ideals and vocal admiration for the U.S., pundits dubbed this edgy outsider who had not gone to the right elite schools, this self-described "little Frenchman of mixed blood," *l'américain*. He took it as a compliment. He began his first day in office jogging in a T-shirt emblazoned NYPD.

He made some right moves. Public sector workers went on strike over his reform of their generous retirement benefits? He faced them down. He correctly identified France's absurd, Socialist-decreed 35-hour work week as an obstacle to prosperity, and took initial steps to end it. The labor market was too rigid; he made it easier to hire and fire. Retirement age was increased from 60 to 62. He ended France's knee-jerk anti-Americanism, bringing it back into NATO's integrated military command.

Sarkozy also got credit for banning the controversial head-to-toe burqa worn by some women in France's growing Muslim community, and cleaning out gypsy settlements that were causing trouble. Along with Germany's Angela Merkel he helped cool Europe's sovereign debt fever and stabilize the euro. Although he initially missed the importance of the Arab Spring, he later prompted the military campaign against Libya's Muammar Gaddafi.

But while this was going on, he was losing contact with the French themselves. For one thing, they couldn't keep up with this man in motion, whose basic political tactic was to keep moving and produce new programs, proposals, and laws as fast as possible. Those initiatives went by so fast in a blur that they were often unperceived and unappreciated. For another thing, the French soon came to find the man's personal style, or lack thereof, repugnant.

They could accept that he was hyperactive, with an endless supply of new ideas and projects—including, unfortunately, doubling his salary to $360,000 and ordering up a fancy new presidential jet modeled on Air Force One. But in this country where the chief of state is endowed with the majestic trappings of monarchy, they could not admit that he appeared grasping, common, gauche. In a word, *unpresidential*. It was Nicolas Sarkozy's political tragedy that a man so in love for decades with the idea of becoming president that he confessed he thought about it every morning while shaving, was unable make the transition to presidential class once elected. Strange to tell, this man with three decades of political experience appeared to lack political instinct.

To start with, there was his turbulent, and very public, love life. Everyone knew that Cécilia, his second wife and mother of their 11-year-old son, left him briefly for another man in 2005, while he consoled himself with a political journalist. But when the capricious lady humiliatingly repeated that caper only weeks after he was sworn in, they were embarrassed. And taking up on the rebound with an Italian model-cum pop singer, an acknowledged man-eater who declared "Monogamy bores me terribly," was a bit much even for the broad-minded French. The derisive giggling began when he giddily announced at a press conference, "With Carla, it's serious." Like some love-sick adolescent. "It's Snow White marrying the dwarf," quipped one comic, wickedly referring to his diminutive stature and tango-dancer elevator heels.

Ever conscious of their image in the world, the French were even more distressed that their president was being mocked in the foreign press. Italy's *La Repubblica* noted with distaste that the man sitting "on De Gaulle's throne" was "a shirt-sleeved president in Hollywood sunglasses who received his ministers with his feet on his desk, using the familiar *tu* form of address with everyone." German newspapers found him "shameless, irritating, narcissistic, a new Napoleon." They noted that Chancellor Angela Merkel disliked his familiar manners, especially the way he hugged and kissed her on both cheeks at every summit. The British press, miffed that he had dared respond to the Queen's formal invitation to visit by cutting his stay a day short, dismissed him as "a soap opera star." Worried a senior advisor at the French Institute for International Relations, "Can he incarnate France with dignity and legitimacy?"

Then, too, the man was just plain unpleasant. Not the sort you would want to have a friendly drink with. Unlike successful politicos the world over, he couldn't even pretend to like people in general. Seemed to scowl more easily than smile. Known for a hair-trigger temper, he stormed out of an interview with CBS when an American journalist dared ask a question he found offensive. His own staff he berated as imbeciles, cretins, and worse. When a member of the public at an agricultural fair declined to shake his hand, Sarkozy tongue-lashed him, "Go to hell, you poor bastard!" Some began to wonder whether the nuclear button was safe with someone so irritable and impulsive. Others wondered what he was smoking.

His popularity plunged from a record 67 percent to a low of 37 in his first year. His own electorate began to turn against him. In the first municipal ballot of his term, some candidates in his UMP party quietly asked him to avoid campaigning for them and deleted the party logo from their leaflets. In a sign of political failures to come, they lost 38 of France's largest cities and towns to the Socialists. It was an early, stinging rebuke to Sarkozy.

Allegations involving dirty money dogged him all during his term. There was the so-called Karachi case, a murky affair centering on kickbacks on a 1994 sale of three French submarines to Pakistan. The money, it was charged, went to fund the 1995 presidential campaign of Edouard Balladur, of which Sarkozy was financial director. His own campaign in 2007 came under official scrutiny due to claims that Sarkozy had received millions in illegal contributions from Lillian Bettencourt, heiress to the L'Oreal fortune and France's wealthiest woman. This spring, a Paris investigative news site published an Arab-language document purporting to prove that he had accepted over $60 million from Muammar Gaddafi to finance his 2007 election. With several investigations ongoing, none of these allegations has been proven. But Sarkozy's need to constantly counter such charges was a frequent distraction from the business of governing—and from campaigning for re-election.

He delayed the start of that campaign until the beginning of this year, far later than his advisors wanted—and months behind the start of François Hollande's campaign—spurring speculation that he might not want to risk rejection due to his unpopularity. When it did begin it was often ill-tempered and belligerent. It also bore the mark of improvisation. Battling a 64 percent disapproval rating and polls that consistently showed Hollande winning by a comfortable margin, Sarkozy erratically changed direction and sprang new programs and promises almost daily. Mainly he veered further and further right in hope of siphoning off votes from the National Front (a disastrous tactic that cost him vital votes from the moderate center and independents), hammering the message that he would save France from Islamists. He would cut immigration by half, closing France's borders, in violation of European Union agreements, if necessary.

Grasping at straws late in the campaign, he attempted, unconvincingly, to cast himself as the people's candidate. He used a video showing him with Barack Obama, suggesting that the American president backed him. He made excuses for his record, claiming that he was distracted early in his term by his failing marriage, and had to deal with the world financial crisis. In the campaign's final days he resorted to that tired old loser's pose: he was the victim of a biased media that hated him. His supporters physically harassed journalists at his rallies.

Sarkozy's last hope was a knockout blow at the single televised debate on May 2 with François Hollande, who was running as a calm, easygoing Monsieur Normal. He and his inept staff thought the Socialist was a creampuff who would buckle under attack. Another miscalculation. It quickly turned ugly as Sarkozy called Hollande arrogant and other names, and repeatedly shouted "Liar! Slanderer!" in reply to his remarks. It didn't work as the Socialist kept his cool and mocked Sarkozy for refusing to stand on his record. A majority of viewers thought Monsieur Normal won.

Having botched his term, Sarkozy has left his UMP party a shambles and France arguably worse off than when he took office. The National Front is now in a position to attract disaffected UMP members and fashion a new conservative party centering on NF programs and values. For the first time in its history, it will likely win seats in the National Assembly in the June legislative elections. As its leader, Marine Le Pen, mockingly asked a crowd of followers, "How does it feel to go from being fascists, racists and xenophobes, to people who are being eagerly courted?"

Sarkozy's legacy to France is a tarnished presidency, a revived, victorious Socialist Party, and an economy burdened with a record debt of $2.24 trillion and counting, some $500 billion more than the day he took office. Unemployment stands at 10 percent and has been growing by the month. Although he tried to hitch France to the German locomotive, the reality is that it is falling further behind Europe's economic powerhouse.

A lawyer by trade, the man himself has little to worry about, except possibly those ongoing investigations for alleged corruption. He said that he would leave politics permanently. Asked during the campaign what he would do after the presidency, he answered, "Make a lot of dough and live *la dolce vita*." Now, rejected by a French electorate he never really connected with, he can be on his way to the life of easy wealth that always seemed to be his goal.

Update: *Sarkozy confirmed that he intended to retire from active politics. After a vacation with Carla and their baby daughter in a villa in Marrakesh on loan from Morocco's King Mohammed VI, he planned to return to law practice at the Paris firm he still partly owns. But he was expected to be called for questioning, either as a witness or potentially as a suspect, in the corruption cases that plagued his years as president. In France, presidents have immunity from prosecution, but lose that a month after leaving office.*

# COLOR FRANCE RED

France's new president looks like a kinder, gentler variety of
Socialist. But his programs are strictly on the left.

Context: *For someone who had no hands-on governing experience at
the national level, much less credible acquaintance with foreign
affairs, François Hollande moved into the French presidency with
apparent ease. Understanding symbols as Nicolas Sarkozy did not, he
spent election day and voted in Correze, his political base in rural
France (one of Sarkozy's handicaps was having no rural roots). He
immediately began introducing some symbolic measures by decree, such
as a 30 percent pay cut for himself and government ministers, and an
increase in a benefit paid at the start of the school year. Other symbols
included taking the train to Brussels for an EU summit, and applying
gender parity in the new cabinet (17 men and 17 women).*

THE OMENS were inauspicious.

François Hollande wanted to celebrate his first day in
office, May 15, by riding up the Champs Elysées in an open-top
car to predictable cheers. It's an old and honorable French
custom, using the grandiose setting of the world's most famous
avenue for a bit of harmless self-aggrandizement. But the
political gods, presumably conservative, chose to greet this
newcomer, a career politico with no government experience who

owed his election largely to the sex scandal that demolished Dominique Strauss-Kahn's candidacy, with a cold shower. The drenching downpour soaked his suit and fogged his glasses as he doggedly smiled and waved, trying to set the tone for a presidency he had promised would be one of "dignity but simplicity." And they weren't finished with him. When he later took off for Berlin and a date with Chancellor Angela Merkel, they struck his plane with lightning, forcing him to return to Paris and take a back-up.

It's a measure of Hollande's low-key, unflappable character that he managed it all with affable aplomb. Indeed, we might be looking at the first president in post-war France who can actually be called—get this—unassuming. But make no mistake: Hollande may seem bland, but he is a dyed-in-the wool Socialist apparatchik who declared during his campaign, "the world of finance is my enemy." His election makes France red all over.

Having won the ultimate prize of the presidency, the Socialists now control the town halls in every big city and all but one of the country's 22 regions. With the conservative UMP party left in disarray by Nicolas Sarkozy's humiliating defeat and abrupt departure from politics, the right is unlikely to keep the majority in the National Assembly it has had since 2002, losing control to a Socialist-led coalition. Polls suggested left-wing parties could get better than 45 percent of the vote in the first-round ballot June 10, while the UMP, with no clear coalition partners, was trailing with numbers in the low 30s. (Parliamentary elections were held after this went to press.)

Holland himself enjoyed a strong 61 percent approval rating in early polls of his presidency. That's less than the 65 percent Sarkozy garnered at the start of his term, but much better than the 54 percent for François Mitterrand, the last Socialist president and Hollande's mentor, when he took over the Elysée Palace in 1981.

At this early point, Hollande looks like a sleeper. After DSK self-destructed in a New York hotel, he came from behind to seize the Socialist Party's nomination last year, overcoming opponents like party leader Martine Aubry and other grandees. Generally considered a 97-pound political weakling (Aubry herself called him "spineless") who had rarely set foot outside France and demonstrated little grasp of foreign affairs, he began his first week in office with a dizzying round of international summitry. During his visit to Berlin he stood up to the redoubtable Angela Merkel. He appears to have convinced her that the recently inked, austerity-based European Union fiscal pact must be renegotiated to include chapters on growth and job creation. That won him applause from other EU leaders resentful of Germany's iron insistence on fiscal rigor as the only solution to Europe's debt crisis.

At each of his following meetings with world leaders—a one-on-one get-acquainted talk at the White House, the G8 at Camp David, the NATO summit in Chicago, an EU conference in Brussels—he surprised with his sure-footed grasp of the issues. And his lack of strutting hauteur. You could almost hear a sotto voce sigh of relief from other summiteers over not having to put up with the aggressive, grandstanding Sarkozy. He came as close as a Frenchman can to being unpretentious. Asked at a Chicago press conference if he felt a bit American, he replied simply, "I try to be a Frenchman, hoping to convince the Americans that we have common interests. I'm just myself." Try to imagine any Fifth Republic president from Charles de Gaulle to Giscard d'Estaing to Jacques Chirac saying that. In Brussels, where he arrived by train as a frugal contrast to the high-living Sarkozy, he ventured to mock the long-windedness of the other EU chiefs of state. "Who knows why some of them talk a good part of the night," he quipped with faux naiveté.

But Hollande's Mister Nice Guy number goes only so far. He immediately began implementing some of his campaign pledges—all tinctured with mainlining Socialism. He had promised to withdraw France's military contingent from NATO's ISAF force in Afghanistan this year? He announced at the Chicago summit, to the muted dismay of the U.S. and other participants, that France's 2,000 combat troops would indeed be out two years earlier than the Alliance's target date for withdrawal, at the risk of destabilizing the established plan to let Afghan forces take over gradually during the next 30 months. (Some non-combat units will remain for training, education and humanitarian missions.)

At home, he swiftly decapitated the French police system, replacing the chief of national police, the Paris police prefect, and the head of the domestic intelligence service with cronies loyal to him. He wowed the feminists with a cabinet staffed equally by men and women in ministerial posts. He pleased his leftist constituents with a symbolic 30 percent pay cut for himself and cabinet members. Workers of the world will unite to applaud the start of Hollande's anti-capitalist witch hunt. That includes requiring top executives of state-controlled companies like the railways and utilities to reduce their salaries to no more than 20 times their employees' lowest wage, demanding that the former head of Air France renounce his $500,000 golden parachute, a 75 percent tax rate on income over $1.25 million, and higher wealth taxes.

The start of the new era of Socialist free-spending is marked by creation of 60,000 new teaching jobs, though exactly why and where these instructors are needed is unclear. Then there is a lower retirement age, bringing it down to 60, a 25 percent increase in the annual welfare payments at the start of the school year—intended to help poorer families purchase school books and children's clothing, but more often spent on smart phones and flat-screen TVs—and a boost to the minimum wage.

Left deliberately vague is how this new spending will be financed in a country whose coffers are notoriously empty—the previous government's premier declared, "France is broke." Hollande's Delphic answer, "We'll find it somewhere," can only be Socialist-speak meaning taxpayers' pockets and higher taxes on company profits. With public spending already accounting for 56 percent of GDP and the IMF forecasting a deficit close to 3.9 percent next year (he has promised to reduce it to 3 percent), Hollande will have very little wiggle room. For one thing, he will have to find an extra $25 billion in savings annually to meet that deficit goal. His new spending alone will account for nearly that much. But there is always that old ploy of a new party in power: the more difficult budget choices will wait until a complete audit of public finances is in. Anybody want to bet against Hollande announcing gravely that the Sarkozy administration was less than truthful about France's finances and he will have to trim back some promises?

Personally, his finances are just fine. In fact, he has amassed a tidy fortune while working for the Socialist Party to improve the lot of the laboring masses. Though the source of his wealth remains vague, it has come out that he is worth something over $1.5 million. That includes his Paris apartment near the Eiffel Tower, two others on the Riviera in glamorous Cannes, a villa in the chic, arty hilltop village of Mougins, where Pablo Picasso used to hang out, and a number of bank accounts. Somehow all this puts the self-declared value of his holdings conveniently under the sum that would make him officially rich, i.e., liable to France's wealth tax.

His private life is just as complicated. On election night, for instance, he addressed massed supporters at Place de la Bastille while flanked on one side by his former mistress, Ségolène Royal, with whom he had four children while never marrying, and on the other by his current one, Valéry Trierweiler, a hard-eyed, 47-year-old, twice-divorced journalist. Marriage is against his Socialist principles. Or as he puts it, "Marrying is not something one does on the pretext of being president." Thus it is that for the first time in France's long history, its chief of state lives with a consort without benefit of matrimony. Call her First Girlfriend.

Scoff if you will, but this has puzzled French diplomats at the Quai d'Orsay losing sleep over how the presidential concubine should be addressed, and how to list her on official invitations. Should it be "Madame Valérie Trierweiler, companion of the President"? How about stretching the truth to "Madame Valérie Trierweiler-Hollande, the president's spouse"? The superlatively tolerant Gauls, of course, shrug this off. As did Michelle Obama when she entertained wives and one French girlfriend at the White House during the G8. But inconvenient protocol could complicate official visits to more traditionalist, less liberal societies like India, Indonesia, and Saudi Arabia, to name a few that come to mind. The Vatican is sure to veto the idea of a joint Papal audience. And when it comes time for a state visit to the United Kingdom of Great Britain and Northern Ireland, how do you explain these living arrangements to the straitlaced old lady who inhabits Buckingham Palace?

There will likely be ample time to work all this out. With the fragmented conservative opposition now marked by post-election squabbling, finger-pointing and infighting, the Socialists can probably look forward comfortably to two five-year terms in the Elysée Palace with a majority in the National Assembly.

Update: *That is a scary prospect for the minority of the French population not living on handouts. With Hollande's declared policy of soaking the rich, many of France's wealthiest families—plus a good many of its professional athletes and show business stars—have been heading for the exit. "It's open season on the wealthy in France," says a happy executive at a Lausanne-based company that offers customized services to those eying a move to Switzerland. "The number of French asking us for assistance has tripled in the last 18 months."*

# PART TWO: *LA CULTURE*

IT'S AN ARTICLE of faith with the French that they have the world's greatest culture. To be sure, there was a time several centuries ago when the Western world looked to France as an exemplar of refinement. With culture and refinement today fighting a losing battle against mass communications, mass travel and the cult of mass man, that time is long gone. But the French cling to the myth and promote it today for all it's worth via organizations like the Alliance Française and the International Francophonie Organization.

You don't have to believe in that to appreciate the awesome magnificence of that monument to Christianity, Chartres Cathedral. Or France's other world-known monument, this one to the Industrial Revolution, the Eiffel Tower. French culture produced the intellectual renaissance of the 18$^{th}$ century Enlightenment, which made its home in Paris, as well as the astonishingly prescient observations of Alexis de Tocqueville. The place serious cultural debate holds in France was exemplified by Jean-François Revel, a sharp thinking free spirit who refused to go along with the country's *intellectuels* when they fell for Marxism and anti-Americanism.

But culture is not only formal high culture. It is also, perhaps primarily, to be found in the everyday attitudes and lifestyle that reflect the soul of a people. This includes details like when it is acceptable to use the familiar form of address, and the mythical status of women, including the notion of seduction. There is real cause for alarm when the cultural values that cement French national consciousness are under attack as the country suffers through a grave crisis of identity due to its transition from a tightly integral society to melting pot.

It was France's international reputation as a capital of culture that made Paris the headquarters of the United Nations' cultural agency, UNESCO. Unfortunately, a close look at that organization shows that its utopian ideal of promoting peace through international cultural cooperation is a much-abused chimera. It also leaves UNESCO open to manipulation by anti-Western, anti-American cliques more interested in politics than culture.

# THE CULTURE PLOY

The death of French culture? Those are fighting words.

Context: *In France a writer can officially list his profession as "Man of Letters." Certain members of the Culture Establishment are honored with a higher place at table than government ministers, just after cardinals and princes of the royal blood. Defying the common fate of mankind, they can even become an "immortal" if elected to the august Académie Française.*

FRANCE ATTACHES great importance to the idea of culture. It's an admirable trait, paying respects to culture heroes the way other countries revere businessmen or players of ball games. It's also one that long attracted talent from the world over. That began with Leonardo da Vinci, who spent his last three years comfortably ensconced in a French chateau on the Loire at the invitation of King François I, leaving behind a painted thank-you note known as the Mona Lisa. The trend accelerated in the early 20th century, when modern non-French artists from Picasso to van Gogh and Chagall did their best work in France, along with American writers from Gertrude Stein and Earnest Hemingway to F. Scott Fitzgerald and William Burroughs.

The official French attitude toward culture changed in the 1960s, when it started to become a political instrument rather than an end in itself. Until then French culture had gotten along nicely without a government ministry to look after it— check out Montaigne, Molière and Monet if you have any doubts. But Charles de Gaulle, a military man, thought culture, anarchistic by nature, needed organizing and subsidizing. He created the ministry of culture as a cabinet-level government job for his favorite conversation partner, the brooding, enigmatic André Malraux.

Although his writings were often incomprehensible to the rest of us, Malraux personified post-war French literary culture. The ministry he founded, true to Parkinson's Law, prospered mightily. Today its 11,000-odd functionaries rain millions in subsidies on everything from movies to museums, archaeology to architecture, public television to public gardens and graffiti artists. The ministry also makes French notions of culture a tool in the country's determined effort to spread its influence in the world, spending about $1 billion a year to promote them abroad.

This culture ploy takes forms like the far-flung activities of the Alliance Française, a global network of some 1,000 centers with language courses, libraries of French publications, and screenings of French films. It also sponsors something called the International Francophonie Organization, stretching membership to include such unlikely countries as Bulgaria and Moldova. Despite the best efforts of the Francophonies, French today is only the world's 12th most widely spoken language, well behind English, Spanish and Chinese.

Another result of government involvement in creativity is France's cultural chauvinism. With nearly half of programming on radio and television now required by law to be French, protectionism against "American cultural imperialism" has followed as night the day. That means high import duties on American films (except, perhaps, those with such French favorites as Jerry Lewis and Michael Moore) and television productions.

Despite official disapproval, American novelists dominate best-seller lists, American films draw nearly half of French cinemagoers—in an access of hysteria, the culture arbiters stigmatized Spielberg's *Jurassic Park* as a "threat to French identity"—American music fills French airwaves. The average Frenchman's idea of a pleasant evening watching television is either an American serial like *Desperate Housewives* or a western, preferably with John Wayne.

All this understandably causes considerable distress to officials trying to promote the country's international claim to a "cultural exception" that bans foreign cultural products while subsidizing its own. Years ago they turned a deaf ear to the late actor and singer Yves Montand, usually a staunch supporter of leftist causes, when he wryly counseled, "Sure, let's bombard the Americans with great novels and films. Let's compete with them intelligently, without demagoguery—if we can."

So far they can't. Today's signs of the times don't bode well for the vitality of French culture.

The art scene is moribund (can anybody name a contemporary French artist?). Paris auction houses have lost most business to New York and London. Creativity in the theater is anemic: the hit of a recent theater season was still another version of an ancient American musical called West Side Story. Publishing? True, hundreds of new novels are published in France every year, but their subjects and treatment are so parochial, obscure, or otherwise boring that only an exceptional few will be picked up by foreign publishers; meanwhile, nearly a third of the fiction in French bookshops is translated from English. Periodicals? The big event this year is the arrival of a French edition of *GQ* magazine. Films? The 1950s *nouvelle vague* that revitalized world cinema is a distant memory. Today the dozens of mostly mediocre, government-subsidized films produced annually go unnoticed by the world at large. The exception is *The Diving Bell and the Butterfly*, which won a Golden Globe as best foreign language film. Its director is American.

On the other hand, French museums, filled with plundered treasures from places like Vienna, Venice and Egypt, still attract crowds. One big museum attraction, though, did cause some concern about the direction of French cultural offerings. The usually staid Bibliothèque Nationale, apparently groping for a blockbuster exhibit, put its secret archive of erotica on public display. Limited to serious researchers until now, the collection included nearly 400 items, ranging from a handwritten manuscript by the Marquis de Sade, to 17th century engravings of sexual gymnastics and flagellation novels. Also on view under suggestive red lights are ever-so-cultural inflated genitalia, sadism, and of course, bestiality.

Meanwhile, the insatiable French craving for Americana reaches improbable heights—or depths. In recent years they have imported, wholesale, Halloween, an American creation with no connection whatever to French history, tradition, or culture. With scary masks and pumpkins filling Paris shop windows in October, some have tried manfully to explain, ex post facto, that it *must* originally have been Breton, or maybe a custom of the prehistoric Gauls. Whatever. And what do we hear now at Christmas instead of the charming traditional hymn, *Il est né le divine enfant?* It's *Jingle Bells*, or better, *Jingle Bell Rock*.

Even those incubators of French culture, the universities, have begun aping their American counterparts. Instead of simply informing successful graduates without ceremony that they have won their degrees, they are contriving commencement exercises copied on the American model, complete with profs in gowns and degrees suitable for framing. "With a little imagination," sighed one Paris newspaper happily, "you would think you were on the Harvard campus."

With polls showing that Americans consider French cooking much more interesting than French culture, it's easy to see why the European edition of *Time* would be tempted to publish a cover story impishly entitled "The Death of French Culture." The reaction was injured outrage. Rather than laughing it off, which would require self-confidence, a sense of humor, and a certain detachment from one's self-importance, the French Cultural Establishment took to the field of honor as one man to strike back.

Righteous rebuttals were fired from all sides. French philosophers like Marcel Gaudchet and René Girard (who?) are very big in the U.S., it was claimed. And despite "Anglo-Saxon hegemony," artists like Buren and Boltanski (ditto) bestride the international art scene. "*Non*, French culture is not dead!" shrieked *Le Figaro* on page one. Such an insolent, perfidious attack could only be the result of still another wave of virulent anti-French sentiment in the U.S., it held. The paper's knockout punch: "This land has been for centuries, and we hope, will be for centuries to come, the land of culture."

Now, you gross, uncouth, culturally challenged Anglo-Saxons, take *that*.

Update: *One area where French culture is gaining fast, is Santa Claus. Having passed Canada in answering children's letters to Santa, it sends out 1.4 million replies to 126 countries. The replies are written,* naturellement, *only in French. "Santa Claus is French, there's no question about that," solemnly explains a government spokesman.*

# MONUMENT TO THE AGE OF FAITH

It outshone every church in Christendom.

Context: *Their cathedral destroyed by fire, the people of 12th century Chartres vowed to build another, even greater. What they created became a coherent expression of transcendent meaning, an architectural demonstration of Christian doctrine that would endure against the ravages of time and the madness of the French Revolution.*

ON THE NIGHT of June 10, 1194, the people of Chartres awoke to see flames and smoke billowing from the town's celebrated Notre Dame cathedral, dedicated to the Virgin Mary. By morning the full extent of the disaster was clear: the Romanesque church, along with much of the town itself, lay in ruins. It was even feared that the fire had consumed the cathedral's most holy relic, the *Sancta Camisa*, the tunic said to have been worn by Mary when Jesus was born.

The Chartrains were bereft far beyond the usual feeling of loss for their homes, businesses and place of worship. For, according to a medieval text, they felt that they, "unhappy wretches, in justice for their own sins, had lost the palace of the Blessed Virgin, the special glory of the city, the showpiece of the entire region, the incomparable house of prayer."

But in this Age of Faith, when everything was filled with rich symbolic meaning, even such catastrophe was soon transformed into miracle. As the Dutch medievalist Johan Huizinga has described this much-maligned period, "There is not an object or an action, however trivial, that is not constantly correlated with Christ or salvation." Thus the citizens of Chartres wasted no time on self-pity. They quickly concluded that Our Lady had actually permitted the fire in order to make way for an even grander sanctuary to be built in her honor.

Exhorted by the cathedral's canons, they were determined that the new structure, whatever it would cost or however long it would take to build, would outshine every other church in Christendom. Their fervor grew when, three days later, it was discovered that the Sacred Tunic had after all been saved by two priests who had taken it down into the crypt and been protected by the Virgin from the inferno above their heads.

It normally took more than a century and many generations of workers to build most of Europe's medieval cathedrals, resulting in a mix of architectural and decorative styles in the same building. But Notre Dame de Chartres was essentially completed by 1220, only 26 years after work began, making it an unusually pure example of High Gothic architecture. The master builder in charge—in some cathedrals the builder's name is inscribed in stone, but we know nothing of the man who constructed Chartres—must have had a considerably bigger workforce than usual.

This bears out the legend that the Chartrains volunteered en masse for the job. Harnessed to carts like dray horses, it is said, they slogged painfully for miles to transport the tons of local purple-grey limestone needed for the enormous structure. As a 12th century account relates, perhaps with some pious hyperbole, "You could have seen men and women moving on their knees through thick mud, chants and hymns of joy being offered to God... Sometimes a thousand men and women or even more, are bound in the traces."

They also strove to lift the massive stones onto walls and into vaults 100 feet high, using crude levers, winches, and cranes driven by wheel-drums 20 feet in diameter turned by the feet of men inside; one slip and the block would plummet, sending the drum spinning and injuring them. But they were rewarded as the spires of Chartres rose and could be seen, as today, far across the wheat fields of the fertile Beauce region 55 miles southwest of Paris. The royal poet William the Breton wrote around 1215, "None can be found in the whole world that would equal its structure, its size and décor... None is shining so brightly."

In the process, they created more than a worthy tribute to Our Lady. Their cathedral became a powerful, coherent expression of transcendent meaning, a compendium of Christian doctrine that would endure, rock-solid, against the ravages of time, the madness of the French Revolution, and the spiritually deadening effects of doubt-riddled secularism. As Napoléon once admitted, Chartres's soaring grandeur would make even the most militant atheist feel uneasy. Today it stands as perhaps the greatest monument we have to the Age of Faith.

In his *Universe of Stone: A Biography of Chartres Cathedral*, the British writer Philip Ball describes in detail the construction and meaning of Chartres. More than that, he shows how spiritual, socio-economic and technical elements fused in late medieval Europe, resulting in a series of unparalleled structures—during the so-called cathedrals crusade from 1050 to 1350 some 80 cathedrals in France alone, plus another 500 large churches and several thousand smaller ones in every town and village—which today, non obstante sterile skyscrapers from Dubai to Shanghai, our lack of conviction makes us impotent to reproduce. Europe's Gothic cathedrals defy our usual version of Western history, "in which the Middle Ages separate the wonders of Greece and Rome from the genius of the Renaissance with an era of muddle-headed buffoonery."

The French architects and artisans of this supposedly benighted age managed to produce nothing less than a stone and glass counterpart to the whole of Christian doctrine as formulated by theologians like Thomas Aquinas, then teaching at the Sorbonne. They accomplished this partly by emphasizing simple numerical relationships like the Golden Mean in laying out the basic design of the cathedrals: a church modeled on rigorous geometrical order in length, width and height reflected the glory of God's orderly universe. As the great French historian Émile Male, put it, in the cathedrals "the doctrine of the Middle Ages found its perfect artistic form, the fullest conscious expression of Christian thought."

Mathematical calculations like the Golden Mean are one thing, actually building a huge, complicated structure successfully is another. Chartres's builders made several technical innovations, starting with a web of intersecting stone ribs to support the vault. They replaced the round Romanesque barrel vault with the characteristic Gothic pointed arches that directed thrust lines more directly downward, limiting the outward force that pushes walls apart. With these techniques, plus outside flying buttresses for additional support, they could build diaphanous walls of vertiginous height that could be opened up with large windows without fear of weakening the structure. (The medieval quest for ever higher walls with ever bigger windows sometimes led master builders to overreach themselves: Beauvais cathedral collapsed twice, the one at Troyes three times.) The architectural innovations at Chartres would serve as the template for the great French cathedrals that came after, such as Reims and Amiens.

Once the basic structure was in place, Chartres was completed with sculptures and stained glass that served mainly to illustrate the Bible and morals to the age's illiterate worshippers. Carved into its stone are some 1,800 images and scenes, including Old Testament prophets and kings, New Testament disciples and saints, the Nativity, Passion, Crucifixion and Resurrection—a virtual library of sculptured books. But medieval piety is again evident in a peculiar quirk: many of the carvings are in fact out of view, hidden in dark nooks and crannies where the artists knew they would never be seen again by human eyes. God was the only audience they needed.

Chartres's crowning glory, its stained glass, casts the nave into a mystical reddish-blue gloom, flooding it with what the poet Paul Claudel called "darkness made visible." Of its original 185 windows, an amazing 152 have survived nearly 800 years of war—they were removed to safety during WWII—political vandalism and acid rain. (Not all the recent windows are entirely French: one in the south transept was financed by the American Institute of Architects.)

Never since surpassed in quality, they were colored with metal oxides while molten, using copper for ruby, antimony for yellow, iron for green. The inimitable *bleu de Chartres* was created with a cobalt compound unknown in northern Europe; it was apparently imported specially from the Mediterranean area. The immense rose windows of the west front, with Jesus sitting in judgment, and the north transept with Mary cradling the Christ Child, radiate starbursts of color as the light changes throughout the day.

Chartres may well have been a model of God's universe and the new Jerusalem, it also existed on a very human level, serving social as well as religious functions. Besides being a temple, it was a town hall, social club and marketplace. A dormitory too, the long nave (built to accommodate 10,000 to 15,000 worshippers) sloping toward the entrance so the floor could be sluiced with water to clean up after the hordes of pilgrims who slept there.

Thus the stone and glass imagery reflected many secular subjects. Sculptured motifs in the south door show the liberal arts—Euclid's figure denoted geometry, Aristotle dialectics, Boethius arithmetic, Ptolemy astronomy—while those in the north portal show signs of the zodiac and months of the year symbolized by figures planting, cultivating, and harvesting, with February showing a sturdy peasant warming his feet by a fire.

Craftsmen from carpenters to wheelwrights and stonemasons contributed windows depicting them in bright colors at work.

Even moneychangers were allowed to set up shop in this temple, the canons carefully stipulating that their dues go to the chapter as a whole and not only to the dean. Many merchants hawked their wares when there was no religious service. Wine dealers, for instance, could sell their products tax-free in the nave. When they broke open a new barrel, one of their cries went, "New wine, just freshly broached, smooth and tasty, pure full-bodied, leaps to the head like a squirrel up a tree."

Vignettes like this of medieval life as it was offer a new appreciation for this period in Western history: the astonishing skill of its craftsmen, the faith-based richness of lives, certainly less comfortable physically than ours, but filled with spiritual meaning.

Update: *Chartres continues to inspire. The atheist Swiss writer and intellectual gadfly Alain de Botton, a London resident, recently proposed a network of temples for atheists, secular spaces for contemplation, starting with a huge black stone tower in London and spreading across Britain. It could be financed, he says, by many small private donations, "just like Chartres Cathedral." Nice idea, but without the powerful faith that motivated the medieval people of Chartres, good luck with that.*

# STILL STANDING TALL

The Eiffel Tower is not only an engineering triumph, it is also colossally beautiful.

Context: *The French were shocked,* shocked, *by the very idea of a 1,000-foot iron tower as the centerpiece of the 1889 world's fair to be held in Paris. It would disfigure the city, the self-appointed arbiters of taste said. More to the point, it was one of the most audacious engineering projects ever undertaken.*

DID YOU HEAR the one about the lady who married the Eiffel Tower? No, really. Erika La Tour Eiffel had had other infatuations with objects, including Lance, the bow with which she became an archery champion, and the Berlin Wall. But, now in her late 30s, she tossed those over and promised to love, honor, and obey the tower in a private ceremony in Paris. She duly changed her name to reflect her marital status. A photo showed the smiling, comely newlywed hugging her riveted husband, who maintained a dignified reserve. Admittedly, said Erika, there is already a bit of a problem in the marriage: "The issue of intimacy, or rather lack of it."

Maybe Erika fell under the tower's spell. Hearts beat faster there, as evidenced by a physiological study done the year it was built. The savants noted that, "On rising by elevator to the third platform, the pulse beats faster, and, especially in women, there is a psychic excitement that is translated by gaiety, animated and joyous conversation, laughter, and the irresistible desire to go still higher—in sum, a general excitement." The people at the TripAdvisor website concur that it inspires romance. After in-depth study, they concluded that the Eiffel Tower is the number one place in the world to propose.

Okay, Erika does live in San Francisco, and maybe this, as the French expression has it, explains that. But the Eiffel Tower has indeed stirred strong emotions ever since its construction for the great Paris World's Fair of 1889. To start with, many in this change-resistant country were scandalized by something so daring and, well, *different*. In 1888, with the tower rising to its ultimate height of 1,000 feet faster than seemed possible, some 40 self-appointed arbiters of taste, including the composer Charles Gounod and the writer Guy de Maupassant, signed a strident petition protesting against "the erection in the heart of our capital of the odious column of bolted metal." Maupassant in particular later sulked that he left Paris because of "this tall, skinny pyramid of iron ladders."

But the public, then as now, loved the tower. Nearly 2 million visited it during the fair. Not only the great unwashed, but also the likes of the Prince of Wales, the King of Greece, the Shah of Persia, and Archduke Vladimir of Russia, not to mention Buffalo Bill Cody. An impressed Thomas Edison rode the elevators to the top and presented Gustave Eiffel, who had a small apartment there where it's said he entertained certain Belle Époque belles, with the first phonograph recording of *La*

*Marseillaise.* Edison dedicated it to "Monsieur Eiffel, the Engineer, the brave builder of so gigantic and original a specimen of modern Engineering."

The crowds kept coming. Over 200 million have visited it since its construction. Today it is one of the most frequented and, statistics show, most photographed monuments in the world, with about 7 million paid visits a year. In France it easily tops the Arch of Triumph, Notre Dame Cathedral, the châteaux of the Loire Valley, and Mont-Saint-Michel in Normandy. It also outdraws comparable attractions in the U.S. such as the Washington Monument and Statue of Liberty.

Still more crowds were attracted by the 2009 celebrations for the tower's 120th anniversary, which was marked by special exhibits at the Paris city hall and on the second platform of the tower itself. Coincidentally it got a new paint job, with 25 men, nimble employees of a Greek company that specializes in painting ships and smokestacks, clambering among its girders to brush on some 60 tons of paint in the subtle shade known as Eiffel Tower Brown. (Fortunately, past French newspaper campaigns in favor of a patriotic tower resplendent in tones of *bleu-blanc-rouge* never got off the ground.)

My own epiphany occurred one evening when I took a stroll on the Champ de Mars, not far from my home in Paris. I found myself beneath the Eiffel Tower and glanced up. Above me the gigantic, intricate tracery of crisscrossing girders soared more majestically than the columns and vaults of any gothic cathedral. I was held, fascinated—awe-struck is not too strong a word. And I was reminded of Eiffel's rebuttal to those who complained that his tower would be ugly: "There is an attraction and a charm inherent in the colossal that is not subject to ordinary theories of art," he insisted. "The tower will be the tallest edifice ever raised by man. Will it not therefore be imposing in its own way? I believe that the tower will have its own beauty."

Artists, poets and philosophers eventually came to agree. The tower has been the subject of paintings by Chagall, Dufy, Picasso, Utrillo, Van Dongen and other icons of modern art. Poets and writers like Guillaume Apollinaire, Jean Cocteau and Jean Giraudoux have rhapsodized about it. Among philosophers, Roland Barthes, grand panjandrum of Structuralism in European and American universities, has done more high-flown double-doming about the tower than any other, devoting an entire book to analyzing it. The tower eludes reason and becomes the ultimate symbol, he posits, by being "fully useless." For him it is "the inevitable sign, for it *means everything*."

Even if it doesn't quite mean everything, the tower often has meant outlandish stunts. The harebrained antics began in 1891 when a Paris baker wobbled up the 347 steps to the first platform on stilts, only to be topped later by a clown named Coin-Coin who bumped down them on a unicycle. Philippe Petit, the tightrope walker who made it between New York's Twin Towers, walked a wire for nearly 800 yards from the Trocadero across the Seine to the second platform to celebrate the tower's centenary in 1989.

Naturally we Americans wanted in on the fun. When Charles Lindbergh approached Paris to complete the first transatlantic flight on May 21, 1927, he homed in on "a column of lights pointing upward." Despite his fatigue, he couldn't resist playfully circling the tower before landing the *Spirit of St. Louis* to a hero's welcome at Le Bourget. Only a few days after American (sorry, I meant *French*, of course) troops liberated Paris and the tricolor again floated above the tower, a B-17 Flying Fortress of the U.S. Army Air Corps zoomed deftly between its legs. Later, Arnold Palmer drove a golf ball off the second platform, getting extra hang time. An ex-Marine pilot who had flown 824 missions over Vietnam aimed a Beechcraft Bonanza down the Champ de Mars and zipped under the tower. Nowadays terrorist crazies have even bigger stunts in mind: intelligence intercepts show the tower is high on the list of things al Qaeda wannabes would love to blow up.

The loss to the world's heritage would be great, for the tower represents a unique achievement. Several thousand-foot towers had been proposed by 19th century engineers to show off their growing technical prowess, notably for London in 1833 and Philadelphia in 1876. Those were never realized, but Eiffel, arguably the greatest engineer of the century, showed it could be done. Working at the forefront of the technology of the age, the man the French call *le magician du fer* had already built iron structures like train stations and railway bridges, including the highest viaduct in the world, from France to Russia, South America to Indo-China. In a spare moment he had also tossed off the internal iron skeleton of the Statue of Liberty.

Eiffel based everything on meticulous pencil-and-paper calculations, with particular attention to wind force. Working from over 5,000 mechanical drawings, he had the tower's massive stone foundations, 15,000 girders, and 2.5 million rivets in place in just over two years with no loss of life —the Brooklyn Bridge, completed in 1883, took 14 years and some 20 lives including its designer John Roebling—and 6 percent under budget. It would be hard to duplicate the feat today.

Update: *It was only in 2004 that two American mathematicians finally broke the complex mathematical code for the tower's shape that keeps it standing tall. It is, they say, a nonlinear, integro-differential equation yielding an exponential profile. Eiffel had figured that out in his head 120 years before.*

# TO *TU* OR NOT TO *TU*

The familiar or the polite? In France the question is fraught with social peril.

**Context:** *The French revel in their cultural complications despite the frequent inconvenience of getting tangled in them. For one thing, it confirms their cherished impression that they are unique, a blest condition known locally as the French Exception. For another, it makes everybody else jump through Gallic hoops to do things their way.*

THE COMPLEXITIES range far and wide. Take the normally simple question of automobile headlights. For decades, French ones were not white, like everywhere else, but yellow. "Much less blinding for oncoming cars," was the official explanation why foreign visitors had to put yellow covers over their headlights at the border. Then in the 1970s France fell in line with worldwide standards and quietly switched to white. The yellow ones, it turned out, had been after all simply a gratuitous complication— although it did have a certain use as a xenophobic tool that made foreigners, always suspect, easily identifiable at night.

Visiting foreigners are also flummoxed by the labyrinth of French closing days before learning that Thursday is the best day to get things done. Why? An unpredictable number of shops are closed on Monday, depending, maybe, on whether they were open Saturday. National museums shut tight on Tuesday, though an indeterminate number of private ones might just be open. Schools are out on Wednesday but in session on Saturday, neatly blocking any plans parents may have for weekend trips. And Friday? Well, that obviously is the beginning of the weekend in a nation with a 35-hour workweek, so your best bet on Friday is just to try a new sidewalk café.

Then there is the problem of what to call an unmarried woman. Anyone with a rudimentary familiarity with French knows that the proper term, from time immemorial, is *mademoiselle. Mais non!* Many single Frenchwomen, especially those in business or of a mature age, now consider that condescending or sexist. Perhaps borrowing a page from their American feminist sisters, they are adamant about being called *madame.* The law is no help, being tactfully unclear on that point, while traditionalist notary publics insist that official documents use *mademoiselle* for unmarried women, executives or not. Then there is the theater, where actresses are uniformly called *mademoiselle*, even if they are icons like Jeanne Moreau or Catherine Deneuve.

Such pettifoggery is all very confusing, not to say annoying, for those of us who consider simplicity a virtue that lets us get on with more important matters.

But of all the complications of French life, none is more perplexing—to foreigners and French alike—than when to use the familiar *tu* or polite *vous* form of address. The delicate, often embarrassing question of when to *tutoyer* a Frenchman is a problem fraught with social peril where one gingerly tiptoes on linguistic eggs. There are no fixed rules for guidance. Make a mistake and you can become an instant boor, make an enemy, or suddenly create a more intimate relationship than you intended. It's enough to make one nostalgic for the protojihadists of the French Revolution. True, they made somewhat excessive use of the guillotine, but at least they decreed that all citizens, being equal, would henceforth use *tu* in addressing each other.

Alas, that good and useful rule fell by the wayside as the 19th-century bourgeoisie replaced the aristocracy and sought genteel status by using *vous* in clannish ways that only they could understand. That left most speakers of French insecure, with nothing to go on but fallible instinct and feel. When they can't figure out which form to use, they have to fall back on turns of phrase, often awkward, that avoid addressing their interlocutor directly. That, of course, can only be a stopgap measure.

It happened to me when my French sister-in-law came for a visit after a long absence. For the life of me, I couldn't remember whether we had previously used *tu* or *vous*. I had to rely on increasingly gauche circumlocution until I could discreetly query my wife about it. "Oh, I've never used *tu* with her husband and she won't with you, so go with *vous*," came the reply. This, despite long being on family terms with the lady.

As one French linguist, Claude Duneton, explains, "All you have to go by are more or less changing usages. There is no rationale to it, and the possible combinations of what form to use in which situation are infinite, depending on the moment at hand and your individual inclination. That's one of the charms of our language."

Especially charming, it seems, in certain situations. As Duneton points out, "During intimate moments, the sudden change from *vous* to *tu* can deliciously increase eroticism." (So *that* is what the bluestocking bourgeoisie has been up to?) Which recalls the old *New Yorker* cartoon of two American tourists chatting in a Paris café. "And then the most wonderful thing happened," one girl says dreamily to the other. "He switched from the polite to the familiar."

But even in France there are sometimes other things to do, like working. And in the office, linguistic confusion generally reigns as everyone tries to sort out how to address each other. In some companies underlings use the respectful *vous* with their superiors, who themselves use the familiar—and condescending—*tu* with them. To avoid this many French firms, especially those in fields contaminated by American mores such as advertising and high-tech, are trying to loosen up the stiff old hierarchical structures by making the *tutoiement* permissible, or even obligatory, along with open-neck shirts and casual Friday. Jacques Séguéla, vice president of a big Paris advertising firm, never uses any form but *tu*. "It's more direct, affirmative and cordial," he explains. "It creates an atmosphere of complicity."

But the idea of using the familiar form with someone older or higher placed in the socio-economic pecking order disturbs France's old feudal reflexes. (Paradoxically, the French say *tu* to God but *vous* to the boss.) Thus contradictions and hypocrisy abound. Dignified chaps like members of the French

Academy say *vous* to each other while at the domed Institut de France, home of the Académie Française, even if they have known each other since childhood. Then they switch to *tu* once they doff their bicorne hats and step outside into the real world.

One group that staunchly holds out against creeping linguistic Americanization is the 20,000 or so families that belong to the former feudal aristocracy and today's *haute bourgeoisie*. Here the second person plural among themselves is de rigueur. Their main object in life is keeping up appearances and transmitting inheritances; the affected *vous* means everyone knows his place, stays within his own class, respects the hierarchy—and keeps everybody else at arm's length.

This can take bizarre forms. I know one family where Madame, proud bearer of "one of the best names in France," as she says, uses the distant *vous* with her children until they obtain their high school diploma. Then, as a treat, she uses *tu* with them. All the while, the children have been using *tu* with her. There is also the case of my good friends Jean-Pierre and Marie-Louise. We have known each other for a quarter-century but we still use *vous*, although they use the familiar with other friends (but *vous* with their son). I gave up long ago trying to arrive at a rational basis for our verbal relationship.

But those sly manipulators of the spoken word, politicians, are the greatest virtuosos of the *tu–vous* conundrum. Among the members of the Communist and Socialist parties, the familiar form is obligatory, reflecting true Marxist comradeship. With conservatives it's more complicated. Jacques Chirac, while president, used the familiar with his longtime political pals, but they replied respectfully with *vous*. At one point he said *tu* to his minister of the interior, Nicolas Sarkozy, but *vous* to Dominique de Villepin, his prime minister, who in turn said *vous* to Sarkozy.

Since becoming president, Sarkozy has become adept at manipulating journalists by using *tu* with them whether they like it or not, the equivalent of George Bush's nicknames. "He makes it hard for me to keep him at the necessary distance to maintain journalistic objectivity," says one newsman at *Le Monde*. "He draws us into a closer relationship than we want when trying to cover the Élysée Palace."

Still, it might be a good sign if ordinary citizens start using *tu* with him. As one sociologist explains the typical subservient French attitude toward the powers that be, "We use *vous* with the president because we're actually still living in a monarchy and you have to respect the king." Now if Frenchmen begin treating Sarkozy as a citizen-president instead of a monarch, we will know that France is indeed venturing onto the terrain—itself complicated enough—of 21st-century democracy.

Update: *Complaining of today's "galloping tutoiement," a displeased* Le Figaro *recently attributed this sorry state of affairs to "the regrettable influence of Anglo-Saxon manners and an egalitarian vision of society." One linguist, Jacques Durand, observes sadly that the disappearing* vous *is another bad sign of leveling in French society. "Some people are even calling each other by their first names," he notes with a certain refined repugnance.*

# TOCQUEVILLE BETWEEN TWO WORLDS

The best book on America was written by a 19th-century
Frenchman.

**Context:** *Alexis de Tocqueville's* Democracy in America *is the most
extensively read, highly revered, and, just possibly, widely
misunderstood book ever done about our form of government. As a
national polestar, it is cited constantly in the public discourse, making
Tocqueville the most quoted Frenchman in the English language. But
was he really pro-American?*

HIS FAMOUS PREDICTION in 1835 that America and
Russia would come to dominate the world seemed uncannily
prescient during the Cold War, when he was seized on as an
alternative to Karl Marx as a theorist of social change in a free
society. The idea of American exceptionalism, due to sui generis
institutions guaranteeing individual freedom and self-
government, had received an endorsement from, of all people, a
French aristocrat.

Today *Democracy* still influences political thinkers,
conservative or liberal—the subtlety, density and complexity of
Tocqueville's thought are such that no party owns him.
Republicans cite his doubts about bloated government and
egalitarianism, Democrats share his distaste for "bourgeois

materialism" and echo his calls for civic engagement. Most scholars seem to agree that it is, as the Harvard political scientists Harvey C. Mansfield and Delba Winthrop have phrased it, "the best book ever written on democracy and the best book ever written on America." Tocqueville reportedly was President George W. Bush's favorite political philosopher; a Tocquevillian think tank may be part of his post-White House legacy.

All well and good. But I suspect that much of the time our take on *Democracy*, which after all is only one of the many volumes that make up Tocqueville's collected writings, is slightly skewed. He was not, in fact, particularly pro-American or pro-democracy.

Tocqueville was, above all, intensely curious about the world's first big experiment in self-government. America, whose people he found generally uneducated and vulgar, was the laboratory where he could examine with clinical detachment the new and—for him and other French noblemen of the day—subversive idea that all men are born equal. As he put it, "If there is any country in the world where one can hope to appreciate the dogma of the sovereignty of the people, study it in its application...that country is surely America." He makes this point repeatedly. "I was looking for the image of democracy itself, its penchants, character, prejudices and passions," he says early in the book. "I wanted to understand it, if only to know what we should hope or fear from it."

Democratic, egalitarian society was not really his cup of tea. Much of Tocqueville's fascinating complexity is his ambivalence toward it. He wrote *Democracy*, he says in an extraordinary passage, "under the impulse of a sort of religious terror created in my soul by the sight of this irresistible revolution on the march." In a letter to his English friend, the philosopher and economist John Stuart Mill, he said that "the main task from now on will be to fight the pernicious tendencies of the new order, not to bring them about." Note the words *fear, terror,* and *pernicious* in the above quotations and you begin to understand Tocqueville's basic stance. Anyone who reads him as a fervent admirer of America or a staunch advocate of democracy had better look again.

Now comes an excellent opportunity to renew acquaintance with Tocqueville the man and his writings. Especially the man, for the British historian Hugh Brogan's masterfully researched, deeply probing new biography, *Alexis de Tocqueville: A Life*, shows Tocqueville in the round, with all his biases, doubts, flaws—and exceptional intellectual honesty and insight—on full view.

Count Alexis Charles-Henri Clérel (Tocqueville does not appear on the birth certificate, in deference to revolutionary sensibilities) was born on the afternoon of XI Thermidor An XIII, which translates as July 29, 1805, in the family's Paris townhouse near the Madeleine church. His father, Hervé, came from a long line of Norman noblemen, one of whom sailed with William in 1066 to conquer England. His mother descended from the prominent magistrate Chrétien Guillaume de Malesherbes, guillotined during the Terror in 1794 after courageously serving as Louis XVI's defense counsel at the

Revolution's kangaroo court. (In all, nine members of Alexis's immediate family were imprisoned during the Terror and five executed; his father luckily escaped the guillotine after ten harrowing months of prison that turned his hair prematurely white at 21.) Interestingly, Tocqueville was also a nephew of one of France's finest writers of the age, François René de Chateaubriand, who visited America earlier and would importantly influence him.

Brogan contends that Tocqueville, proud to belong to the *fine fleur* of old France, remained "a noble to the end of his days, and cannot be understood unless this is recognized." He made no bones about it. "I have an intellectual taste for democratic institutions," he wrote at one point, "but I am an aristocrat by instinct, that is, I fear and scorn the mob." He was immediately at ease with a fellow noble, feeling that they spoke the same language even if they had nothing but good blood lines in common. Thus Brogan's convincing assertion that Tocqueville was "caught between two worlds, unable to repose in the one where he was born, unable to go forward confidently into the one he saw rising inexorably before him."

Alexis grew up to be short and slight, with abundant curly black hair, a fine, expressive face with luminous brown eyes and, with chronic stomach problems, frail health that caused him long periods of illness. Painful anxiety and doubt dogged him all his life. That was possibly brought on by the dramatic *crise de conscience* he suffered at 16, when he lost his Catholic faith, a terrifying experience during which he felt as if the walls and ceiling of his room were shaking.

Following in the footsteps of Malesherbes, he studied law, became a junior magistrate at Versailles, and entered politics in 1839. Tocqueville helped write the Second Republic's constitution, served as vice president of the National Assembly, and was named foreign minister briefly in 1849. But his career in politics was limited by his anxiety-induced deficiencies as an orator. Worse, his ingrained aristocratic disdain meant that he disastrously lacked the necessary backslapping touch, especially with his fellow deputies in the National Assembly: "I treat them as commonplace," he commented dryly. "They bore me profoundly."

Tocqueville's sentimental life was often difficult. To put it simply, our man, a sexual democrat, had a short fuse with the opposite sex. Unconfirmed rumors spoke of an illegitimate child sired by him on a maid-servant during his adolescence. He had several youthful affairs, and may have fought a duel, before falling for an attractive, resourceful English woman living in Versailles. Mary Mottley, six years his elder, had three strikes against her: she was English, Protestant, and middle-class, all things his aristocratic family despised. But Tocqueville had a maverick streak (he eschewed the title of count) despite his proper upbringing. He found the available young noble Frenchwomen insipid and boring, and Marie, as he always called her, provided the mothering and emotional support his health and nerves required.

Their marriage in 1835 endured despite temperamental differences—he once threw her plate of pie on the floor because she ate too slowly for him—and his wandering eye, a "blind instinct which from time to time drove him crazy." In a letter to a friend, Tocqueville asks, "How could I manage to stop that sort of boiling of the blood that meeting a woman, whatever she may be, still causes me, as it did twenty years ago?" The Tocquevilles had more than their share of marital crises as a result.

When Tocqueville decided to travel to America in the spring of 1831, his motives were decidedly mixed. Officially he was going to study the American penal system and report back on possible applications in France. The real reason was to put some distance between himself and an uncomfortable political and professional situation following the fall in 1830 of the Bourbon king Charles X, to which the Tocqueville family was close. There was also the example of his favorite uncle, Chateaubriand, who had sailed for America in 1791 to avoid a similar spot of political trouble during the Revolution; his resulting book, *Voyage en Amérique*, had declared that "The establishment of a representative republic in the United States was one of the greatest political events in the history of the world."

Here might have been the germ of Tocqueville's masterpiece, just the topic he needed. And he needed a topic because his true vocation apparently was not politics, but writing. He worked hard at it, burnishing his prose until it was supple, simple, often ironic and always to the point. His 17 volumes of output are a monument of French literature.

He was 25 when he set out with his lifelong friend and fellow magistrate at Versailles, Gustave de Beaumont, who later married a granddaughter of La Fayette. They sailed on April 2,

1831 on the American ship *Le Havre*, making it to Newport, RI, in a relatively swift 37 days. During the crossing a charming American lady, Miss Edwards, helped them brush up their English, which was sorely in need of it.

New York was a shock. Instead of a primitive backwoods people, Tocqueville found the city's smart set, including the Knickerbockers, showering him with invitations to worldly parties and balls, prompting an urgent letter to his brother Édouard for a supply of silk stockings, cravats, and 24 pairs of kid gloves. Most disorienting to the young noblemen were their first vignettes of raw democracy: Governor Enos Throop staying in a simple boarding house like theirs and receiving them in the parlor; Americans writing to President Andrew Jackson as "Dear Sir;" waiters even sitting down at table with their customers. And when they later met Jackson in Washington, they were distinctly underwhelmed. The American president lived in a house "infinitely less magnificent than those of our ministers," and, with no lackeys, actually served their glasses of Madeira himself. "Formerly he was known chiefly as a duelist and a brawler," sniffed Beaumont.

At first, Tocqueville fell back on familiar French clichés to make sense of it. In letters home full of broad generalizations, he described American women (all chaste because American men were too busy for sex), American manners (unpleasantly vulgar), political parties (non-existent as far as he could tell), and gastronomy and the arts (in their infancy, *hélas*). But by the time he left New York after seven weeks, he had found his grand theme. "We are heading towards unlimited democracy," he noted. "I don't say this is a good thing...on the contrary it won't suit France, but we are driven by an irresistible force."

Tocqueville did his legwork. Over the next seven months he swept up through Buffalo and the Great Lakes to the frontier states of Michigan and Wisconsin, then doubled back to Boston, Philadelphia and Baltimore before again heading west to Cincinnati, south to Nashville and New Orleans, visiting Washington just before sailing home from New York. Along the way he and Beaumont nearly drowned in the icy Ohio River when their steamer hit a rock, and stayed in a log cabin so cold that water froze before they could drink it. Once when they complained of the discomfort of an open buckboard in Tennessee, the driver shot back, frontier style, "Go ahead, moan. The other day one of our passengers broke an arm, and another a leg."

Despite roughing it, Tocqueville scrupulously kept recording his thoughts. Before landing in America, he held the standard French view, still a basic tenet in France today, that only an elite could govern a nation's affairs. But sometime during his visit to Ohio, intellectual honesty compelled him to admit that "the middle classes can govern a state. In spite of their petty passions, their incomplete education, their vulgarity, they can demonstrably supply practical intelligence, and that is enough." This was Tocqueville's watershed moment.

Publication of the book's first volume in 1835 (the second was in 1840) made Tocqueville an instant celebrity in Paris. Accolades showered, from the Legion of Honor to membership in the French Academy. Two major works followed, *The Old Régime and the Revolution*, in which he perceptively described a France prisoner of its past and prey to class hostility, and *Souvenirs*, a sardonic, psychologically astute look at the mediocrity of French political leadership during the revolution of 1848. His poor health finally caught up with him: at age 53 he was interred in the churchyard of the Tocqueville fief on Normandy's Cotentin peninsula.

Update: *Among Tocqueville's continuing lessons for today is his contention that while freedom is indeed the natural destiny of man, "I would think it a great misfortune for humanity if liberty had to take the same form everywhere." Only by long, careful preparation and education of the people in its practice can it take root. He was thinking of France, but Americans can easily see its application to other parts of the world and its implications for the dangers of nation building, however well-intentioned it may be.*

# REVEL: FRANCE'S MAVERICK FREE SPIRIT

He told the French some unfashionable truths about America—
and themselves.

Context: *Anti-Americanism became the most ubiquitous form of racism in the latter part of the 20th century. And if you don't agree with that, your argument is not with me, but with Paul Johnson, whose judgment it was in his masterful history,* Modern Times.

FOR the European Left, those were heady days: vociferating against fascist American neo-colonial imperialism and the Viet Nam war, denouncing American companies worldwide as bloodsuckers, treating American troops in host countries like a nuisance at best, occupiers at worst. This peculiar racism, largely envy-based, continued after 9/11, with many European chattering intellectualoids and media touching bottom with cheap shots. Terrorists were justified in attacking the United States, the line went, because its ostentatious wealth and success was a provocation.

I recall this reflexive anti-American environment to point up the intellectual courage of Jean-François Revel. Like the little boy and the emperor's new clothes, he dared tell his fellow Europeans some simple but deliberately overlooked home truths. Their sanctimonious criticism of America as fascist was just a bit much, he thundered in articles and books, given that the U.S. was "a land that in over 200 years has never known a dictator, while Europe has been busy creating crowds of them." He pugnaciously rubbed European noses in things they preferred to forget: "We Europeans invented the great criminal ideologies of the 20th century," he reminded, "forcing the United States to intervene on our continent twice with its army."

As for his home country, Revel lectured the French that their irrational, endemic bitterness over American success was due to their loss of status—real or imagined—as a great power. Both left and extreme right detested America because, he observed, they hated democracy and the market economy that goes with it. He skewered leftist French thinkers from Jean-Paul Sartre to Michel Foucault for "an ideology of falsification" and accusing free societies of the flagrant flaws of totalitarian ones. The notorious French hang-up on Marxism, at a time when no other developed country will have anything to do with it? "Many French are still unable to digest the reality," he commented matter-of-factly, "that communism and socialism, the equivalent for them of a secular religion, failed."

Revel's death in the spring of 2006 at the age of 82 deprived France of one of its last great free spirits, and the U.S. of one of the last prominent French intellectuals who refused to run with the pack of yapping anti-Americanism. A man for all seasons, he was a philosopher, art critic, member of the wartime Resistance, connoisseur, bon vivant, journalist, polemicist and member of the French Academy, the closest thing to a universal man that his country has produced in a very long time. In his way, he certainly was more important than that other candidate for the title, the endlessly self-promoting André Malraux.

Ever eclectic, Revel's 30-odd books include such varied works as a three-volume history of Western thought, a literary history of food from antiquity to today, and a dialogue on philosophy and religion with his son, Mathieu Ricard, a Buddhist monk. But his most renowned works were those that took up the cudgels in favor of individual freedom. They gained him fame and, in France, dark accusations of pro-Americanism.

In a land of Jesuitical casuists, Revel, with his well-fed frame, bull neck and bullet-bald head, stubbornly stood for reasoned, fact-based analysis and, above all, intellectual independence. He shunned all ideologies and pre-mixed, one-size-fits-all systems of thought. For him, the search for truth was a full-time job involving exhaustive research and firsthand knowledge. That was what led him to look more closely, and comprehendingly, at America than any French observer since Alexis de Tocqueville.

Most French never did quite figure out what to make of Revel. He was simply too independent and original a thinker. Because his consistent theme, first strongly articulated in his 1970 best-seller, *Without Marx or Jesus*, was that political democracy and free-market economics were the only path to progress, it is tempting to consider him a conservative, what the French call a *libéral*. But he tended to shun that notion, as he did the label pro-American. Revel always thought of himself as a man of the moderate Left, a socialist with a lower-case "s." In fact, after attacking Stalinism in all its forms, from "pidgin

Marxism" to Maoism, he early on called for nothing less than global socialism based on the decline of the nation-state and reformed capitalism.

As his political evolution developed in the 1950s and '60s, Revel began by uncritically accepting the then-current French view of America as the land of McCarthyism and the execution of the Rosenbergs, of racism and fat-cat, stogy-smoking capitalists. He wrote a few speeches for a certain François Mitterrand in France's 1965 presidential election. But he was soon disgusted by Mitterrand's opportunistic rapprochement with the Communist Party. His epiphany occurred during a 1969 coast-to-coast visit to the U.S. "I was thunderstruck by how false was everything that Europeans said about this country," he later recalled, explaining his break with the organized left that stunned the hermetic French intellectual world.

But it was Revel's bombshell the following year that won him worldwide recognition. "The revolution of the 20th century will take place in the United States," he stated at his polemical best in the opening sentence of *Without Marx or Jesus*. "It can take place nowhere else." And he seemed to take pleasure in insisting that this revolution, based on individual freedom, technological innovation and free markets, would take place not in the Left's darling Cuba, but in California. Liberals from Paris to Palo Alto were shocked, *shocked*.

French media immediately caricatured Revel as a hard-line conservative, or worse, a *réactionnaire*. And as it was translated around the world, the book got almost universally hostile reviews, despite becoming a best-seller. His Swedish publisher could not obtain a single television interview for him; his Greek publisher, setting a new record for craven political correctness, actually added a preface to the book apologizing for issuing it.

Revel kept hammering at his theme that today's great conflict is not between classes but between totalitarianism and freedom. In *The Totalitarian Temptation* he tore into Europe's so-called neo-communism, "a mishmash of Marxist-Leninist and Marcusian ideas, along with third world claims that the industrialized nations are guilty of all the planet's ills." In *How Democracies Perish* he tough-mindedly mused that democracy may, after all, be only a parenthesis in man's political history. Moreover, that era might be now closing because democracies hate to take the unpleasant action necessary to defend themselves, even justifying the victory of their mortal enemies.

In his last book, the post-9/11 *Anti-Americanism* (its original French title, *L'Obsession anti-Américaine*, is more to the point), he castigated his compatriots for daring not criticize the likes of Qaddafi, Castro and Saddam, while spewing contempt for Ronald Reagan and George W. Bush. He also anticipated by several years the fiasco of the cartoons of Muhammed, pointing out lucidly that Muslims demand that "all humanity respect the imperatives of their religion, while they themselves owe no respect to any other religion."

After being taken to task for decades by him, many in the French Establishment still paid Revel tribute in death, with President Jacques Chirac praising him as "an indefatigable defender of human dignity." More important than such boilerplate statements, though, is his lasting influence. Jose Maria Aznar, the former conservative Spanish prime minister, said he drew much of his political courage to resist pressure groups and ideological dogmas from reading Revel.

We will all miss Revel's gutsy independence and his flair for provocative polemics. I fear that we shall not look upon his like in France again.

Update: *Revel's influence continues to be felt. As one of France's premier columnists, Ivan Rioufol of* Le Figaro, *told me, Revel was his model: "I adopted his method of getting the facts, calling a spade a spade, and not worrying about being politically correct," he said. "He was the heir of the Enlightenment, a cultivated free-thinker, a specimen rare today in France."*

# THE DARK SIDE OF THE ENLIGHTENMENT

With its view of life without transcendent meaning, it helped create bleak existentialism and justify state-sponsored terror.

Context: *Atheism is trendy—again. Over the centuries it periodically raises its head, from the ancients like Epicurus and Lucretius, who blithely described a purely material, pleasure-based, godless universe, to Europe's 18th-century Enlightenment. And now something called New Atheism is clamoring for attention in America.*

THE ZEITGEIST favors it. Consumption-oriented young Americans are dropping out of religion at a historic rate: fully 22 percent of 18 to 29-year-olds now claim no religion, twice the number in 1990. The American Religious Identification Survey reports that those with no religion are growing in every corner of the country, from secular Northeast to conservative Bible Belt. New Atheism believers are egged on by the movement's so-called Four Horsemen, Sam Harris, Richard Dawkins, Daniel C. Dennett and Christopher Hitchens. Their idea of a good bedtime book bears a title like *The End of Faith, The God Delusion, God: The Failed Hypothesis,* or *God is Not Great.* They loudly and proudly put their faith in no faith at all.

Now from Europe comes a candidate fifth horseman. Philipp Blom's *A Wicked Company: The Forgotten Radicalism of the European Enlightenment*, is an erudite, detailed account of the Paris literary salon where the wealthy Baron Paul Henri Thiry d'Holbach wined and dined some of the most passionate of the Enlightened. Blom, a German-born, Oxford-educated historian and novelist who lives in Vienna, is also author of a history of Europe from 1900 to 1914.

The forgotten radicalism he celebrates refers to the most anti-religion, anti-revelation, anti-God theorizing done during this period of ferment, when bold new thinking in science, mathematics, religion and politics was in the air all over Europe. (The French called it the *Siècle des Lumières*, Germans the *Aufklärung*.) Blom gladly embraces the desolate world conceived at Holbach's intellectual bull sessions, "a world of ignorant necessity and without higher meaning, into which kindness and lust can inject a fleeting beauty."

Gathered on Thursdays and Sundays in Holbach's elegant town house across the Seine from the Louvre to enjoy multi-course meals—30 dishes often filled his groaning board—were not only the French philosophes like Denis Diderot, creator of the famous *Encyclopédie*, the father of Romanticism Jean-Jacques Rousseau, and the sharp-tongued opponent of tyranny, Voltaire. From the 1750s to the 1770s the salon was also a must for foreign visitors to Paris who wanted to make the avant-garde scene.

English historian Edward Gibbon dropped in occasionally, as did the skeptical Scottish philosopher David Hume and his fellow Scot, the free-market economist Adam Smith. The great English actor David Garrick puckishly dubbed

Holbach's group "a wicked company." When Benjamin Franklin arrived in Paris in 1776, one of his first requests was, "Take me to the philosophes." He had already heard that the salon was a place where intellectual sparks flew, cold, pure reason prevailed, the ignorant, church-going masses were despised, and a good time was had by all. The Irish-born English satirist Laurence Sterne noted that "Every man leaves the room with a better Opinion of his own Talents than when he entered." Holbach knew how to flatter an intellectual.

Usually organized by aristocrats for their amusement and prestige, the literary salon was a Paris institution in these heady decades before the French Revolution. It was a stage where budding, rebellious philosophes could show off their wit and sing for their supper. It was also a way to circumvent the harsh censorship laws under Louis XVI. Penalties for publishing anything considered critical of the monarchy or the Catholic Church ranged from symbolic tearing and burning of the book by the hangman of Paris, to doing time in the Bastille, or public torture and execution. Diderot, once imprisoned for his writings, later disguised his atheistic thinking in fiction.

Holbach was born in Germany, became a naturalized French citizen and wrote in French. His most popular book, *Système de la nature* (*The System of Nature*), derided religion and an afterlife as mere superstition. (He published it in Holland under the name Mirabaud.) Man was simply a machine devoid of free will. As for belief in God, that could only be due to ignorance and fear. Another book, *Le Christianisme dévoilé* ( *Christianity Unveiled*), proclaimed Christianity to be harmful nonsense, "in no way different from all other superstitions with which the universe is infected."

This was the dark side of an Enlightenment whose most radical theoreticians were misfits who held a contemptuous, ultra-cerebral, exclusively materialist view of the human condition. Dark as it may appear to some of us, it was catnip to the likes of Denis Diderot, a sybarite with alley cat morals who agreed wholeheartedly that God and religion interfered with the Good Life. In his case the wish obviously was father to the thought.

Diderot had attended a Jesuit school and became a tonsured *abbé* headed for an ecclesiastical career until piety yielded to lust. As he tells it, "I was going to take a doctorate in theology. On my way I meet a woman beautiful as an angel; I want to sleep with her, and I do." His marriage to the simple seamstress was mainly a façade for affairs with a succession of women, including a threesome with two sisters. (No doubt good writer's research for his two erotic novels.) His succinct philosophy, shorn of all the philosophical claptrap: "There is nothing dependable but drinking, eating, living, loving and sleeping." Somehow all that living, loving, etc. did not interfere with his day job editing the monumental 28-volume, 20 million-word illustrated *Encyclopédie*.

His sometime friend Jean-Jacques Rousseau, the great Romantic, agreed. Civilized societies with their religion-based ethics, he held, enslaved men and perverted them from their "crude but natural" morality based on immediate desires and needs. Rousseau's own desires and needs would have barred him from polite society anywhere but Holbach's group. They ranged from obsessively describing how he had watched a man "manipulating himself" to seeking women willing to spank him (his subtle technique consisted of haunting alleys and dropping his pants to moon likely prospects).

To his credit, even the unbalanced Rousseau was uncomfortable with bleak reason as the only basis for a philosophy of life without meaning or spirituality of any kind. Increasingly paranoid and given to rages, convinced that Holbach and Diderot were plotting to destroy his reputation, he broke with them. Voltaire, a moderate deist, was also wary of godlessness for his own reasons: as he said, he wanted his servants to believe in God so they wouldn't rob him blind, and his wife to be pious so he wouldn't be cuckolded.

No matter. Holbach's well-fed coterie became the dreaming flower children of the 18th century. Their favorite hallucination was a brave new world where "desire, erotic and otherwise, would make their world beautiful and rich... In this godless universe there would be no more sin, no reward or punishment in an afterlife, only the search for pleasure and fear of pain." Just as today's New Atheists are opinionated and preachy, the hard-core Paris Enlightenment scorned those who disagreed. Edward Gibbon, though a skeptic, was revolted by the "intolerant zeal" of the philosophes, who "preached the tenets of atheism with the bigotry of dogmatists, and damned all believers with ridicule and contempt."

To be sure, Europe's Enlightenment was an important development in Western intellectual, moral and political history.

Its critique of the arbitrary, authoritarian state and demand for individual freedom led to nothing less than the French and American revolutions with their insistence on the right to self-government. Most mainstream Enlightenment thinkers had the good sense to distrust the human and social implications of the more radical philosophes' ideas.

But some of those ideas lent themselves to disastrous distortion. Rousseau's utopian notions of an ideal society, ultimately based on ideological manipulation and political oppression, were later used by totalitarian lunatics. Maximilien Robespierre seized on them to justify brutally de-Christianizing France during the revolution and controlling its population with state-sponsored terror. In the 20th century, Lenin and Cambodia's murderous Pol Pot, who studied Rousseau in Paris in the 1950s, cherry picked his philosophy of a society based on guilt and paranoia.

**Update:** *Ironically, the radicals of the French Revolution rejected the two arch-radicals of the Enlightenment. Robespierre and his Jacobin henchmen found the notions of God and religion, grotesquely secularized into the Goddess of Reason and worship of an abstract Supreme Being, more useful in manipulating the citizenry than outright atheism. Thus it was that the remains of Holbach and Diderot finished not in Paris's Pantheon, final resting place of France's official Great Men, but in unknown graves, their paeans to godlessness forgotten.*

# IN SEARCH OF LOST IDENTITY

The French begin to wonder what it means to be French.

Context: *What used to be one of the most integral cultures in Europe is in the throes of unwillingly becoming a melting pot. The strains are showing as a way of life is lost and is replaced by social Sturm und Drang.*

IT WAS ALMOST a century ago that Marcel Proust began publishing his 4,300-page opus, *In Search of Lost Time*. From his manuscript-strewn bed in a cork-lined room, he grappled with the conundrum of how an individual can recapture his vanished past. The time/memory puzzle is a tough one to crack, but what would Proust have made of his country's vanishing identity? Most likely he would have found the notion simply too absurd for words.

After all, he lived in a time when France had a strong, unquestioned fix on its self- image, as attested even by its very nomenclature: the people of a country called France, proud descendants of the medieval Franks, were themselves called French, their language was French, their currency the franc. Thanks to centuries of nation building and ruthless repression of minorities by French monarchs and Napoleon, this was the most tightly integrated nation in Europe when Germany and Italy were still loose collections of provinces. It was said, proudly, that French schoolchildren everywhere opened the same book to the same page on the same day, and read the same history lesson beginning, "Our ancestors, the Gauls."

Small wonder then that the basic French attitude has long been an insular, self-absorbed composite of preening pride, often frankly chauvinistic, in being French, and barely concealed dislike, bordering on fear and loathing, of change. As a people they advance reluctantly toward the future, eyes fixed firmly on the past. Then too, most French are only one or two generations removed from village life and penurious peasantry. Their mentality and manners still reflect this in their feeling for *le terroir*, or soil, their avarice and cunning, their suspiciousness of others, their distrust of modernity. The national culture has never been open to the melting pot idea.

Then came the humiliations of WWII, the loss of their colonies, the subsuming of national sovereignty in the Common Market/European Union, and hurried, catch-up modernization of the economy. Even before globalization began diluting its essence, France had changed more in recent decades than even the protean U.S. In a few dozen years it went from an agricultural country where 20 percent of the population were peasants and telephones and decent plumbing were luxuries—in Paris, I once waited three years to get a phone line—to one with a cell phone in every pocket, high-speed trains rocketing through the countryside, and three-quarters of its electricity derived from nuclear power. With this came the future shock angst of a lost way of life.

The most unwelcome change has not been economic, but socio-cultural as France has tried, and largely failed, to integrate the rapid influx from its former North African and sub-Saharan colonies. That includes some 6 million Muslims, making Islam officially its second religion. Many French whose ancestors were indeed Franks or Gauls look on with dismay as their country, once considered the eldest daughter of the Catholic Church, is covered with dozens of mosques. Its second-largest city, Marseilles, now at least 25 percent Muslim, began building the biggest one in April 2010, a $33 million-dollar structure with an 80-foot minaret that will compete for skyline with cathedral spires that now seem so hopelessly out of sync with the new France.

The consequences of France's failure to deal with its ethnic problems were driven home in December 2005, when angry, alienated minorities burned some 10,000 automobiles and trashed schools and public buildings, causing $300 million of destruction. To war cries of Allah Akhbar, they attacked arriving police with everything from Molotov cocktails to pickaxes. As wake-up calls go, it was a humdinger.

But in its autistic self-satisfaction, Paris officialdom didn't get it. France is still averaging about 40,000 cars burned annually. And the French national anthem, the *Marseillaise*, has been booed and jeered before international football matches— not by fans of opposing teams, but by ethnic Arabs born and raised in France.

The inevitable backlash is beginning. A member of President Nicolas Sarkozy's own UMP party and mayor of a town in northern France told his constituents flatly that the immigrant problem had been swept under the rug for too long. "It's time we reacted, or we'll be eaten alive," he said. "There are already ten million of them, ten million who are getting handouts for doing nothing."

More ominously, Muslims showing up recently at the main mosque in Castres, a normally quiet town of 40,000 near Toulouse, were shocked to find two pig's ears nailed to the door, the animal's mutilated snout hanging from the doorknob. The French equivalent of "White power," "France for the French," and *Sieg heil* in German were sprayed on the desecrated building's sides.

With danger signals like that flashing, the government's reaction has been a gaggle of gadgets: suggesting job seekers use anonymous CVs to give the Kemils and Mohammeds a better chance against the Jean-Pierres and Gérards; pushing schools to teach the *Marseillaise* and respect for national symbols; urging TV channels to hire multi-ethnic presenters; banning the Muslim head scarf in public schools and outlawing the head-to-toe burqa; asking France's elite colleges, the so-called Grandes Ecoles, to reserve 30 percent of their enrolment for minorities (the schools, bastions of the exclusive, self-perpetuating haute bourgeoisie, said forget it).

One of President Nicolas Sarkozy's gadgets was a vast debate on national identity so the French could discover that *je ne sais quoi* that makes them special. He launched it with an editorial in *Le Monde* acknowledging the basic verity that people "don't want their way of life, their mode of thinking and social makeup, to be distorted." It had to be admitted that "the French feel they are losing their identity." In speeches he liked to say he was elected "to defend French national identity."

Organized in town halls all over the country, the grand national talk-fest quickly became a vehicle for uninhibited immigrant-bashing. Nearly one-fifth of the comments online had to be erased as xenophobic, i.e., politically incorrect. Samples of the more publishable ones: "Being French means being white, that's all." "To be French you have to have French blood." "Being French means having to park your car in a closed garage to keep it from being burned by Arabs." When one contributor of the Islamic persuasion ventured, "We Muslims have the right to our religion and minarets," the quick response was, "France taught you to read and write so you could express your opinion. You should thank her instead of foaming at the mouth."

Sarkozy was playing with fire in an attempt to siphon off right-wing votes from the National Front party. At a town hall meeting in the eastern city of Troyes, police had to be called in to stop the screaming and scuffling; several participants singing a full-throated patriotic *Marseillaise* were dragged out as the rest of the audience joined the melee. A similar donnybrook occurred in a middle-class Paris suburb when an invited speaker, a historian, criticized his host for holding the debate, calling it Vichy-style propaganda to stigmatize immigrants.

The great identity debate that nobody asked for shows every sign of boomeranging on Sarkozy.

Update: *The populist National Front is predictably turning the debate on national identity to its political advantage. In this it has some unwitting help from neighboring Switzerland, where a referendum banned the construction of tall minarets on mosques. "Nicolas Sarkozy has involuntarily woken up the French people," says a Front leader. "Immigration is ruining French life, its finances, its security, its employment and its educational system."*

# THE DECLINE OF THE BEST

Its cuisine is one of the glories of French culture. Can it resist the general lowering of standards?

Context: *We have it on the authority of none other than President Nicolas Sarkozy that France has the best gastronomy in the world. So convinced is he that he pushed UNESCO to declare French cuisine part of the world's cultural heritage, something with outstanding universal value right up there with the Taj Mahal, Chartres Cathedral, the pyramids of Giza and the Statue of Liberty.*

WHATEVER the international functionaries at UNESCO think, there is no doubt that over the centuries France has created one of the world's most artful, complex, and enjoyable forms of preparing food, teaching the rest of us how to cook— and eat—in the process. The French preoccupation with eating well has benefited us all. As the great epicurean Brillat-Savarin put it in his *Physiologie du goût* in 1825, gastronomy is our last pleasure as we grow older, the one that consoles us for the loss of all the others.

Has French cooking now become another victim of the zeitgeist and its assault on values, standards, and excellence? Michael Steinberger, *Slate*'s longtime wine columnist and unrepentant gourmand, toured French restaurants and chefs to see whether their cooking still measures up. He concludes regretfully in his new book, *Au Revoir to All That: Food, Wine, and the End of France,* that it does not. French chefs, he finds, have been content to rest on their laurels while others, including the likes of Spanish cooks, have surpassed them in some respects.

To be sure, finding fault with French cuisine is an old story. The writer Alexandre Dumas *père* was already lamenting in 1869 that excessive haste was beginning to mar French cookery, with fewer chefs willing to spend the necessary hours tending a boiling *pot au feu.* A. J. Liebling, who held that the first requirement of a professional food critic was a good appetite—he qualified handsomely—complained in 1939 that there was a decline in the quality of Paris restaurants. "The decline, I later learned, had been going on even in the '20s," he wrote. "We are headed for a gastronomic Dark Time."

Maybe Liebling was prescient and the Dark Time is now at hand. The deterioration of French cuisine fits into the overall context of the country's palpable decay in everything creative, from literature to films, the fine-art trade to fashion and the once-admired educational system. The state of gastronomy may seem a frivolous topic when the world economy is in a mess, but it augurs nothing good for what used to be called civilization. Time to reread Spengler's classic *The Decline of the West.*

France's economic torpor of the last 30 years, with its weak growth and high unemployment, has meant less money in French pockets to spend on restaurant meals. In recent decades the number of cafes in France has been divided by five. Bistros have gone out of business by the thousands—becoming so relatively rare that one in Paris's 16th arrondissement is now classified a historic monument. Per capita wine consumption has dropped 50 percent, ruining scores of vintners.

Incredibly, the French no longer care that much about food. In good part that is because French women, doubtless inspired by Simone de Beauvoir's exhortations to liberation, increasingly prefer flirting in the office to preparing meals and nurturing the appreciation of good food that is the foundation of a national cuisine. The legendary family meal, that used to average an hour and a half, is now over in 38 minutes. Even that is often at a McDonald's, where over 1 million Frenchmen eat every day, apparently lovin' it. (After initial resistance, France has become McDonald's biggest market outside the U.S., with over 1,000 outlets.)

Neighborhood butchers, bakers and cheese shops have been going out of business in droves, replaced by trendy clothing stores. Cavernous hypermarkets with 40 or more checkout lanes account for three-quarters of retail food sales, and internet food shopping is gaining fast. Perhaps most ominously for the French restaurant scene, future chefs are no longer required to know how to truss chickens, open oysters, or make a béarnaise sauce to qualify for their professional certificate. Rather, they are tested on techniques for using processed, powdered, frozen and prepared foods.

Some of France's most famous chefs, particularly Paul Bocuse and Alain Ducasse, are no longer involved in their métier. Steinberger has lunch with Bocuse at his restaurant near Lyon and comes away depressed. "The food was awful," he remembers. "I was dumbstruck by how bad my lunch was, a parody of Escoffian cuisine." It was Bocuse, one of the prominent creators of *nouvelle cuisine* in the 1970s, who became the first international celebrity chef, opening restaurants abroad and leaving the cooking to underlings. "Truant chefs," became the norm in the 1980's and '90s, busier opening restaurants in Japan and New York than sticking to their stoves. The quality and creativity of French haute cuisine could only suffer.

The most flagrant truant today is Alain Ducasse. With over 20 restaurants on four continents bearing his brand, along with a cooking school, publishing imprint, and over 1,000 employees worldwide, Ducasse no longer even pretends to be anything but a businessman. He epitomizes much of what is wrong with French restaurants today: absentee chefs, money-motivated self-promotion, a lack of sincere devotion to good cooking. (Even Americans, we of short attention spans and burger-dulled palates, saw through Ducasse's New York restaurants, the town's food critics reacting indignantly to their flashy vulgarity and outrageous prices.)

Where the author does find gastronomic hope is in Spain's *nueva cocina*, with its "hunger for innovation, openness to new ideas, and desire for creative freedom." But innovation for its own sake can turn into self-caricature. Instead of relying on their own taste, talent, and respect for local produce to refine and reinterpret traditional dishes, Spanish chefs began treating cooking as a form of chemistry. They accordingly filled their kitchens with test tubes, syringes, pH meters and lasers. The result: "a riot of strange powders, foams, jellies, flash-frozen dishes, and unusual flavor combinations." This produced dishes like pistachio truffles frozen with liquid nitrogen, coconut ravioli in soy sauce, Parmesan ice cream sandwiches, and exploding strawberry milkshakes.

In nodding approval of such culinary clowning, Steinberger comes across as a foodie liberal taking the neophiliac approach to haute cuisine: make it novel, make it fun, surprise us. Creativity is certainly important, but, pace nouvelle cuisine and *nueva cocina*, it is not the be-all and end-all of fine cooking.

He also neglects that indefinable thing called taste, an admittedly old school notion including judgment, discernment and refinement. It is not to be confused with tasty. Otherwise, three stars would go to Denny's Super Grand Slamwich with two scrambled eggs, sausage, bacon, shaved ham, mayonnaise, and American cheese on potato bread grilled with maple spice spread and hash browns. Not very epicurean, but tasty—and creative— as hell.

The food people eat and the way they prepare it, like other elements of traditional culture, is the tangible expression of a nation's soul. Brillat-Savarin also wrote, famously, "Tell me what you eat, and I will tell you what you are." By that measure the French, and by inference we as well, have become hurried, harried, undiscriminating, and largely incapable of nuanced pleasure.

But the end of France? Come now. The France where you couldn't get a bad meal ended decades ago when it, alas, began to join the Modern World. That doesn't mean you can't still, with patience, research and luck, find good dining. On a recent journey to the South of France I stopped off at La Pyramide, a restaurant in Vienne that was once one of the pinnacles of gastronomy under its famous chef, the late Fernand Point. It's not what it used to be—what is?—but the current chef, Patrick Henriroux, respects his heritage and does a creditable job at the stove. I started with a creamy bisque of succulent crayfish and stuffed mushrooms, followed by perfectly cooked lamb chops breaded with white poppy seed and garnished with spinach gnocchi, and ended with a Grand Marnier soufflé that nearly floated off the plate. No creative breakthroughs or exploding dishes, but a memorable dining experience.

Update: *Unfortunately good reasonably-priced restaurants are increasingly hard to find, especially in Paris (the best are in the provinces). It is now advisable to practice what I call defensive eating: after very carefully choosing a restaurant, you then order the most conservative, traditional, least exotic dish on the menu. And hope for the best. Meanwhile, the newest delicacies on French supermarket shelves are Oreo cookies, just down the aisle from the Coca-Cola Light, Gatorade, Skippy peanut butter and Kellogg's cereals.*

# CHERCHEZ LA FEMME

Why women's lib has never been very popular in France.

Context: *The role of women in society is an important part of the popular culture. If it is true that femininity is essentially role-playing, as Simone de Beauvoir argued in her feminist bible,* The Second Sex, *it must be admitted that the Latins play it with flair. The French in particular developed it to the point where women, with eager male complicity, have historically held sway over their menfolk to an outlandish degree.*

THE IRONY of the women's lib campaign for empowerment by Beauvoir and her short-sighted ilk, is that French women already had it all. Not for nothing did the French coin the expression *cherchez la femme* as the universal solvent of male motivation.

A millennium before Jean-Paul Sartre's lover graduated from the Sorbonne, amorous French knights were on their knees swooning before ladies of the court, putting them on an absurdly high pedestal (from which, to be sure, most scurried down as fast as their voluminous skirts allowed). The nominally celibate clergy followed suit, idolizing the Virgin Mary and covering the landscape with churches dedicated to *Notre Dame*. Ever since, influential *dames*, if not dames, have wielded power behind, and often on, the scenes theoretically dominated by susceptible, lovesick French males.

The tradition remained through monarchy, empire, and republic. It became official in 1444, when Charles VII acknowledged the beauteous Agnès Sorel as his extracurricular squeeze, thereby adding a *maîtress en titre* to French kings' perks. As befitted the Sun King, Louis XIV had three mistresses, Mesdames de la Vallière and De Montespan for fun and, after he publicly renounced pleasure, the pious Madame de Maintenon for consolation.

These ladies typically had their royal paramours wrapped around their little fingers, particularly Madame de Pompadour and Madame du Barry, respectively Louis XV's first and second official playmates, whose pillow talk is credited with improving his taste in art. France has even exported its mistresses, like some national specialty. Brittany-born Louise-Renée de Keroualle, for example, was sent across the Channel in the 17th century to seduce Britain's King Charles II and influence his policies toward France, becoming Countess of Fareham, Baroness Petersfield in the process.

Napoleon, a romantic sort, first fell for the sister of his brother's wife and wrote a sappy short novel about it. He was later infatuated to distraction with Joséphine, putting up with her extravagant spending and wandering eye, alternately throwing jealous tantrums and making her empress of France before finally divorcing her. Then there was General Georges Boulanger, wildly acclaimed as the savior of France by a Paris mob one evening in January 1889 and urged to stage a coup d'état; he preferred to keep a date with his mistress, the felicitously named Madame de Bonnemains. Ten years later, President Félix Faure died suddenly of cardiac arrest in the Élysée Palace, a smile on his face and rigid fingers still gripping to his lap the curly head of his alarmed lady friend.

But in contemporary France it took a Socialist president, François Mitterrand, always looking out for the good of the people, to actually set up a parallel wife and daughter in a Paris apartment at public expense during his 14-year tenure. Even that wasn't enough to sate Mitterrand, who occasionally visited three lady friends of an evening, chivalrously referring to them as his "hors d'oeuvre, main course, and dessert." His successor, Jacques Chirac, admitted he had loved many women "as discreetly as possible." The presidential chauffeur dutifully drove him to his trysts while First Lady Bernadette kept house.

Enter Nicolas Sarkozy, elected on a platform of change, indeed, *rupture* with the past. Sarkozy's personal life, too, marked a turning point in French mores. Gone was the conventional presidential couple-cum-mistress in the Élysée Palace. With his stylish wife Cécilia and their five handsome children from a total of three marriages, Sarkozy formed the very model of a modern major family. They brought the sort of brief, shining, Camelot moment the French have secretly yearned for ever since they went into raptures over John and Jackie in the White House. He told friends on election night in May, 2007, "If you liked Jackie Kennedy, you'll love Cécilia."

But for all his pugnacious, macho modernity, Sarkozy has one thing very much in common with Frenchmen past and present: he is just as *toujours l'amour* dotty about women as any of the most besotted of them. The only difference is that, instead of the usual division of labor in these matters, he treated Cécilia as both wife and mistress.

The harsh reality was that Cécilia had telegraphed her intention to leave him for months, if not years. They had already broken up in 2005 when Sarkozy was interior minister and she took off for New York with a French executive; he retaliated by taking up with a lady political journalist.

Cécilia's justification for leaving him only weeks after his election was redolent of Romantic Feminism. Rebelling against a destiny that pushed her into the unwanted spotlight of public life, she was unwilling to live a lie, she told an interviewer. For sympathetic women's magazines she was a frustrated Marie-Antoinette, Flaubert's suffocating Emma Bovary, a Princess Diana lonely in a public marriage. But many French thought that she was, after all, more midinette than mistress.

Rumors inevitably were rife about the steroidal president who didn't mind being called a *chaud lapin*, or hot rabbit, always a much-sought accolade among French politicians. The most persistent one concerned a willowy model-turned-pop singer whose previous companions reportedly include Mick Jagger and Donald Trump. Whatever else he did for France, Sarkozy is the best thing that could have happened to the country's avidly read gossip columnists. All of whom are delighted to play *cherchez la femme* at the lovelorn Élysée Palace.

Update: *The willowy model-turned-pop singer was, of course, the Italian-born Carla Bruni, whom Sarkozy, on a very public rebound, quickly courted and wed. Like her husband, she was never liked or accepted by the French. Indeed, that contributed to Sarkozy's unpopularity and ultimate defeat in his bid for a second term. That was a problem that France's libidinous kings didn't have.*

# HERE'S LOOKING AT YOU, KID

The greatest cultural treasure in Paris is Italian.

Context: *From the Champs-Elysées to Saint Germain des Près, the Bastille to posh Passy, Paris is the undisputed capital of girl watching. And with their pert presence, sense of style and fashion flair, the ladies in question are indeed well worth a look. But who is the fairest of them all?*

THE CITY has even turned girl watching into a spectator sport of sorts—besides fiddling with cell phones, what else are all those sidewalk cafés for? Especially in summer, when café tables overflow to the curbs with goggle-eyed male patrons looking their fill. But *la Parisienne*, for all her many assets and attributes, is not actually the most ogled woman in the city. That title goes to an aloof Italian beauty who neither flounces by nor makes with the saucy repartee. She merely gives gawkers an enigmatic smile.

For a look at her, you shun sidewalk cafes and start an epic journey in a cavernous crypt beneath a glass pyramid. You climb worn, crowded stone stairs of an ancient palace now known, for reasons no one can remember, as the Louvre. On the second floor you invariably come across a horde jockeying and elbowing as close as they can get to a bullet-proof, air-conditioned showcase. If you can squeeze your way in, you are entitled to a harried look at Lisa Gherardini, a.k.a. Mona (a variation of Madonna, Lady) Lisa, the wife of a wealthy Renaissance Florentine merchant, Franceso del Giocondo.

Louvre officials estimate that fully 80 percent of the museum's 6.6 million annual visitors come mainly to look at Leonardo da Vinci's 500-year-old portrait. The question is, why? One answer is that like most celebrities, Mona Lisa is famous for being famous. Another is that they come to see the cultural archetype that has provoked more esoteric analysis, crass imitations and common commercialization than just about anything else in the world.

If there was ever any doubt about her world-class status, that was laid to rest in January 1963, when Mona Lisa arrived in America. A formal President John F. Kennedy and an elegant Jacqueline officially welcomed her to Washington's National Gallery of Art, where U.S. Marines stood guard around the clock and crowds waited for hours. It was the same mob scene later at New York's Metropolitan Museum. In all, more than 1.5 million Americans looked over Mona Lisa.

What they saw is defined by that tight-lipped smile. After looking carefully, the art critic Bernard Berenson considered that Leonardo's subtle *sfumato* technique of modeling light and shade reached its apex here, carrying "facial expression perilously close to the brink of the endurable." For centuries many an artist has tried to equal it. One, the mid-19th century French artist Luc Maspero, threw himself out the window of his

Paris room, leaving a farewell note: "For years I have grappled desperately with her smile. I prefer to die."

These days we don't need suicidal artists to analyze the dreamy, diaphanous atmosphere that seems to envelope her. We can use an x-ray fluorescence spectroscope, as technicians at the Louvre have done. With this they were able to detect dozens of layers of translucent glaze, each only one or two micrometers thick, that give her face a sense of depth and reality. Leonardo's *sfumato* technique was well known before, but this is the first scientific explanation of exactly how he did it.

But beyond mere technique, the question remains of what it all means. The Marquis de Sade, for one, found Mona Lisa full of "seduction and devoted tenderness," and "the very essence of femininity." Walter Pater, leader of the 19th century English Aestheticism movement, was even more overwrought at the sight of her. "She is older than the rocks among which she sits," he swooned, "like the vampire, she has been dead many times, and learned the secrets of the grave; and has been a diver in deep seas."

Sigmund Freud, too, went into raptures. Terming Leonardo an obsessive neurotic in *Leonardo da Vinci, A Study in Psychosexuality*, the Viennese supershrink decided that Mona Lisa's expression could only resemble the mysterious smile of the artist's mother: "This picture contains the synthesis of the history of Leonardo's childhood." As for Mona Lisa herself, he proclaimed her nothing less than "the most perfect representation of the contrasts dominating the love-life of woman, namely reserve and seduction, most submissive tenderness and the indifferent craving, which confront man as a strange and consuming sensuality."

Over at the Louvre, they have a more playful view. What if a pun lay at the heart of Mona Lisa? After all, *Giocondo* in Italian, like *Joconde* in French, means cheerful, merry, joyous, as does "jocund" in English. "He was punning on Mona Lisa's married name when he gave her a subtle smile in *La Joconde*," a curator of 16th-century French and Italian painting at the Louvre once told me, using the usual French term for the painting. "What we really have here is an idea, more than a realistic portrait, the idea of a smile expressed in a painting."

The question inevitably arises of how much the painting is worth. King Francis I added Mona Lisa to his royal collections for 4,000 gold écus, or about $128,700, after Leonardo's death in 1519 at Francis's chateau of Amboise. Louvre officials say simply that Mona Lisa's monetary value is inestimable. Such a valuation has naturally given rise to temptation, and in 1911 it was the object of the biggest art heist in history—*Time* recently ranked it one of the most famous crimes of the last 100 years.

That was when an Italian laborer named Vincenzo Perugia walked out the door with it one evening. When Perugia naively proposed the original to a Florence art dealer he was promptly pinched. Mona Lisa, undamaged, returned to France on December 31, 1913, riding like royalty in a special compartment of the Milan-Paris express, escorted by a squadron of policemen, politicians, museum officials, and artists.

Somehow the caper rubbed off some of her mystique. The age of Giocondoclasm had begun. With irreverence and reaction against "bourgeois" values the new order of the day, the painting became the ideal target for desperately modern iconoclastic artists. Marcel Duchamp, leader of the Dada anti-art movement, summed up the new zeitgeist in 1919 by brushing in a pointy mustache and goatee on a postcard representation of the sacred face. The Art Establishment was duly shocked.

Today Mona Lisa is the ultimate in kitsch. Collectors have catalogued nearly 400 advertising uses of the image and counting, along with at least 61 products called Mona Lisa in 14 countries, from rosé wine and chocolate to cigars, cheese, hairpins, potatoes, corsets and beer.

Jean Margat, has his own answer to the painting's mythic status. A retired geologist, Margat from his home near Orleans presides over The Friends of Mona Lisa, a club of serious collectors of Giocondiana. His own vast, house-filling collection includes everything from Mona Lisa T-shirts and posters to condoms and panty hose. "There's no way you can get away from it today," he told me cheerfully. "Mona Lisa has an enormous recognition factor. For better or worse, I'm afraid she still symbolizes Western art."

Well, it could be worse. She's really pretty good looking.

Update: *She continues to fascinate. A resident of Ipswich, England, spent years studying the Mona Lisa and decided Leonardo was a Mason who incorporated Masonic symbols like the compass and square in it. He also claims to have discovered hidden faces, several chalices and a high priest of the Knights Templar. Scholars are skeptical. Meanwhile, experts at Heidelberg University library said they found a book in the archives confirming that the sitter was Lisa Gherardini, something most experts had already deduced. Korean Air wrapped a Boeing 747-400 flying the Incheon-Paris route with the image of Mona Lisa. "We expect the plane to open a new era of global culture marketing," an airline official said.*

# THE GREAT SEDUCERS

The French are obsessed with seduction, and there's nothing
frivolous about it.

Context: *Voltaire wrote that "It is not enough to conquer, one must
also seduce." And the French really work at it, considering it an
important component in their way of life. To the rest of us, though, it
might seem manipulative. Maybe that's why it doesn't work so well
in America.*

IN FINE OLD American families where tradition holds an
honored place, the wisdom of the ages is passed down from
father to son. One early dictum, when sonny is still in short
pants, is the time-honored, "Never pass up the chance to take a
leak." When he starts school and has trouble with the inevitable
recreation bully, the advice is likely to be, "The first stiff right to
the nose usually wins." Then, as adolescence arrives with its
raging hormones, it's time for delicate, tactful counsel on
relations with the opposite sex. Here the only admonition better
than "Always treat a broad like a lady, and a lady like a broad," is
surely the classic, "Candy is dandy, but liquor is quicker."

The French, of course, do things differently in the area
of gender relations, as in most others. To help us understand
their sly, convoluted approach, we now have *La Séduction: How*

*the French Play the Game of Life* by Elaine Sciolino. A longtime
Paris correspondent for *The New York Times*, Sciolino holds that
the key to just about everything in France, from romance to
business, style, gastronomy, diplomacy and politics, is seduction.
We might have suspected as much. Along with *élégance*, the
most overworked and overused word in the French language is
*séduction*. No subject is safe from it. When the pope visited Israel
in 2009, for example, the French press had him "seducing" the
Palestinians with a call for an independent state.

In our simple-minded way, we might think this
obsession with seduction means the French are badly in need of
a few sessions on the analysts' couch. But no, Sciolino explains,
this isn't necessarily about sex. "In French, the meaning is
broader," she says. "The French use 'seduce' where Americans
might use 'charm' or 'engage' or 'entertain.' Seduction in France
does not always mean body contact." Still, it is always used with
the intention of winning over someone in a given situation, a
mental form of arm-wrestling. As a line in an old film by the
great French director Eric Rohmer goes (young man to young
woman), "I love seduction for the seduction. It doesn't matter if
it succeeds. Physically, I mean." At least he wasn't a flatterer.

Dominique Strauss-Kahn, we now know, is an extreme
example of *le grand séducteur*. Long before he went to
Washington to head the International Monetary Fund, many in
France quietly admired him for having such an active, er, social
life. This didn't seem to trouble his wife, Anne Sinclair. Asked
in 2006, well before his sordid caper in a New York hotel, if she
suffered because of her husband's reputation, she answered, "No,

if anything I am quite proud! For a politician it's important to seduce. As long as I seduce him and he seduces me, that's good enough."

Clearly the French give considerable thought to this. The celebrity philosopher Bernard-Henri Lévy says, "Seduction is more than a driving force. Life is seduction. Civilization is seduction. What distinguishes men from animals is seduction." Lévy's wife, the Franco-American actress Arielle Dombasle, chimes in, "Seduction is not a frivolous thing. No. It's war."

French schoolchildren learn the tactics and strategy of this daily social warfare early. One of the first things they get is that their grades can vary by up to 40 percent depending on their looks and manner. (The French were shocked by the Monica Lewinsky affair, but not because of Bill Clinton's behavior in the Oval Office; it was her pathetic lack of style they couldn't take.) As time goes on, they master the tools of seduction.

One is *le regard*, a way of locking someone's eyes with a deep, smoky look hinting at mysteries to be explored. And never wink. It turns out that French women not only don't get fat— they would rather get hit by a truck than put on pounds—they don't wink either. "It disfigures your face," warns one seduction expert.

Another weapon is words. Nimble verbal banter is crucial, conversation being less a means of imparting information than a form of stroking. The frontal approach is to be avoided at all costs, being just too, *too* vulgar. The voice is kept soft and low—which is why Americans in Paris often seem loud to the natives. Private coaches can be hired to teach professional women how to eliminate unsophisticated chirpiness from their voices, and men to cultivate those irresistible lower tones.

Adolescents from good families can polish their seduction technique in the *rallyes*, ultra-chic parties where they can mix with their own kind without interference from the riffraff. Besides engaging in subtle banter with plenty of double entendre while locking eyes, they learn the fine art of the *baisemain* and its inflexible rules: never kiss a gloved hand or the hand of a young girl; kiss only the hand of a married woman; do so only indoors. And the lips should *not* touch skin, merely come close.

The basics acquired, apprentice *séducteurs* turn to the necessary accessories, starting with an alluring perfume. The theory is that the seduction target will be lured by irrational feelings inspired by a subtle—never, please, strong or obvious—scent, and be driven by emotion. Thus the French spend over $40 per man, woman, and child annually on fragrances, more than any other people in the world. (Americans spend about $17 on average.)

Just as important is the right lingerie, for which French women spend nearly 20 percent of their clothing budget. The goal here is the peek-a-boo effect of concealment, or, as the connoisseurs of seduction say, hiding to show better. Arielle Dombasle, for one, declares she would "never, never, never" appear entirely naked before her husband, Bernard-Henri. Such gaucherie would be anti-erotic.

Lucky man, you might think. But not on his trips to the United States. Lévy, who spent months traveling in the U.S. to research a book on Alexis de Tocqueville's time there, finally gave up on American women. "They don't like being seduced," he concludes with a shrug and little moue of disappointment. "I realized that in the U.S. I had to force myself to avoid showing a woman that I found her seductive, because I knew that instead of creating complicity between us, it would create a barrier."

French politicians have to be considered seductive. It goes with the territory. Jacques Chirac did everything he could while mayor of Paris, and later president, to promote the idea that he was hot. His *baisemain* technique was notoriously defective—instead of letting the kiss properly hover in the air, he planted it moistly on the knuckles—but no complaints were recorded. He deliberately let it be rumored that he had had the comely Italian actress Claudia Cardinale as mistress. True or not, the idea that he was a practiced if hasty ladies' man was firmly held by the fair sex. "Chirac?" whispered knowledgeable Parisiennes. "Three minutes. Shower included."

Giscard d'Estaing also worked hard on his image as an irresistible male. During his seven-year term as president, he boasted, "I was in love with 17 million French women." One technique was to stare at them individually with a smoldering look when working a room or a crowd. "Was there some method or trick in this to influence and seduce?" he mused. "Presumably." Giscard later published a novel relating the violent passion between a French head of state and a British royal, suggesting he might have had an affair with Princess Diana. Le tout Paris giggled.

President Nicolas Sarkozy is an exception to the rule. Indeed, the most likely answer to the frequent question, "Why don't the French like him?" is that he was slow in mastering the art of appearing seductive. It didn't help that this second wife, Cécilia, dumped him weeks after he took office, leaving Sarkozy, a teetotalling workaholic who's not much fun anyway, looking lonely and forlorn.

Even the woman who followed his presidential campaign for a year before the 2007 election and then wrote a book about it, Yasmina Reza, was surprised that he hadn't tried anything. "It's almost insulting to spend an entire year with a man," she later said, "without him trying to seduce you." But things have improved since he wooed and married Carla Bruni, pop singer, former model, and indisputable prize catch for any seducer. She loyally fosters his new image with comments like, "His physique, his charm, his intelligence seduced me."

It may well be that Voltaire, that archetypal Frenchman, was right when he wrote, "It is not enough to conquer, one must also seduce." But to those of us woefully lacking in the seductive arts, it will always seem that there is something sneaky, deceptive, manipulative—in a word, *phony*—about seduction. It is, after all, an insecure way of getting around people rather than being upfront.

Even Sciolino, who admires French seductive prowess, admits it has its drawbacks. "Seduction is the best that France has to offer," she concludes. "When it works, it's magic... But it can also entail inefficiency, fragility, ambiguity, and a process that at any time can end badly. When the game comes up against the cold, hard wall of reality, when it reveals itself, seduction fails."

Q.E.D. There couldn't be a better argument for the superiority of liquor.

Update: *There's no escaping seduction in France, so it's best just to relax and enjoy it. Museums try to "seduce" new visitors with blockbuster exhibits. Milk producers don't go on strike, they are said to be on a "seduction mission," while the interior of a new car is touted as filled with "the spirit of seduction." A politician reaching for first-time voters is trying to "seduce the young." And so on, ad infinitum.*

# THE UNITED NATIONS' ROGUE AGENCY

With the admission of Palestine, UNESCO shows again it is over-politicized and running out of control. The U.S. should head for the exit.

Context: *With its widely accepted—and much promoted— reputation as a world capital of culture, Paris was the choice in 1946 to be the home of the United Nations' specialized cultural agency. The UN Educational, Scientific and Cultural Organization had as its stated purpose the promotion of peace and security through international cooperation. As the American writer Archibald MacLeish wrote in the preamble to UNESCO's constitution, "Since wars begin in the minds of men, it is in the minds of men that the defenses of peace must be constructed." This high-flown, utopian ideal has never been achieved and never could be. It is too vague and open to political manipulation. It does not help that the organization has been taken over by anti-Western cliques.*

WE HAVE ALL heard the jocular remark about the inmates taking over the asylum. But I had never actually witnessed that unnerving event until October 31, 2011, when I spent an afternoon in the press gallery of the United Nations Educational, Scientific and Cultural Organization in Paris. The vast conference hall was not quite a madhouse, but it was noisy, agitated, and full of wild surmise. Hundreds of delegates from member states milled about, chattering excitedly as the president of UNESCO's biennial general conference plaintively called for them to take their seats and get on with the business at hand. To wit, voting on a request by the Palestinian Authority for membership—and with it, the first recognition of its statehood by a United Nations agency.

The stakes were high. In its quest for statehood without making concessions to Israel, the PA had applied for full membership in the UN in September, but it was obvious that the U.S. would veto that ploy in the Security Council. So PA President Mahmoud Abbas was targeting a weak link in the UN system where the veto does not exist. He knew that UNESCO, with its fuzzy cultural mandate, was as open to political manipulation now as it had been when it was an ideological battlefield in the Cold War.

The U.S. had made abundantly clear that, due to laws dating from the 1990s, admitting Palestine to any UN agency would mean an immediate cutoff of American funding. In UNESCO's case, this amounted to fully 22 percent of its budget. There was no leeway for interpretation, no possibility of waiving the laws' provisions. Perversely, that seemed only to sharpen the delegates' appetite for admitting the Palestinian Authority. As the roll was called, it became obvious that they relished thumbing their collective nose at the U.S. and the handful of member states that held this was the wrong place to decide the issue of Palestinian statehood. Cheers greeted votes in favor by delegations from Africa, South America, the Middle East,

Russia, China and, of course, France. Joining the fun was the ambassador from Uzbekistan, the beauteous 32-year-old Lola Karimova-Tillyaeva, socialite daughter of President Islam Karimov, whose use of torture against dissidents, including boiling to death, the UN itself has termed "systematic."

A sprinkling of moans or boos rippled through the assembly when the U.S., Germany, Holland, and a few others voted against. The president repeatedly called for a bit of decorum. Not a chance: now the grinning, gibbering, gesticulating inmates had indeed taken over. The final vote was 107 in favor to 14 against, with 52 abstentions. For anyone who still believed in UNESCO's mission, it was an appalling spectacle. With that frivolous, self-defeating act, UNESCO signaled to the world that, once again, it was becoming the UN's over-politicized rogue agency.

It was a lose-lose move both for the Palestinians and UNESCO itself. After the grandstanding, Palestine was no closer to statehood and possibly further away, hardening positions and jeopardizing the peace process. "It was an extremely reckless and callous move by Abbas," one dismayed Western ambassador to UNESCO told me later. "There are no winners in this. Abbas has alienated some of his most important supporters." The State Department and both parties in Congress quickly denounced the vote. As Texas Republican Kay Granger, chair of the House State and Foreign Operations Appropriations Subcommittee had warned, "I have made it clear to the Palestinian leadership that I would not support sending U.S. taxpayer money to the Palestinians if they sought statehood at the United Nations. There are consequences for short-cutting the process, not only for the Palestinians, but for our longstanding relationship with the United Nations."

UNESCO immediately began suffering those consequences, starting with the loss of America's contribution of about $80 million to its budget for 2011, 2012, and perhaps indefinitely. "We have to take drastic action and take it now," the Bulgarian director general, Irina Bokova, said unhappily. "We are reviewing all activities in all areas, including staff travel, publications, communication costs, meetings and the rest." Some 20 of its 57 field offices might have to be closed.

It is paying the logical price for letting politics trump its cultural/educational mandate, and demonstrating that UNESCO lends itself, systemically, to this kind of abuse. Those who cannot remember the past are condemned to repeat it, as the man said, and this fiasco reminded me of the bad old days of the 1980s. UNESCO was then a hotbed of vicious anti-Western ideology complete with strident condemnations of America. Instead of concentrating on fostering "full and equal opportunities for education for all, in the unrestricted pursuit of objective truth, and in the free exchange of ideas and knowledge," it became a political tool wielded by the Third World and the Soviet bloc. "If you don't like what we are proposing," an African delegate once shouted at Westerners, "we will jam it down your throats until you choke!"

One notorious program promoted a socialist-lining New International Economic Order. Its undeclared purpose was to redistribute Western wealth to a global welfare state; private enterprise was dismissed as "an economy of waste." Educational grants were funding violent Marxist movements like the Palestine Liberation Organization and the Soviet-armed South-West Africa People's Organization. Another wayward project was euphemistically called Communication in the Service of Man. In reality it promoted a New World Information and Communication Order with state licensing and codes of correct conduct for newsmen. When in 1983 France expelled 47 KGB spies, a dozen were under cover at UNESCO.

The director general was one Amadou-Mahtar M'Bow, a volatile, irascible Senegalese who ran it like a profitable personal fief. Official funds were used to stroke his supporters. All job appointments and promotions were personally approved by him and based on ideology and nationality. When a planned U.S. audit of financial irregularities was announced, a mysterious fire destroyed key files. Disgusted and demoralized, competent senior staff fled, one protesting in writing "the destruction of professionalism." The U.S., too, left: Ronald Reagan finally had enough and pulled America out of UNESCO in 1984.

With no perceptible repercussions on American citizens except tax savings, it stayed out for 19 years. In 2003 George W. Bush took America back in "As a symbol of our commitment to human dignity." The organization had been reformed, he noted hopefully at the time, "and America will participate fully in its mission to advance human rights and tolerance and learning." Laura Bush later became, and remains, a UNESCO goodwill ambassador. After all, idealistic America has always been an important part of this organization with utopian visions, beginning with its creation. The first American member of the executive board, the writer Archibald MacLeish, wrote the high-flown preamble to UNESCO's constitution: "Since wars begin in the minds of men, it is in the minds of men that the defenses of peace must be constructed."

Today it has grown to 195 member states, more than any other multinational organization including the UN itself. Its staff of some 2,000 toil in half-a-dozen buildings at its sprawling Paris headquarters and field offices. They handle a biennial budget of $653 million, plus millions more in extra-budgetary contributions. At its best, it can be useful for monitoring and standard-setting in fields like education, science, and information. Member state delegations I spoke with voiced many complaints about UNESCO—especially its growing politicization—but mostly like its education programs. American officials generally praise its efforts for universal literacy and clean water, women's education, and disaster preparedness. One of its largest American-supported education projects is in Afghanistan, with literacy centers for both civilians and Afghan police officers.

Membership can also be good for American business. Companies like Apple, Cisco, Intel, Google and Microsoft are cooperating with UNESCO because it opens access to global markets. As David T. Killion, U.S. ambassador to the organization, told me, "We think there are critical American interests at stake here: moral, cultural, national security, even economic interests. We think this is a strategic piece of real estate in the international system. It can get us to places we couldn't get to otherwise."

But Killion has been publicly critical of the political manipulation that goes on. Formerly a leading voice on international organizations with the House Foreign Affairs Committee, he made the rounds of delegations trying to dissuade them from voting for Palestinian admission. During the executive board's debate on the question he took the floor to express America's "strong opposition." He added, "We are profoundly disappointed that this issue has injected a difficult political issue into this organization, and believe that it has the potential to undermine severely the organization's ability to carry out its critical mandate." In 2010 he protested UNESCO's tendency to single out Israel for criticism. "This undermines UNESCO's credibility," he said. "The US strongly encourages the executive board to seek an alternative to highly politicized decisions and seemingly permanent agenda items focused only on one country."

If the organization keeps hammering Israel, it is due to its aggressive Arab-African regional bloc of members. Its influence over UNESCO can be seen in ways large and small.

There was the scandal over World Philosophy Day. UNESCO inexplicably decided the 2010 conference would be held in Teheran, capital of that beacon of free thought, Iran—an inexcusable choice by an organization supposedly dedicated to freedom and human rights. Shocked academics around the world declared a boycott, calling the confab a propaganda exercise for a brutal regime. "It's as if they decided to hold a philosophy conference in Berlin in 1938—with Goebbels as its head!" said Dr. Ramin Jahanbegloo, an expatriate Iranian philosopher teaching at the University of Toronto. Backpedaling, an embarrassed UNESCO first said the conference would go ahead as scheduled, then tried to dissociate itself from events in Teheran by holding a parallel meeting in Paris. Confusion all around, along with red faces.

UNESCO's warped attitude toward Israel showed again in its ham-fisted condemnation in 2011 of a political cartoon. Published in the Israeli newspaper *Haaretz*, it showed Premier Benjamin Netanyahu and his defense minister briefing pilots before an imaginary attack on Iran, telling them to target UNESCO's office in the West Bank on their way back—a joking reference to Netanyahu's anger over the admission of Palestine. Within hours, a UNESCO assistant director general solemnly summoned Israeli Ambassador Nimrod Barkan and handed him an overwrought official protest saying, preposterously, that the cartoon "endangers the lives of unarmed diplomats." Barkan merely reminded him that Israel enjoys a free press. "We've heard of Islamists raging against supposedly disrespectful cartoons," an Israeli Foreign Ministry spokesman commented, "but UN officials going down the same road, that's a whole new ballgame."

That blunder was only a peccadillo compared with the ludicrous mess in 2011 over filling an opening on the UNESCO committee that deals with human rights issues. The mind-boggling choice: Syria. No matter that the UN's own High Commissioner for Human Rights recommends that the regime of Bashar al-Assad be prosecuted in the International Criminal Court in The Hague for crimes against humanity. That includes slaughtering thousands of demonstrators, including children, and arresting thousands more in its crackdown on opposition protests.

This grotesquerie was created by manipulating the organization's skewed procedural rules. Syria was elected to the executive board in 2009, and all members have the right to sit on its committees. Once the Arab bloc decided for its own reasons to put Syria on human rights, it was a done deal. "It's shameful for the UN's prime agency on science, culture and education to take a country that is shooting its own people and empower it to decide human rights issues on a global scale," said Hillel Neuer, executive director of the Geneva-based UN Watch, an independent human rights monitoring group. Commented Florida Republican Congresswoman Ileana Ros-Lehtinen, who chairs the House Foreign Affairs Committee, "UNESCO continues to outdo itself with stunning displays of irresponsible and dangerous behavior. The selection of Syria to serve on a UNESCO committee responsible for human rights is an affront to those suffering at the hands of tyrants all around the world. The Administration must continue to follow U.S. law and withhold funds to UNESCO so our tax dollars are not used to support this increasingly irresponsible agency."

Attempting to distance itself from the gaffe, UNESCO quietly let it be known that Director General Bokova actually disapproved of the choice but had her hands tied. That only underscored that Bokova, a soft-spoken, graying, grandmotherly lady of 60, has a tiger by the tail. In reality the organization is run by the volatile, unpredictable, pliant general conference, and the 58-member executive board that sets the conference agenda. The Arab-African bloc has an automatic 20 votes on the board, and can easily find another 10 from emerging nations for a majority to push through policies predictably anti-Western, or utterly irrational like the vote on Palestine. However well-intentioned, Bokova is powerless to control or prevent its rogue actions.

Elected in 2009 as UNESCO's first woman director general, Bokova was a member of Bulgaria's Socialist—formerly Communist—Party as well as ambassador to France and UNESCO itself. She had served as Bulgaria's foreign minister under Premier Zhan Videnov, who did little to clean up the country's post-communist cesspool of organized crime and corruption. She is a convert to press freedom—she certainly did not learn it from her father, who edited Bulgaria's main, party-lining communist newspaper. Like many of the privileged of her generation, she studied at Moscow's State Institute of International Relations, later doing stints at the University of Maryland and Harvard. "I am from this cold war generation that lived through this period; we didn't choose it," Bokova told *The New York Times* defensively before her election. "I have nothing to be ashamed of."

Her election was symptomatic of the penchant of multilateral organizations for choosing the least common denominator. She is certainly not the strong, decisive leader UNESCO needs to keep the rambunctious executive board and general conference from riding roughshod over it. But in one respect at least, Bokova's election helped UNESCO avoid another spectacular calamity.

Her only rival for the position, backed by the Arab-African bloc, was the Egyptian culture minister Farouk Hosny. Hosny's record for promoting culture and defending human rights was of the Middle Eastern variety. He had declared he would personally burn any Jewish book found in Egypt's great Alexandria library. He also boasted he had helped organize the 1985 escape of the Palestine Liberation Front hijackers of the *Achille Lauro* cruise ship, the charmers who shot the disabled American Leon Klinghoffer and shoved him overboard in his wheelchair. This being UNESCO, Hosny almost became its director. Arm twisting and threatening, Egypt and its allies on the executive board managed to push the election to five rounds of voting—unprecedented in the organization's history—before Bokova narrowly won. That a thug like Hosny could come within a hair of UNESCO's top job speaks volumes.

Its official priorities are also revealing. Number one on the official list is Africa, followed by gender equality. Only then come proper core activities like education, ethics, and intercultural dialogue. So no one should be surprised if the African tail wags the UNESCO dog. Official documents are peppered with the phrase "especially in Africa." Its Cultural Commission considers that intercultural dialogue mainly means raising awareness of the slave trade, slavery, and the African diaspora. The general conference last November proudly expressed its official satisfaction with the publication of the eight-volume *General History of Africa*, "making this masterpiece of UNESCO one of the major intellectual achievements of the 20th century (sic)."

This order of priorities can lead to the occasional crack-up. Most spectacular in recent memory was the $3 million UNESCO Obiang Nguema Mbasogo International Prize for Research in the Life Sciences, set up in 2008. Never awarded, it was suspended in 2010 after protests ranging from Nobel laureates and press freedom groups to human rights defenders around the world. How could such a generous, euphonious, impressively named prize with the worthy goal of encouraging scientific research cause such a brouhaha?

Consider the donor. President Obiang, who has ruled Equatorial Guinea with a despotic hand since taking power in a coup 30 years ago, is justly renowned for rigged elections, arrest and murder of opposition leaders, muzzling the press, and what a UN special rapporteur termed "inhuman conditions" and "systematic torture" in the country's prisons. Along with this goes, naturally, unabashed corruption in the use of the country's abundant oil wealth for himself and his family. Appropriately enough, the $3 million prize money was reportedly delivered to UNESCO in cash.

When protests over this transparent attempt to improve a brutal dictator's image became too embarrassing, Bokova called for the prize to be withdrawn in 2010 and said she would not be involved with it. Furious backroom politicking followed. Western diplomats, typically scared of looking colonialist or, *quelle horreur*, anti-African, took a back seat and left it to the sub-Saharans to annul the prize and return the money, presumably in small-denomination banknotes. The Arabs said they would support any decision by the Africans. Those worthies said the prize must be awarded.

There things stand, with UNESCO still holding the $3 million—Obiang refuses to take it back. Bokova, being against the prize after being for it, was left looking compromised. As a longtime secretariat member told me privately, "There was a very strong feeling here that it was wrong to accept it, just as we were against admitting Palestine. But these things get done anyway, despite what we feel is right." Clearly out of control, it's anyone's guess what this outfit's next caper might be.

Compared with the missteps of priority Africa, priority gender equality looks innocent enough. Of course women and girls should be taught to read and write, and UNESCO has programs in that field. And they should certainly be protected from discrimination, though it's hard to see what UNESCO does about that except preach the good word. But in its effort to please feminist zealots, the organization inevitably ends up looking more than a bit silly. As when it slavishly altered UNESCO's slogan to read, "Building peace in the minds of men *and women.*"

It has become a one-stop shop for everything on the feminists' shopping list, plus some pleasant surprises. Do media women in the Maghreb need courses in "gender sensitive scriptwriting"? It held a workshop in Casablanca for that. Do downtrodden female philosophers need to "write free from the looming gaze of an imaginary, universal, male reader"? There's a Women Philosophers' Journal where they can. And while writing, they can refer to the UNESCO Guidelines on Gender-neutral Language pamphlet, with its gross cartoons showing male chauvinists ruthlessly dominating helpless females. It is surely helpful to women raising children amid poverty and disease to know that "human power" is better than "manpower," "wife and husband" preferable to "man and wife," "intrepid child" tops "Tomboy."

Of all UNESCO's countless programs, the World Heritage List is by far the best known. The 936 properties in 153 countries, including 21 in the U.S. from Yellowstone to the Statue of Liberty, are selected as being "of outstanding universal value." When the Convention Concerning the Protection of the World Cultural and Natural Heritage was adopted in 1972, it was to ensure that important natural and manmade sites were not wantonly endangered—a worthy cause to be sure.

But today UNESCO has twisted its meaning to satisfy as many of its client activists as possible. The new slogan of its flagship program is World Heritage *and Sustainable Development*, thereby pleasing the greens and those who view UNESCO primarily as an economic development, not cultural, agency. (Just for the record, culture properly understood has nothing whatever to do with economic development, as many an impecunious writer can attest.) As Irina Bokova said in a recent speech announcing the upcoming 40th anniversary celebrations of the convention, "Heritage stands at the crossroads of climate change, social transformations and processes of reconciliation between peoples. Heritage carries high stakes—for the identity and belonging of peoples, for the sustainable economic and social development of communities." Anybody feel left out?

To be sure, with a headquarters staff of 80 running the program, the World Heritage Committee can sometimes help avoid damage to important sites. When in 1995 Egypt planned a new highway near the Giza Pyramids which might have blighted the site, negotiations with the Egyptian government found a solution. And when the archaeological site of Delphi in Greece was threatened by plans for an aluminum plant nearby, the Greek government was persuaded to find another location.

But many observers are increasingly unhappy with the way the World Heritage Committee operates. They accuse it of inappropriate politicization and, ultimately, corruption of its original mandate. This came to light publicly at the general conference in November 2011, when the Estonian ambassador, Marten Kokk, stood up and said aloud what many insiders were thinking. "We regret to say," he declared, "that the increasing operational problems and politicization of the World Heritage Committee compromise the credibility of the [1972] Convention and the World Heritage List." He also criticized conflicts of interest on the committee, with members abusing their positions to win selection of candidate sites in their home countries.

Interviews with other delegations made clear what Kokk was concerned about. "Several delegations are unhappy with the way the Committee is selecting sites for its list," the ambassador of one Nordic country told me. (Delegations I interviewed insisted on anonymity when voicing criticism.) "Too often, the decision is made not on the grounds of a site's historical or esthetic value, but for political reasons. As a result, the committee's choices diverge more and more frequently from the professional advice of the outside experts who make recommendations. This is against the very raison d'être of the 1972 Convention." A member of a different delegation, who sat on the committee for four years, confirmed this. "It's clear that, for political reasons, the World Heritage Committee is not complying with the recommendations of the experts in selecting sites," he said. "There are many obvious cases. We regret this very much." A recent report by an external auditor confirms the program's corruption. It notes that in one recent year, six candidate sites that the experts did not find "of outstanding universal value" were selected as heritage sites anyway for political and economic reasons.

Member states obviously consider that it is worth doing whatever necessary to get as many World Heritage sites as possible. They mean prestige, jobs, and economic development in the form of increased tourism. Travel agencies tout package tours focused on World Heritage-listed sites, manna from heaven for poor countries. "Is the World Heritage Committee politicized?" asked one disabused Western ambassador I talked with. "Everything at the UN is politicized. Should the committee be overturning the recommendations of the experts? Absolutely not, and we have to put pressure on member states not to do that anymore." A committee official says that it is now considering the growing criticism and issuing new operational guidelines. "We hope these reforms will correct anomalies," he says, without saying how.

Some locations with World Heritage sites are learning that it's not an unmixed blessing. The German city of Dresden, known for its splendid baroque and rococo architecture, won heritage status in 2004 for its restored city centre including palaces, churches, opera houses and museums. Then in 2006 UNESCO's culture police frowned on the city fathers' decision to build a four-lane bridge across the river Elbe, over a mile away from the historic center. They gravely "delisted" the city in 2009 for refusing to obey orders not to build. The citizens of Dresden now enjoy their new bridge and somehow continue to thrive in one of Germany's fastest-growing cities.

Latest target of UNESCO intrusion is Liverpool. The English city on the Mersey, home of the Beatles, founded in 1207, was granted World Heritage status in 2004. Alas, a three-day visit by UNESCO inspectors in 2011 concluded with the warning that it would lose its status unless it made radical changes to the $9 billion Liverpool Waters project to regenerate its northern docklands. The project, a half-mile from the historic center, includes offices, a shopping mall, cruise liner terminal and other job-creating features. "This project is absolutely vital for the future of the city," the head of the Liverpool city council, Joe Anderson, told me on the phone. "We have a 29 percent unemployment rate, and this will create jobs both now and for generations to come. Plans dating back 100 years show our forefathers wanted a similar docklands development. And now we have these outsiders trying to tell us how to shape our city."

He still hopes for a compromise, but Liverpudlians will get their new docklands.

The intrusions can get worse. Maladroitly designating a World Heritage site can actually spark warfare, a rather serious unintended consequence for an organization striving for a "culture of peace." That happened on the Cambodia-Thailand border after the Preah Vihear temple was selected in July 2008 in response to a Cambodian request. This reignited a longstanding border dispute over that area. Within weeks the first Thai and Cambodian soldiers were being killed in firefights, while thousands of civilians fled. The 1,000-year-old temple itself was damaged. The military standoff continues while the International Court of Justice considers the case.

Meanwhile, UNESCO's boffins recently created a functionary's dream: a program that is, literally, infinite. If you liked physical, measurable World Heritage, they reasoned, you'll love the *intangible* heritage that can exist simply in the minds and habits of certain people. This can mean everything from oral traditions, performing arts, social practices, quaint rituals and festivities, to "knowledge and practices concerning nature and the universe."

There are already 267 intangible heritage items, but, as an expansive program official explains, "There exist in the world thousands, even billions of potential practices that could be on the list. It's unlimited and infinite. The only limit is our capacity to handle it." You can bet that will be growing. Meanwhile, recent additions include the Mibu no Hana Taue rice planting ritual in Japan, Mexico's mariachi music, French cooking and horseback-riding, and Croatia's Nijemo Kolo, a silent circle dance from the hinterland of Dalmatia. The only really important heritage ritual still missing from the list is the Texas Two-Step, though it does unfortunately involve a man leading a woman.

Less than a decade after the U.S. rejoined, UNESCO, with the Palestinian flag now flying at its headquarters, has shown convincingly that it is back to its old political games. Whatever the best intentions of the secretariat, political infighting will always trump good works. Africa, the Middle East, and the emerging nations own it. They may individually contribute one percent or less to the budget, but their vote equals America's. Without weighted voting according to contributions, or some safety valve like the UN's Security Council, they will stay in the driver's seat. It is unrealistic to think the U.S. can significantly influence UNESCO's direction, as the futile campaign to block the admission of Palestine shows.

The organization does have worthwhile programs in literacy, tsunami warning systems, clean water, post-disaster relief, and others. But unlike some other UN agencies that occasionally have quantifiable, visible results, most of UNESCO's activities are impossible to assess objectively and are oriented to pleasing its activist clients. Moreover, in the absence of any sunset clauses, vested interests can keep asinine or downright undesirable programs, all with overwhelmingly self-important names, running indefinitely.

Britain, far more tough-minded toward ineffective UN agencies than the Obama Administration, did its own independent assessment of UNESCO in 2011. Among other failings, the study found it "is unable to identify its impact. Systematic results reporting and evaluation is not adequately practiced... UNESCO is under-delivering significantly in its leadership of the education sector... Long-lasting historic underperformance now means much of UNESCO's mandate is often done elsewhere." Without improvement, the UK threatens to cut its funding, as it has already to UN Habitat, the UN International Strategy for Disaster Reduction, and the International Labor Organization.

Do useful programs in education and the like require a heavy, inept, expensive international bureaucracy? Or could unilateral foreign aid, along with ad hoc groupings of nations, nongovernmental organizations, and corporate sponsors do the job more efficiently?

The question is rapidly becoming academic for the U.S. By cutting off its funding to UNESCO, America has de facto begun heading for the exit. It is not an option to humiliatingly lose all moral authority there by trying to remain a member without paying our dues. (Internal murmuring against the U.S. on this score has already begun.) Washington policymakers must accept the logic of this situation and either change the laws that created it or declare America's official withdrawal. Bokova's December, 2011, trip to Washington to lobby the Hill changed few minds. Her argument, that U.S. influence abroad will be reduced without its voice at the culture palace on the Seine, pales beside UNESCO's endemic flaws.

"UNESCO is easy to criticize, even to mock. How could it be otherwise? Here we have an organization which has set out to influence the educational, scientific and cultural activities of the world—no less. Obviously ridiculous and laughable! Yet would it not be more helpful to suspend judgment at least until the facts have been looked at as a whole?" Those words were written in 1951 by a former UNESCO staff member, the British psychical researcher, bibliographer, biographer, and translator Theodore Besterman, in the first book ever published about the organization. It shows that the UN's cultural agency, with its ill-defined, infinite utopian mandate, has been open to abuse and invited criticism since the beginning. The difference is that now the facts are in.

Update: *The organization continued to struggle with the tainted Obiang Prize. While wrangling over it went on at the executive board—the African-Arab bloc insisting it be awarded—investigations in America and France revealed how corrupt the donor's playboy son, Teodoro Nguema Obiang Mangue, known as Teodorin, was, thanks to Equatorial Guinea's dirty money. He moved over $100 million into those countries, using it to purchase lavish homes in Malibu and Paris, and fleets of luxury automobiles. And the executive board voted in the spring of 2012 to keep Syria on the human rights committee, despite vigorous efforts by the U.S. and Britain to have it removed. In the face of such irresponsible, provocative behavior, America's continued membership appeared ever more undesirable.*

My article predictably provoked replies from a number of readers. Following are those by two prominent ones.

### *From Ambassador David T. Killion, U.S. Permanent Representative to UNESCO*

Joseph A. Harriss' recent article expresses appropriate concern about certain recent events at UNESCO. At the same time, the piece mischaracterizes events that are portrayed as stains on the organization when they were actually triumphs for UNESCO—and U.S. interests.

For example, Harriss alleges that the election pitting Mubarak's corrupt henchman Farouk Hosni against other candidates was a black mark on UNESCO's reputation. On the contrary, due to intense and vigorous pressure by the United States, Hosni was defeated and instead the organization elected Irina Bokova, who in my view has been a superb Director General. Without U.S. active membership in UNESCO, this would not have happened.

Similarly, the controversy over Iranian sponsorship of World Philosophy Day ended in a U.S. victory and Iranian defeat. Director General Bokova played a statesmanlike leadership role during this crisis, making a clear decision to cancel the plan to hold World Philosophy Day in Tehran. Without U.S. active membership in UNESCO, this would not have happened.

Third, the piece makes the classic mistake of conflating the organization with its Member States. This is the world. The United Nations and organizations like UNESCO reflect the full spectrum of its membership—democracies, dictatorships, failed states, emerging powers. We can either be engaged and active in fighting for our values and interests, or we can find a seat on the bench while other players dictate the game.

UNESCO's conduct and constitution are profoundly influenced by the United States. Its mandate to promote education, science, and culture to advance universal respect for justice, rule of law, human rights, and fundamental freedoms reflects American values. Our active engagement is absolutely critical to ensuring that the organization stays on track.

Mr. Harriss also gets it wrong when he suggests that UNESCO doesn't do anything to fight discrimination against women except to "preach the good word." To cite just a few examples, UNESCO is on the front lines in Egypt and Tunisia, educating women about their rights and supporting their participation in political processes. In the Democratic Republic of Congo, UNESCO works to prevent violence against women through school and community-level programs. These programs help create stable, democratic societies that are more resistant to extremism and violence.

Of course, Harriss is right to be outraged about Syria's reappointment to the UNESCO committee that deals with human rights. But the story isn't finished. In early February, thirty countries from around the world, including the United States, requested that UNESCO's Executive Board review the issue when it meets in late February/early March. With active U.S. engagement, respect for human rights and dignity may triumph once again.

If we follow the author's advice to withdraw, we would be unable to pursue the Syrian issue and many others fundamental to our interests at UNESCO. American leadership is crucial at UNESCO and this is true now more than ever. Without it, UNESCO -- an organization that has enjoyed widespread bipartisan support -- could very well become a "rogue agency."

### From Mr. Neil Ford, Director, Division of Public Information, UNESCO

If only UNESCO could embalm the brain of Joseph A. Harriss. It contains a perfect example of cold war mentality from around the time of the Cuban missile crisis—definitely a cultural artifact worth preserving. Harriss is so busy looking for communists and defending U.S. global hegemony that he can't see the modern UNESCO. We are the UN agency that:

- Teaches police in Afghanistan how to read and write;
- Leads global research in Tsunami warning systems;
- Ensures that the Holocaust is never forgotten; and
- Spearheads Education for All, the movement for universal schooling.

And yes, we're the first UN agency to admit Palestine. What Harriss misses is that—put to the vote—every UN agency would make the same decision, except for the General Assembly in New York where the U.S. has a veto through the Security Council. At UNESCO, he blames this new global reality on the "aggressive Arab-African regional bloc" and comes dangerously close to racism when he talks of "grinning, gibbering, gesticulating inmates" "taking over the asylum." Does he always have such an extreme reaction when a vote goes against him? I'm surprised *The American Spectator* agreed to print such bigoted, undemocratic cant.

But never mind. No one's perfect, certainly not UNESCO. We're in the middle of reforming our business processes and management systems so that the excesses Harriss so exhaustively describes can never happen again.

Actually, there's a lot that someone with his perspective should be cheerful about. The old UNESCO tried to stifle media through the New World Information and Communication Order. The new UNESCO defends media freedom by protesting every time a journalist is killed in the line of duty. Isn't that what was supposed to happen when America won the cold war?

*My replies:*

I was delighted when the editors told me they had received letters reacting to my article on UNESCO. I expected that they would be the sort of serious, constructive discussion of the organization's problems and what to do about them that the article was intended to stimulate. They did, after all, come from Mr. Neil Ford, UNESCO's director of public information, and Ambassador David Killion of the U.S. Mission to UNESCO. Imagine then my disappointment on discovering that their letters, except for Ambassador Killion's, contained only spiteful vociferation and personal attacks.

First, to answer Mr. Ford: After a brief flash of wit concerning the desirability of embalming my brain, he launches into a snide tirade, beginning with preposterously trying to paint me as a commie hunter of the old Cold War school. He also says

I cannot see the modern UNESCO. On the contrary, his reaction indicates that I have seen today's UNESCO only too well. More to the point, a close reading of the article will show that there is no "looking for communists" or "defending U.S. global hegemony," though clearly Mr. Ford, in keeping with the prevailing UNESCO attitude toward America, certainly does not favor the latter. It is distressing that the UNESCO director of public information, surely an intelligent, articulate gentleman as one would expect, resorts to a cheap ad hominem attack. Indeed, his whole missive is devoted to assailing the author, rather than responding concretely to the facts and issues mentioned in the article. He might usefully even have pointed out errors, if any.

His statement that every UN agency would also have admitted Palestine is a spectacularly unsupported allegation. If he has any, Mr. Ford would do better to give us his empirical evidence for that assertion. That would have gone far to refute, if possible, the point that Palestine chose UNESCO, not some other agency, because they knew it was the weak link in the UN system.

He refers to the Arab-African bloc being a "new global reality." This does indeed reflect the official UNESCO line and its day-to-day reality on the ground. But what concerns me is that he comes dangerously close to calling me a racist, the lowest of low blows, to which I do not take kindly. But in all due Christian charity, I forgive him. I understand that, in the absence of seriously contesting points I raise, and being unable to express himself with the sort of verbal elegance one might expect of a high UNESCO official representing what claims to be the world's premier cultural organization, he has no choice but to fall back on guttersnipe rhetoric.

He asks, oddly, whether I always have such an extreme reaction when a vote goes against me. While I am flattered that UNESCO might have been voting for or against me personally, the vote actually had nothing to do with me. It was against the member states that considered UNESCO was not the proper forum for deciding the question of Palestinian statehood. Besides the United States, these included such considerable nations as Australia, Canada, the Czech Republic, Germany, Israel, Lithuania, the Netherlands and Sweden, among others. Your argument about the vote is with them, Mr. Ford, not with me. I am only the messenger of the bad news.

When he refers to an ongoing reform of the "excesses" I describe, I can only accept and applaud Mr. Ford's candid admission that 1) my article was indeed exhaustively researched, and, 2) that these "excesses" need to be corrected. QED.

As to America's winning the Cold War, I fail to see the connection between that and the fact that UNESCO has again become dysfunctional due to the political and, occasionally, economic corruption made clear in my article. More likely, such incoherence is simply another example of Mr. Ford's regrettably angry reaction due, no doubt to a sensitive nerve having been touched. Perhaps he would like to cool down and make a positive contribution to a discussion about what can be done to reform that organization? Just a thought. But the present reality is that such reform, as in the 1980s and '90s, will probably be possible only as a result of the salutary shock of America's complete withdrawal.

As to Ambassador David Killion's contribution, I salute his sincere engagement in his task, as do many other ambassadors to UNESCO I interviewed. The problem is that he understandably—and, I am sure, sincerely—wants to portray these setbacks as victories. My research makes it necessary that I disagree, as my article demonstrates.

His contention that the defeat of Farouk Hosny as director general was a triumph is unconvincing. At best, this is barely snatching victory from the jaws of defeat. But, while the U.S. Mission's role here was indeed exemplary, that is not the point, which is that Hosny's very candidature and near victory demonstrates the systemic failure of the organization.

Ditto the embarrassing mess over World Philosophy Day in Iran. The question is not whether the U.S. and other member states were at the last moment able to change that incredibly stupid decision, but why on earth UNESCO decided to hold it in Iran in the first place. Systemic, self-perpetuating failure is the answer.

Ambassador Killion argues, as anyone in his position must, that engagement in such an organization is the only way to influence it. The unfortunate reality is that most of the time, it's a losing game for the U.S., as the vote on Palestine admission and the corruption of the World Heritage Convention decisively demonstrate.

His argument that UNESCO has programs that promote democracy fails to pass the test of results. UNESCO, as

I have pointed out in the article, has many high-flown programs with impressive names, and indeed programs within programs. The problem, as the thoroughgoing British evaluation last year says, is showing convincing results. I see very few, as do the British.

Yes, there is the promise to review the disastrous decision to include Syria on the committee that treats human rights. Nice try again, Ambassador, but Syria's appointment to that committee would never have happened if UNESCO were not dysfunctional. The whole episode illustrates its systemic failure.

Lastly, Ambassador Killion argues with some heat the need of American participation and engagement to keep UNESCO from becoming a rogue agency. Dear Ambassador, it is *already* a rogue agency, as anyone who reads my article can see. The U.S. can do nothing useful about that except to make the ultimate protest of withdrawing. History shows, as it did during our deliberate 19-year absence, that only that will concentrate UNESCO's collective mind on the root and branch reform that could make it, once again, a worthwhile enterprise worthy of American support.

# PART THREE: *LES AFFAIRES INTERNATIONALES*

PARIS has long been my base as a correspondent, but because foreign bureaus are notoriously short-handed, I have had to keep an eye on European and international affairs as well. No single journalist could claim to be an expert on both of these endlessly complex subjects; I certainly don't. But France, being at the geopolitical heart of Europe, is a good observation post for viewing things like Europe's tentative efforts at creating a union of sorts.

Thus this section on affairs beyond France's borders includes several articles on Europe past and present. That gets into relations between Europe and America, including the role Americans have played in helping Europe overcome its debilitating tangle of centuries-old rivalries and antagonisms, not to mention the after-effects of WW II. The Cold War, for instance, would have resulted in the tragedy of Soviet domination without vital U.S. assistance, with the Berlin Airlift the most spectacular example. Still, that has not kept thinkers from Oswald Spengler to Jean-Paul Sartre from declaring the end of Europe as we have known it. The historian Walter Laqueur worries that it may end up a cultural theme park.

Based on its results so far, the so-called European Union will not be enough to prevent that. The main achievements of this Eurofudge have been to subsidize French farmers and redistribute wealth to the poorest areas of Spain, Portugal, and

Greece—inadvertently leading to Europe's grave current debt crisis and just possibly the end of the euro. Indeed, very few Europeans still believe that the funny money called the euro can promote prosperity. It is instead a strait jacket preventing EU members from competing in the global marketplace, thereby destroying jobs. But mentioning that is taboo in Europe. So taboo is it that Brussels Eurocrats refuse even to discuss plans to deal with problems created by the euro.

One of the EU's more preposterous claims is that it has produced peace in Europe for half a century. If that were true, maybe the Europeans wouldn't need the tens of thousands of American troops still stationed there. On the other hand, it is questionable whether the 60-year-old North Atlantic Alliance, NATO, still serves any purpose. A close look at its clumsy management and command structure shows that it has outlived its usefulness. Saying that, too, is taboo. I think that's all the more reason to say it.

# PRESENT AT THE CREATION

Contrasting America and Europe.

Context: *A look at political developments in America and Europe during the years from 1788 to 1800 is like being present at the creation, when the modern world was being painfully born. While much of monarchical Europe was engulfed in an orgy of warfare, the U.S. got on with the business of peacefully setting up a radically new type of society based on government by the people.*

"THE CONTRAST between the United States and Europe is too striking not to be noticed by even the most superficial observer." To that typically understated comment by George Washington in the earliest, uncertain days of our republic, one can only add a fervent, thank God for the difference. If that seems unduly churlish toward our European friends, then I invite you to dip into Jay Winik's new book, *The Great Upheaval: America and the Birth of the Modern World, 1788-1800.*

This look at the momentous events crowded into the last years of the 18$^{th}$ century leaves one overarching impression: how those people in Europe could hate. Lurching from one vicious bloodletting to another they shot, slashed and eviscerated each other with glorious abandon as centuries of feudal brutality and institutionalized slaughter came to a frenzied head.

While America got on with the unprecedented task of peacefully transferring executive power and setting up government of the people, by the people, for the people, Continental Europe was consumed by a continuing orgy of violence. As Winik puts it, "In 1792, the most striking feature of the Western world, old as well as new, was the hideous death rattle of the war engulfing Europe." Small wonder that millions of Europeans began heading en masse for the New World, inspired by a document that began, "We hold these truths to be self-evident, that all men are created equal..."

It was a world in Promethean tumult as subversive ideas about individual freedom fermented in many countries simultaneously—with drastically different outcomes. It was these relationships and interrelationships, as much as any one country alone, that laid the foundations for the world we know today."

This situation was created by in good part by the same factor that produces much of our cultural, political and economic climate today: the age's new mobility. Ideas and men began freely crossing borders, leading inevitably to the dilution of conviction, whether in religion or government. Doubts about long-held beliefs such as divine right and hereditary privilege were raised by the French trio of *philosophes*: Voltaire and his fight for intellectual freedom, Montesquieu on the necessary separation of powers and limited monarchy, and Rousseau with his insistence that republican liberty would return man to his basic goodness. These were the intellectual underpinning and motive force for one of the greatest events in history, the creation of the American nation. To be sure, they were spread far and wide by the age's unprecedented cross-fertilization of cultures— from far-off France Montesquieu and Voltaire intrigued Russia's Catherine the Great. But only New World vessels were ready to receive the new wine of freedom.

It's worth recalling that this exchange of ideas worked both ways. If the Founding Fathers were well read in the *philosophes*, and the Enlightenment informed thinking at the Constitutional Convention, America also influenced the Old World. Russian reformers like Nikolai Ivanovich Novikov and Alexander Radishchev studied the ideas of Franklin, Jefferson, and Washington. Jefferson and Thomas Paine strongly colored French republican thought. And Gouverneur Morris, a signer of the Declaration of Independence, advised Louis XVI, unfortunately too late, on how to modernize French society.

As a result, by the end of the 18th century it was clear to opinion leaders on both continents that the past was only prologue to what was coming. Many, like Lafayette, enthusiastically welcomed the coming change. Others, like Catherine the Great, finally rejected it furiously after initial fascination. In any case, this proved to be America's hour.

It was an hour full of unpredictable peril. Tension and drama marked the Constitutional Convention of 1787 and the nation's first steps toward the democratic transfer of political power. A handful of audacious men representing vastly different vested interests attempted to invent a diverse nation from scratch in only four months. The peril was clear to Benjamin Franklin, who warned, "Our detractors believe that we are here only for the purpose of cutting one another's throats," and to Washington, who sighed, "The event is in the hand of God."

The document they produced was one of the most creative moments in the history of political thought. Washington's later stepping down as president of his own volition in March 1797, rather than clinging to power like a European monarch, was another unprecedented event. As King George III had commented cynically, "If he does that, he will be the greatest man in the world." He did. He was.

The uniqueness of America's accomplishment becomes clear when compared with what was happening simultaneously in France, where the U.S. Constitution was hailed as a portent of things to come. Maximilien Robespierre, he of the later Terror, called Franklin "the most brilliant scholar in the universe." On July 14, 1790, the first anniversary of the storming of the Bastille, Thomas Paine and John Paul Jones were invited to carry the American flag at the huge "freedom festival" staged on Paris's Champ de Mars, symbolizing the passage of the spirit of American freedom to France. But it all turned tragic when the French Revolution ran madly out of control, producing what Margaret Thatcher once called, with tart reduction, "a pile of corpses and a tyrant."

The period's events in France, from the beheading of Louis XVI and Marie Antoinette, to the infighting among Robespierre, Danton and Marat, came to be known as the Terror. It is viscerally vivid in such details such as the executioners' assembly-line approach to beheading—surely that should be *de*heading—to satisfy the vindictive bloodlust of the

Revolutionary Tribunal: honing their skills with the newly invented guillotine, they went from 22 heads in 36 minutes to 32 in 25 minutes, finally reaching 12 heads in five minutes, or 144 per hour. In all, some 40,000 French citizens would feel "the razor of the republic" on their necks. Louis XVI himself was certainly indecisive and often weak, but few monarchs in history are as underappreciated. Few would leave this world with such dignity, nobility, and grandeur.

Unlike America's one durable constitution and uninterrupted two centuries of democracy, the end result of France's errant quest for escape from its feudal past would be two empires, three kingdoms and five republics. Perhaps part of the explanation lies in the innate difficulty of the French to turn cerebral theory into everyday practice. One is reminded of the reaction of John Adams, the quintessential down-to-earth American pragmatist, on reading a treatise by the French philosopher Destutt de Tracy, founder of the school of *idéologie*. "What was this delightful piece of French rubbish?" Adams asked. "What did 'ideology' stand for? Does it mean idiotism?"

Update: *More than 200 years later, and despite the best efforts of the globalizers, Europe and America remain as far apart in their institutions and basic attitudes toward life and its possibilities as they ever were. However much the Europeans would like to imitate the American model—and they mimic everything they decently can, collectively and individually, of the American way of life—they can never duplicate the American way. The thin façade of the so-called European Union notwithstanding, they remain riven by their cultural differences, by their class consciousness, by their inability to assimilate newcomers..*

# AND THE REST ALSO RISE

America's decline has become the fashionable new orthodoxy.

Context: *The European powers that for centuries had created and defined Western civilization were bled white at the end of the First World War. It pushed the young American nation onto the world scene in 1918, even though Americans, as Teddy Roosevelt lamented, had no "stomach for empire." By 1945 the Europeans were on their knees, kaput as international powers, thanks to one last irrational orgy of tribal bloodlust. Suddenly the U.S. not only dictated the rules of the game, it was the game.*

SOME SAID said it was a permanent new world order, the end of history. But that vision of history and our place in it contradicted what philosophers and historians had long been telling us: *sic transit gloria mundi* applies always and everywhere, no exceptions. Oswald Spengler's elegiac, monumental *The Decline of the West*, appropriately published in 1918, argued that the creative period of our culture was over and it was downhill from there. Arnold Toynbee's *Study of History* showed the rise and fall of civilizations and the nations that produced them to be the inevitable norm.

Declinism went into high gear two decades ago with Paul Kennedy's much-discussed *The Rise and Fall of the Great*

*Powers*, which developed the concept of relative politico-economic decline due to constantly shifting patterns of wealth, innovation, and military strength, with its obvious implications for the erosion of America's dominance. More recently, Robert Kagan's *The Return of History and the End of Dreams* gave us a stiff dose of reality with its warning that international competition and conflict were alive and well. Patrick Buchanan told us in *The Death of the West* that the breakdown of religious, cultural and moral values threatened our collective soul.

Inspired by ominous events like the tanking dollar and credit crisis, the story line of America's decline has become today's new orthodoxy, with the likes of Thomas Friedman opining that "We are not who we think we are. We are living on borrowed time and borrowed dimes." It was the talk of Davos at a World Economic Forum; Goldman Sachs issued its so-called BRIC report showing that Brazil, Russia, India and China are coming on strong; the Pew Global Attitudes Project has found that majorities in Western Europe believe either that China will replace America as the leading superpower—or already has. It also found that 31 percent of Americans think the same thing.

All this makes Fareed Zakaria's *The Post-American World* something of a late-comer to declinology. But late-comers often have an advantage, and his is that he can build on the others and do some summing up. He finds a balance between dire views of declining American influence and hopeful scenarios for the future. He points out that since America emerged victorious from the Second World War, Nervous Nellies have often worried about losing the number one spot. First we fretted over being behind the Soviets in space after they put up Sputnik, then the oil shocks of the early 1970s convinced us Saudi Arabia and Europe were the future, and in the 1980s we were going to be eaten alive by the Japanese. Time and again, America's resiliency and resourcefulness made such notions look silly.

The "rise of the rest," is the third big power shift of the last 500 years. It began with the rise of the Renaissance Western world, followed in the late 19th century by an industrialized U.S. becoming the most powerful nation since imperial Rome. Today Zakaria observes a move away from American dominance in every dimension—industrial, financial, educational, social, cultural—except military power.

This post-American world is one shaped by many people in many places, multipolarity with a vengeance. Taipei has the world's tallest building, Mexico the richest man, China the largest publicly traded corporation, Europe is building the biggest passenger plane, and London becoming the leading financial center. Most of the industrialized world has better cell-phone service than the U.S., computer connectivity is faster and cheaper, with America rating about 16th in broadband penetration per capita. The most richly endowed investment fund is in the United Arab Emirates, the biggest shopping mall in Beijing, largest movie industry in India. And, in case you were wondering, the largest Ferris wheel is in Singapore.

The good news is that globalized capitalism is hugely successful and millions are escaping poverty. And this success is all America's doing, because for the last 60 years it has been urging the world to open up to free markets and develop new industries and technologies. It has trained their best and brightest in its universities, and it worked: the natives have gotten good at capitalism.

China and India are the world's current success stories. But while India—handicapped by messy democracy—will have the third-largest economy by 2040, China's astonishing rise is already here, having compressed 200 years of Western industrial development into 30 and still growing faster than any major economy in recorded history. Some of the results of that rise: exporting as much in a single day as it did in all of 1978; making two-thirds of the world's photo copiers, microwave ovens and shoes; average Chinese personal income rising 700 percent in the last 30 years. Thus has the world's largest country also become its largest manufacturer, second-largest consumer, biggest saver, and probably, second-largest military spender. Development on such a scale adds an entirely new dimension to the international system.

One aspect of that, for better or worse, is that the world is moving from anger toward the U.S. to indifference, from anti-Americanism to post-Americanism, from Yankee Go Home riots during presidential visits abroad to a bored, consumption-drugged shrug. And the newly confident and assertive rest won't be talked down to any more: Chinese officials publicly lecture Washington on its "warped conception" of market regulation that created the sub-prime crisis, and denounce its "hostility" and "discriminatory attitude" on allowing foreign investments.

Zakaria points out uncritically that two of China's "advantages" today are autocratic central planning ("not having to respond to the public has often helped Beijing carry out its strategy"), and the Chinese not believing in God. A foreign multinational wants an attractive, well-located production site that inconveniently is already occupied by buildings and people? No problem, they can be cleaned out within months. And a tolerant Confucianism frees the authorities from having to worry about petty ethical problems created by Christian morality.

Still, for all their new dynamism the rest are not 10 feet tall. America's per capita GDP remains 25 times that of China. Of the 35 largest companies on the Shanghai stock exchange, 34 are either wholly or partly owned by the government—hardly the best path to efficient management. Besides that, China is the world's worst polluter, regional differences are widening, and socio-economic inequality is rising to dangerous levels, as is corruption among high Chinese officials. In India some 836 million live on less than 50 cents a day, while Indian democracy is problematic at best: nearly one-fifth of the members of the Indian parliament have been accused of crimes including embezzlement, rape, and murder.

Today dominance by an "enfeebled" America may be over, but it can be argued that the world is increasingly going our way. Prosperity, open markets, and democracy are spreading, we live in a relatively peaceful era by historical standards, al-Qaeda and rogue states are fading into blips on the radar screen. America's advantage in higher education is overwhelming and its demographics are better than Europe's.

But with hegemony finished, consultation, cooperation and compromise with the rest is the way to go as we dodder off to retirement. We can always aim at being the world's chairman of the board guiding a group of independent directors. The elder statesman, in effect. Not a bad role, though far from a Roman imperium. And get used to a second-best Ferris wheel.

Update: *It's worth recalling that slightly over 100 years ago a bold Canadian prime minister confidently declared that while the 19th century was America's, the 20th would surely belong to Canada (sic). Gloomy predictions aside, the hard fact is that today we continue to inspire and fascinate with our openness, opportunity, flexibility and dynamism. America remains the default power, as one German commentator recently put it. "Who else will take care of global business?" he wondered. Until further notice it's still the last, best hope of mankind.*

# WHEN THE PARTY WAS OVER

For Americans in Paris from 1920 to 1940, it was very good
while it lasted.

Context: *Despite what I have said about the irreconcilable
differences between American and French institutions, individual
Americans and Frenchmen generally get along very well. Indeed, I'm
convinced that we have more in common, temperamentally, with the
French than with the British cousins.*

LIVING IN PARIS is one of our oldest traditions. It started in
1776 with Ben Franklin, who spent eight delightful years
wrangling loans, military aid and diplomatic recognition from
France, becoming the homespun darling of many powdered and
perfumed young ladies. Thomas Jefferson replaced him in 1784,
representing the U.S. at Versailles, opening French markets to
American products—and for five years thoroughly enjoying the
local art, wine, and food (while warning American tourists to
stay away from Parisian luxury and sinfulness). John Adams,
Thomas Paine and James Monroe spent important time in Paris,
with Adams's wife Abigail vocally sad to leave. Even that
quintessential American poet Walt Whitman imagined himself
"a real Parisian."

The tradition continued throughout the 19th century as American financiers, socialites, artists and mere adventurers made the city home. In the 1920s Gertrude Stein and her "lost generation" acolytes Hemingway, Scott Fitzgerald, Dos Passos, et al., made Paris a must for American creative types of all stripes. Saint Louis-born Josephine Baker starred at the Folies Bergère with her scandalous *danse sauvage* and her song, "*J'ai deux amours, mon pays et Paris.*" A cliché, an-American-in-Paris, was born, later to be incarnated by Gene Kelly in the musical of that name.

For many Americans who lived here between 1920 and 1940, Paris was one long party. As the journalist Eric Sevareid, who did time at the *Paris Herald*, recalled, "The permanent American colony in those days divided quite sharply between those who worked for a living like newspapermen, and those who kept country châteaux and moved between Paris and various spas." The level of implacable frivolity can be measured by the casual note in the *Paris Herald* as German troops closed in on the city in late May 1940: "Owing to unsettled conditions, the racing card scheduled for this afternoon at Longchamps has been called off."

Many more things would be called off in coming months and years, as Charles Glass reminds us in his new book, *Americans in Paris: Life and Death under Nazi Occupation 1940-44.* Glass, who has spent much of his career as a foreign correspondent, mines a lode of diaries, war documents, letters and police files from the period to portray some of the more interesting Americans who stayed in the wartime city. As he puts it, "Americans in Paris under the occupation were among the most eccentric, original and disparate collections of their countrymen anywhere—tested as few others have been before or since." For them, the party was over.

Ambassador William Bullitt advised Americans to leave when Britain and France declared war on Germany for invading Poland in September 1939. Many of the 30,000-odd American colony in Paris, the largest in Europe, hesitated for family or professional reasons. Others simply loved the place (the feeling was reciprocal, it then being acceptable for Frenchmen to openly like Americans), and were convinced that the Maginot Line would hold. The approximately 2,000 who remained after Wehrmacht jackboots hit the Champs Élysées on June 14, 1940, were protected by official U.S. neutrality for another 18 months.

But when Hitler unilaterally declared war on the U.S. four days after Pearl Harbor, Paris Americans suddenly became enemy aliens. The White House and State Department urged Bullitt himself to get out. "No American ambassador in Paris has ever run away from anything," he cabled FDR, "and that I think is the best tradition we have in the American diplomatic service." After the French government turned tail and fled south, the embassy was one of the few governmental organs of any stature still functioning in Paris; Bullitt became in effect the city's provisional mayor. (His haggling was key to convincing the Germans not to bombard the city.) But he could not prevent over 1,700 American citizens being rounded up and interned for varying periods at Frontstalag 122, 50 miles north of Paris.

For the next four years Americans shared the hardships of other Parisians. They counted their ration coupons, scrounged for bread and other essentials, suffered malnutrition and anemia. They got around on bicycles if lucky enough to own, or steal, one. They shivered in darkened, unheated apartments due to coal and electricity shortages. During the few hours a day the Metro ran, its cars were so crowded that, as one wrote, "a sardine box is spacious and deliciously perfumed by comparison... passengers have their clothes torn off, children are trampled underfoot, fist fights common." Neighbors settled old accounts French style, by denouncing each other to the Gestapo.

Paris Americans during the occupation were a disparate group. They included the likes of Ohio-born Countess Clara Longworth de Chambrun, a cousin of Franklin Roosevelt and the wife of Count Aldebert de Chambrun, Washington-born and a direct descendant of Lafayette. An accomplished Shakespeare scholar and author of 16 books, eight each in English and French, the indomitable Clara brooked no insolence from the Nazis. As wartime head of the American Library, she established a wary working relationship with Dr. Hermann Fuchs, the Bibliotheksschutz, or protector of libraries in German-occupied Europe. That and her fierce determination kept the library open as a unique beacon of American culture during those dark years.

Other American books were available from Sylvia Beach, originally of Baltimore, who owned the Shakespeare and Company bookshop. For 20 years her small Left Bank establishment had served as a club, mail drop and forum for

American writers in Paris. It was also a valued source of books for French writers like André Gide and Paul Valéry who there developed an appreciation of American literature. When an occupying Wehrmacht officer, angry because she refused to sell him her last copy of James Joyce's *Finnegan's Wake,* threatened to confiscate the shop, she spunkily closed it permanently and hid all the books in a friend's apartment before he came back with troops. Rounded up and interned for several months, Beach was later "liberated" in August 1944 by Earnest Hemingway and his self-styled Hem Division of four jeeps on his way to the Ritz Hotel bar.

Charles Bedaux was a naturalized American and self-made businessman married to the well-connected socialite Fern née Lombard of Grand Rapids. An advisor on productivity to hundreds of corporations around the world, Bedaux was variously tagged "a Mephistophelean little Franco-American efficiency expert" (*Time*) and "The Mystery Man of international intrigue" (*The New York Times*). High society contacts like the Duke and Duchess of Windsor, who were married at his Renaissance château, enabled him to consort and deal with both French officials of the Vichy regime and Nazi rulers of the occupied zone. Curious about his dealings with the Germans, Washington put him under surveillance by Treasury, State, the Office of Naval Intelligence, and the FBI. Arrested in 1942, he committed suicide before being tried in the U.S. for treason and trading with the enemy.

Dr. Sumner Jackson, an outstanding example of civilian American heroism in occupied France, was head surgeon at the

American Hospital of Paris. When not treating hundreds of wounded Allied soldiers and American civilians, Jackson secretly worked with resistance networks to spirit downed British and U.S. airmen out of France. His French wife Toquette and 15-year-old son Philip also aided, the boy even infiltrating a German submarine base at Saint Nazaire to photograph U-boat pens for later bombing. The Gestapo arrested all three just two weeks before D-Day and sent them to concentration camps. On May 3, 1945, the day after the Nazi surrender in Berlin, Jackson, his son and thousands of other prisoners were herded onto ships in Lubeck harbor; an RAF squadron, assuming the ships were transporting German soldiers, attacked. Philip survived, as did Toquette in a separate camp. But Jackson died in a particularly tragic case of friendly fire.

Today's American community (estimates run as high as 50,000), composed largely of itinerant businessmen, spouses of French nationals, students, retirees, and the usual diplomats, is humdrum by comparison with these, as well as with the colorful *entre deux guerres* Yanks who made Paris synonymous with overseas eccentricity and hijinks. Many old American social and professional clubs cut less of a swath.

As for the American press corps, you can still tell the recent arrivals by the new trench coat, but their swagger and ranks have diminished drastically with the decline of foreign bureaus. *Time*, where I once toiled as part of a large squad of correspondents supported by a brigade of researchers, chauffeurs of Mercedes sedans, and factotums in the plush Time-Life

Building near the Champs Élysées, now has one lonely reporter—and the building has been sold off.

Update: *We who live here as tolerated foreign residents blend in inconspicuously, looking for what's left of the good life in the city that the novelist and playwright Irwin Shaw, after a sojourn, termed the urban ideal. It's only Paris, after all, but it's become something like home.*

# FUTILE HEROISM AT DIEN BIEN PHU

There were to be no white flags.

**Context:** *The French generals' plan looked good on paper, but when he saw it, Dwight Eisenhower was horrified. The Battle of Dien Bien Phu was one of the biggest blunders in military history. Although it was also the scene of heroic resistance in the face of overwhelming odds, France's defeat there deeply affected its political scene and heralded the end of its vast colonial empire.*

FOR Ho Chi Minh, né Nguyen Sinh Cung, peripatetic professional revolutionary and alumnus of the Soviet Union's University of the Toilers of the East, founder in 1941 of the Vietminh independence movement against French colonial rule in Indochina, it had been a long wait. Some 50,000 French *colons* had ruled for decades over Vietnam's native population of 20 million Annamites, creaming off the profits from the land's rubber, coal, tin and tungsten. Now at last he smelled blood. French blood, in the broad, mountain-ringed valley known as Dien Bien Phu.

As he saw it, the situation was simple. To illustrate it for a visiting journalist, Ho turned his pith helmet over on the austere bamboo table that served as his desk. Placing his hands in the bottom of the hat, he said, "That's where the French are."

Then, running his fingers around the helmet's rim, "That's where we are. They will never get out."

Simple indeed, and you have to wonder whether only a delusional French general would fail to get it. Certainly President Dwight Eisenhower, a man of some military experience, had to agree with Ho on that point. "Finally, [the French] came along with this Dien Bien Phu plan," he wrote in his memoirs. "As a soldier, I was horror-stricken. I just said, 'My goodness, you don't pen up troops in a fortress, and all history shows that they are just going to be cut to pieces.'"

But French generals, shifting arrows on wall maps back at headquarters, decided this godforsaken spot in the northwest corner of Vietnam was just the place to get General Vo Nguyen Giap's hit-and-run guerrillas into the sort of conventional, set-piece battle the French could win after eight years of harassment. The plan had the additional advantage, in their eyes, of drawing the Vietminh away from the important Tonkin Delta and cutting off their advances toward nearby Laos. Not incidentally, a victory at Dien Bien Phu might just win back some flagging public support among the French public for the Indochina war. The first French paratroops dropped into the valley on November 20, 1953, and began setting up their base.

The generals were wrong, as we know. Why and how they could be so wrong, committing one of the biggest and most costly blunders in modern military history, is the subject of a book by Ted Morgan. A French-born naturalized American citizen formerly known as Sanche de Gramont, Morgan recounts the 56-day battle itself in horrific detail. Thanks to newly opened archives in France and China, and recently declassified top secret U.S. documents, the extent of Chinese aid to the Vietminh and how America was gradually, reluctantly, controversially drawn into the Vietnam War become clear.

It was 55-year-old General Henri Navarre, appointed overall commander of forces in Indochina in May 1953, who chose Dien Bien Phu for the French stand. A career intelligence type, not a combat officer, and with a preference for the European theatre, he protested that he had never served in Asia and knew nothing about Indochina. Paris's answer: "Someone has to do it... You will see it with fresh eyes... Find an honorable way out." When Navarre flew to French army headquarters in Hanoi to work out final details with his commanders on the ground, they unanimously rejected the plan. Drop paratroops over enemy-held terrain? "You're going to lose 50 percent of your men," they told him. In his later memoirs, Navarre baldly writes, "No unfavorable opinion was expressed before the battle."

The augurs were never good. To start with, Navarre immediately requested more troops, but France's pusillanimous Fourth Republic government refused. Of the nearly 15,000 in the garrison, only a minority were French. The rest were from France's pickup colonial armies of Algerians, Moroccans, Laotians and Vietnamese, plus mostly German members of the Foreign Legion. The latter were especially useful, because "They never complained, and when they were killed, no one claimed their corpses."

Then there was Navarre's questionable choice to command the stronghold. Colonel Christian de Castries was a cavalry officer. When offered Dien Bien Phu, he replied candidly, "If you're thinking of setting up an entrenched camp, this isn't my line. I'd rather you picked somebody else." Too bad. So an officer used to carrying the battle to the enemy and operating in the open field of rapid tank advances was ordered to head what was, in effect, a defensive Maginot Line. All the initiative would be left to the Vietminh guerrillas.

Castries soldiered on, repairing the small airstrip that the Viets had previously pitted with holes. Until it was ready, everything had to be parachuted in, from canned cassoulet to bales of barbed wire and a six-ton bulldozer in two parts. Then eight fortified "centers of resistance" were created. There were underground surgical units—and two *Bordels Mobiles de Campagne* (Mobile Field Bordellos), one with 11 Algerian women and the other with five Vietnamese, each with its own madam.

All this was closely observed by two very interested parties: General Giap and the Eisenhower administration.

Giap had his own plans for Dien Bien Phu. The French assumed he would be unable to bring in artillery on the region's narrow, twisting mountain roads. But Giap mobilized brigades of coolies for the seemingly superhuman trek. Working in gangs of hundreds, they manhandled in mortars, 105 mm. cannon, recoilless rifles, anti-aircraft guns and 12-tube Katyusha rocket launchers, much of it provided by Communist China. He had nearly 150 artillery pieces securely dug into the sides of the mountains, compared with 60 French pieces exposed in the valley. Advised of this, Navarre was already having doubts in January 1954. "Two weeks ago I was one hundred percent sure of winning at Dien Bien Phu," he reported to Paris, "but given the new means our intelligence is announcing… I can no longer guarantee success."

The Eisenhower administration, unlike Giap, was divided over what to do. On one hand, Ike, like every administration since Franklin Roosevelt, was loath to help the French in a colonial war. On the other, the domino theory had been dogma in Washington since at least April 1950. That was when President Harry Truman signed off on NSC 64, which held that if the French could not contain Ho's forces, the rest of Asia would go communist. (The American chargé in Saigon was even more alarmist: If Indochina fell, "most of the colored races of the world [sic] would in time fall to the Communist sickle.") In May Truman approved $10 million in aid for Indochina and sent a military assistance group. At this point the tragedy of Indochina became the shared responsibility of France and the United States.

Having just gotten the U.S. out of the Korean War, Ike considered any direct American armed intervention in Vietnam unacceptable. "No one could be more bitterly opposed to ever getting the United States involved in a hot war in that region than I am," he told a press conference. But in January 1954, Ike approved sending 700 tons of military equipment to Vietnam aboard a squadron of C-119 Flying Boxcars with French insignia, piloted by American civilians under CIA contract. By

March the U.S. was actually paying for fully 80 percent of France's Vietnam War.

Giap attacked on March 13. His artillery quickly made the airstrip unusable, so all French reinforcements and supplies had to be parachuted in despite thick anti-aircraft flak. After his troops had dug trenches to within a few hundred yards of the garrison, they advanced in human waves, starting with "death volunteers" who threw themselves at French positions with 20 pounds of TNT strapped to their chests. Reports and letters home give vivid descriptions of the carnage. One Legion officer wrote to his wife of "human waves of Viets drunk on *choum* (rice alcohol) marching over their own dead and attacking with flamethrowers. Our men have bloodied uniforms and ravaged, ghostlike faces." Another described an artillery barrage: "It was like the end of the world. I thought the sky was falling. We were glued to the ground." A German Legionnaire summed up, "We kill them but they just keep coming. *Alles kaput!*"

On a single day early in the siege, doctors performed 23 amputations, plastered 15 broken ribs, sewed up 20 open abdomens and chests. As one surgeon described it, "Piles of hands, arms, legs and feet mixed together as in some foul bouillabaisse. Maggots swarmed in bandages and plaster casts." Machine guns were manned by amputees who urinated on their red-hot barrels to cool them. As morale declined, Castries's chief of staff had a nervous breakdown and had to be evacuated. His artillery commander, who had boasted he would easily wipe out Giap's guns, held a grenade to his body and pulled the pin. Hundreds of deserters, mainly colonial troops, fled to the banks of the Nam Yum River and lived off the plunder from errant air-dropped supplies and stripped corpses.

With no avenue of retreat, only surrender was possible. By May 7, the battle had cost France 16 battalions, two artillery groups, and a squadron of tanks. (Vietminh losses were heavier, but Giap had a virtually inexhaustible supply of manpower.) Castries got his headquarters in Hanoi on the radiophone to say he was sending out negotiators to meet the Vietminh. "Listen, *mon vieux*," replied his delusional chief, "I realize it's all over, but avoid any form of capitulation. That is forbidden. We must have no white flags." Some 10,000 French prisoners were taken. Those who survived forced death marches spent months in camps where mortality rates ran over 60 percent.

Then began the diplomatic games at the Geneva Conference, which opened April 26 and lasted almost three months. There the U.S., Britain, France, Soviet Union, China and the nations of Indochina (Cambodia, Laos, North and South Vietnam) debated and jockeyed for position over what had been a colonial conflict and became a superpower proxy war.

Secretary of State John Foster Dulles took a hard line and earned the enmity of Britain's Anthony Eden, who feared that Dulles wanted to bomb China. (Prime Minister Winston Churchill privately called Dulles "a stupid sermonizer.") Chou En-lai sought the spotlight to raise China's standing as a world power. The French dithered, intellectualized, and drove the others crazy with their shifting positions. In internal memos Britain's Foreign Office lamented the excessive "mental dexterity" of the French, "the hopeless instability of French thought."

The conference ended July 21, 1954, with the partitioning of Vietnam at the 17th parallel, costing France "the crown jewel of its colonial empire." Some of the French press tried to turn defeat into victory. The weekly *Paris Match* called Dien Bien Phu "the capital of heroism." But most saw it clearly, like *Le Figaro*, which editorialized, "During these nine years of war, opportunities to win…were lost because of our weakness… we fought this war shamefully."

The domino effect hit France itself. The humiliating defeat at Dien Bien Phu contributed to the fall of the Fourth Republic and the return to power of Charles de Gaulle. Next to topple were France's West African and North African colonies. Despite the desperate heroism of its troops, the spectacular blunder at Dien Bien Phu weakened France's self-confidence and hastened the end of its colonial empire.

Update: *Today Dien Bien Phu boasts the Victory Statue, a splendid example of grandiose neo-Stalinist style. Dedicated in 2004 to commemorate the battle's 50th anniversary, the metal work is already rusting and cracked. The Vietnamese bureaucrats who oversaw the project are accused of using inferior materials and pocketing the difference, faking documents to embezzle, and taking bribes.*

# EUROPE WAS YESTERDAY

Welcome to the world's biggest theme park.

Context: *Could the obvious exhaustion of Europe's creative juices— today virtually all its popular culture, as well as its social, economic and political thinking, comes from America—its second-rate universities, high unemployment, hand-out mentality and rising violent crime be the signs of a deep-seated malaise?*

OFTEN DECLARED in its death throes over the last 200 years, Europe has been a long time dying. France in particular, bled white by Napoleon's wars, was considered down for the count following its defeat by the Prussians in 1871, and again after the humiliating capitulation of 1940. Twentieth-century European historians and philosophers from Oswald Spengler to Jean-Paul Sartre saw no future for it following the determined destruction and mass slaughter of that century's two European wars. More recently articles with titles like "The End of Europe" and "The Decline and Fall of Europe" have appeared regularly in American media. But Europe has continued to show signs of life, creating seeming prosperity and welfare for all, plus six-week vacations.

Still, what if an insidious cancer, long ignored, covered by taboos, too late detected, really did threaten the Old World?

From being a leader in 1900, when it boasted far-flung colonies, great military power, the strongest economy and a population six times that of the United States, is it destined to become "a cultural theme park, a kind of Disneyland on a level of a certain sophistication for well-to-do visitors from China and India"?

These are the questions that the veteran historian Walter Laqueur poses in his latest work, *The Last Days of Europe: Epitaph for an Old Continent*. European-born, polyglot author of more than 20 learned books, he decided that it was time, he writes, "for a summing up, as the Europe I have known is in the process of disappearing... The general direction seems to be clear, and it is not one that fills my heart with great joy... I hope it will be more than that of a museum."

Recent developments seem to have changed Laqueur's mind considerably about Europe. The rosy picture he painted 15 years ago in his *Europe in Our Time* was full of praise. "The history of postwar Europe," he wrote then, "unlike many other periods in the history of the continent, reads almost like a Hollywood movie of the old-fashioned kind, with all kinds of tensions and conflict but a strikingly happy ending." A spirit of freedom reigned, it had become a civilian superpower and once more a partner in world leadership. He devoted barely two pages to problems posed by new immigrants. Muslim fundamentalism got short shrift. Terrorism was the home-grown variety of Basques, IRA and Italian Red Brigades, not Islamic jihadists.

That was yesterday. Today finds Europe's economy plagued by slow growth and high taxes, while the European Union is stumbling and trying to find a second wind after the failure of its draft constitution and ill-considered enlargement to 27 members. But worse are its demographic decline in the face of uncontrolled immigration, and the turbulent rise of militant Islam.

The face of Europe is changing fast. In Brussels over half of the children born in 2004 were of immigrant, mainly North African, parents. Bangladeshis are taking over the East End of London, a.k.a. Londonistan, while in Germany's Ruhr over half of the cohort under 30 will soon be non-German, mainly Turkish, in origin. (Note to travelers: a world atlas published by London's *Times* carefully identifies the country's languages as German and Turkish.) North Africans are turning large swaths of Paris suburbs into no-go zones as their private halal preserve. Not only big cities are being submerged by the wave of newcomers. Places like Britain's Bradford, Burnley and Oldham are also gradually coming to resemble North Africa and the Middle East.

Immigration is old news. But these immigrants are radically different from either the growing ethnic minorities in the U.S. or the repeated waves of migration of European history. In America, an immigrant nation by definition and one used to pluralism, newcomers typically want to be assimilated; they are not bent on imposing their religion or way of life on others. In northern Europe, the postwar guest workers from Spain, Portugal and Italy mostly came for a few years and returned home with their money.

But Europe's new immigrants from the Middle East, Africa and Asia who replaced them had neither the intention of going back nor any desire to be assimilated into European societies. They came largely for the welfare benefits that obliging European social workers showed them how to obtain and manipulate. These galloping demographic changes are not going to go away. As Auguste Comte, the father of modern sociology, put it, in the life of a nation, demography is fate.

Since the vast majority of these new populations are Muslims, they have constructed their mosques—today over 2,000 each in France, Germany and Britain, and counting—frequented their halal butchers and grocers and lived among themselves in isolated enclaves, obeying the Islamic commandment to shun the infidel, the *kufr*, like very sin. From London to Paris, Brussels to Berlin, former working class neighborhoods have become strongholds of Muslim fundamentalists, mostly illegals and many criminals, their preachers and rappers spouting hatred for their host country. They are spreading exponentially and have every intention of imposing their religious law on the local populations. An apprehensive Dutch minister of justice admits that if a majority ever votes for the sharia, that will become Holland's law of the land.

Today's Europe, offering easy mobility, free health care, and financial support in the form of housing and cash payments, has become a gigantic safe house. This is perfect for terrorists like the Muslim Brotherhood and Hizb al Tahrir, which have been banned in most Arab countries. Statistics show these people are already a criminal plague: 80 percent of crimes committed on the London Underground, for instance, are by immigrants; 30 percent of them in Berlin have a criminal record; fully 70 percent of France's prison population are young Muslims, many of whom have been torching tens of thousands of cars each year. In their neighborhoods they pressure non-Muslims to leave, and intimidate non-Muslim girls into conforming to sharia dress rules like the hair-covering veil or full-body burqa.

So what, we may say, every country has its social problems. But a sampling of recent incidents hints at what this means for Europe in terms of individual freedom, particularly free speech: when a French philosophy teacher writes a newspaper op-ed piece criticizing Muhammad and the Koran, he has to go into hiding under police protection after death threats; there are violent street demonstrations throughout Europe and the Muslim world when a Danish newspaper publishes satirical cartoons of Muhammad; after a storm of protest, Berlin's Deutsche Oper delays plans to stage a Mozart opera with a scene of The Prophet's severed head; Pope Benedict XVI apologizes after a Muslim uproar over a speech they didn't like; and Mohammed Bouyen stabbed, shot and tried to behead the Dutch film-maker Theo van Gogh because he made a film about the abusive treatment of Muslim women.

Europe's weak political leaders authorize the lavish distribution of entrance permits to so-called asylum seekers whose status cannot be verified, shunting them into welfare programs from the day of arrival. This failure of nerve, along with Europe's prevalent cultural and moral relativism, may be due to guilt for its aggressive nationalism of the past. This contrasts sharply with more self-confident nations like Japan, China or Singapore, where illegals are sent back within days, if not hours, to their country of origin.

It's all a far cry from the heady days, not so long ago, when some American observers were predicting that the 21st century would belong to Europe. They were impressed by a burgeoning EU, its social safety net, and its sophisticated wielding of soft power and subtle diplomacy. That think-tank view was based on wishful thinking on the part of Euroenthusiasts in their dream world. Soft power was a nice, cuddly idea as an alternative to military power. But Europe, unwilling to make the effort to create credible clout, did not have much of either. This lack of political will, combined with malignant demographic/social changes, means the end of Europe as a major player in world affairs.

For many of us who have long known and appreciated Europe, the saddening impression is that it is changing permanently for the worse: the preening European emperor is dangerously, if not terminally, naked.

Update: *It is not only Europe's social fabric that is ripping apart under the strain of uncontrolled immigration and resulting crime. The economic crisis that began in 2008 has revealed growing cracks in its façade of institutional and monetary unity. The euro currency is seriously threatened as countries from Ireland to Greece, Spain and Portugal struggle with excessive debt. Rising populist parties from Finland to Italy demand more say in local affairs, raising the specter of fragmentation rather than unity.*

# "EUROPE" AT 50

Are we having fun yet?

Context: *In case you didn't notice, in 2007 the European Union, a.k.a. "Europe," celebrated the 50th anniversary of its founding Treaty of Rome. Don't feel bad if you missed it, most Europeans didn't pay any attention either.*

THE BRUSSELS EUROCRACY threw a party and nobody came. Pity, that, considering how hard they worked at it, spending over $11 million on forced jollity.

The alleged fun included free buns for the Danes! Tree plantings for the Estonians! A marathon run for the Czechs! Naturally the French produced a *toujours l'amour* TV film about a Parisian barmaid and a former German occupation officer, and, perhaps most appropriate, there was a giant puzzle for the Spaniards to figure out. British pop star Kim Wilde even sang her hit, *You Came*, reflecting the general gush of ecstatic joy.

Or it might have referred to the leaders of the EU's 27 member states, who came to Berlin to wine and dine, attend a gala concert and slum at street parties. After Jacques Chirac had gallantly nibbled at hostess Angela Merkel's knuckles they were supposed to sign the Berlin Declaration, one of those vacuous statements of grand principles steeped in the self-satisfaction and moral superiority "Europe" is so good at.

On second thought, they decided not to. Even though it studiously avoided any mention of the controversial, now-defunct EU constitution (the Brits and Czechs wouldn't hear of it), the 27 still couldn't agree on the text. The Poles, backed by Pope Benedict XVI, fought for some reference to a Christian heritage, but were reminded that Europe is now in its post-Christian era. Germany eschewed God but wanted to plug a new constitution. The French wanted to laud the European social model guaranteeing plenteous welfare for all. In the end, only three persons—Merkel and two EU functionaries—signed as the others headed for the exits.

Thus goes European unity. The EU can decree the regulation shape of a Eurocucumber or the permissible number of bacteria in a camembert, but can't formulate a position on questions concerning the real world. Things like how to deal with Russia's aggressive play to dominate the European energy market, or the swift rise of China, or whether Turkey is European enough to become a member, or the alarming swell of a potentially explosive Muslim minority. And, given the EU members' inability to agree on their fraught relationship with the United States, it was wonderfully symbolic how dithering about deployment of the American anti-missile defense shield loomed over the self-congratulations in Berlin. Of course, EU leaders knew the U.S. would end up defending them anyway, so they could afford the luxury of pretending independence, some even parroting Putin's anti-American line of "Encirclement of Russia" and "New Cold War."

It's hard to suppress an amused smile at the way "Europe"—the italics distinguish the artificial, calculated, soulless creation from the genuine home of Western civilization—defines itself by contrast to the U.S.. Socially, economically, politically, it poses and preens as everything we are not. And yet its creative exhaustion is glaringly visible in the way the EU constantly apes America in its search for national symbols: its frequent references to its "founding fathers" (haven't I heard that somewhere before?), the proclaimed goal of "ever closer union" (shades of the Constitution's "more perfect union"), a hastily designed flag with—guess what—stars on a blue background. Even the feckless Berlin Declaration begins, "We the citizens of the European Union..." (now where do you suppose they got that?). Fifty years old indeed. The EU acts more like an insecure, defensive teenager struggling for identity.

This kind of juvenile gaucherie is pardonable. But when "Europe's" flacks claim that its greatest achievement is to have single-handedly preserved peace and brought prosperity to the Continent, it's a bit much.

Can the sophisticated, courtly Europeans be so inelegant as to make no mention in this year's anniversary celebrations of America's extraordinarily generous support for European recovery and unity, all the while protecting it from the Soviet ogre? They can. Could the polished, classy Continentals possibly be so crude as to not even invite the United States to send a representative to the Berlin festivities? They could.

So let's jog European memories with a bit of reality, starting with Winston Churchill's description of postwar Europe as "a rubble heap, a charnel house, a breeding ground for pestilence and hate." That was the situation when on June 5, 1947, Secretary of State George C. Marshall proposed the European Recovery Program to get Europe off its bloodied knees after yet another perverse attempt at collective suicide. Over the next four years the Marshall Plan rained some $13 billion of American money on 17 European countries, boosting their economies by up to 25 percent. This, friends, was 10 years before "Europe" was even a gleam in the eye of "founding father" Jean Monnet, French cognac salesman by trade.

When the Soviets responded in 1948 by using their 40 divisions in East Germany to close access to West Berlin, America took up the gauntlet. The Berlin Airlift kept the city alive for 11 months, delivering over 2 million tons of food, fuel and other supplies by plane at a cost of $224 million. But that was a stop-gap. The Soviets and their Warsaw Pact allies, showing remarkably little interest in rebuilding Europe, understood only force.

So America cobbled together the NATO defensive alliance in 1949 and backed it up with the threat of nuclear retaliation. The tab for that was $3 billion in the first 20 years alone, meaning the Europeans could save that much on their defense budgets and spend it on things like creating, and enjoying, the Club Med. Later, with a war on its doorstep in Bosnia and Herzegovina, the EU boldly declared in 1995 that "Europe's time has come." It would step up and settle this little matter itself. When, predictably, it failed to act, it took U.S.-led NATO air strikes against Bosnian Serbs to save Sarajevo.

Aside from the fraudulent claim of producing peace and prosperity all by itself, "Europe" takes pride in having created a free trade area. Whether this is worth replacing beloved national currencies with the hated, misbegotten euro that sent prices soaring and consumers' heads reeling, or opening borders—a nation's immune system—to allow illegal immigrants and organized crime to circulate freely, or creating a 20,000-strong unelected, entrenched Brussels Eurocracy to run it, is the question many Europeans openly pose today. Some are even wondering if they really want the most massive redistribution of wealth ever attempted this side of the Soviet Union and Communist China, with subsidies to just about every special interest except the long-suffering middle classes.

Instead of an "ever closer union," European citizens have surrendered their national sovereignty for an ever more clumsy, unwieldy, and basically undemocratic organization answerable to no one and riddled with scams—in 1999 the hanky-panky was so rampant in Brussels that the entire executive Commission had to resign. Virtually every program lends itself to woggish corruption. Free trade? Crooked importers collect the value added tax from cross-border commerce and then conveniently forget to pass it on to governments, costing them some $130 billion a year in lost revenue. Subsidies? Even the EU's own auditors refuse to sign off on its accounts, citing scams like phantom cattle declared by Slovene farmers to get grants, non-existent subsidized olive groves in Italy and Greece, and $10 billion worth of subsidized Italian hospitals that have never treated a patient (though one was put to good use as a Mafia weapons stash). The list goes on and on.

But you can't fool all the Europeans all the time. Every chance they get to express an opinion, they show their monumental indifference, when not outright hostility, to "Europe." The French and Dutch contemptuously shot down the proposed EU constitution in 2005. Even before that the Danes had voted against the Maastricht treaty creating the European Union in 1991, and the Irish nixed the important Nice treaty in 2001. Each time the Eurocracy ordered them to vote again (and if necessary, again, and again) until they got it right. When a majority of British and French respondents recently told pollsters they thought life had gotten worse under the EU, the Euro Elite Oligarchy magisterially dismissed them as "nostalgic and insecure."

Update: *This arrogant, top-down construction without grassroots support staggers on despite deepening cracks resulting from an economic crisis for which it was never prepared. Europe is facing a serious political testing, thinks Charles Kupchan, a professor of international relations at Georgetown University and senior fellow at the Council on Foreign Relations. In fact, he says that the EU just might already have reached its high-water mark. Well, at least 50 is a nice round figure.*

# WAR BY OTHER MEANS

When a game became a proxy war between the superpowers.

**Context:** *It's mostly forgotten now, but there was a time in mid-20ᵗʰ century when chess matches were front-page news and grandmasters were household names. At stake was nothing less than national prestige.*

WITH its virtually limitless possible moves and combinations, chess has meant many things to players since it appeared in India about the 6ᵗʰ century: casual pastime or embarrassing school of humility, challenging mental workout or, in the case of a number of grandmasters, sanity-threatening maniacal fixation. The Austrian writer Stephan Zweig, author of the great chess story *The Royal Game*, whose chess-obsessed protagonist goes crazy, puckishly defined it as "thought that leads nowhere, mathematics that adds up to nothing, art without an end product, architecture without substance."

For Daniel Johnson, chess is nothing less than a mega-metaphor for the late Cold War. Indeed, in *White King and Red Queen* he argues persuasively that, with its "abstract purism, incipient paranoia, and sublimated homicide" it became a proxy war between superpowers prevented by the nuclear balance of terror from engaging in direct hostilities.

Long a favorite of Russian intellectuals and rulers— Peter the Great took along special campaign boards of soft leather while battling Turks or subduing obstreperous serfs— chess was turned into a tool of the revolution by Marx and Lenin, who were avid players. (They were also very bad losers: Marx would rage when put in a difficult position; Lenin got depressed if he lost and finally gave the game up because it distracted him from the revolution.) They and Stalin made it an instrument of the all-embracing communist state. It was, they considered, both a demonstration of dialectical materialism and good mental training for war both hot and cold.

By the mid-1920s Moscow launched a nationwide program with the declared objective of dominating the chess world. What better propaganda for the New Soviet Man? "We must organize shock brigades of chess players and begin immediately a 5-year plan for chess," declared Nikolai Krylenko, Stalin's commissar of war and founder of the Red Army, who himself headed the new All-Union Chess Section. With a multi-million ruble budget, Krylenko created a vast, tentacular infrastructure of 500,000 players by the 1930s. That number would eventually peak at some 5 million. A systematic training program spotted promising players early in communist youth chess clubs and rewarded them as they matured with rare treats like foreign currency earnings and travel abroad. At one point the Ukrainian province of Chernigov alone had over 10,000 players, more than the entire U.S.

The first great Hero of Soviet Chess was Mikhail Botvinnik. A meticulous, methodical product of the Russian chess machine, he developed a rigorous pre-match procedure that became standard for Soviet masters preparing for international competition: three weeks' confinement in a country dacha with intensive training games, plenty of exercise and fresh air, stringent analysis of all the opponent's past games, four openings devised for both White and Black, concluding with five days of rest without chess just before the match.

After Botvinnik won a big international tournament in 1936, the ministry of heavy industry rewarded him with an automobile. Stalin himself signed an order providing him 250 liters of gasoline. Except for the vehicles assigned to the nomenklatura, Botvinnik's may well have been the only private car in the Soviet Union. When he entered a theater, the audience gave him a standing ovation; his studious, bespectacled face glowered from propaganda posters; Foreign Minister Vyacheslav Molotov, he of the eponymous cocktail, personally intervened to ensure that Botvinnik had plenty of time off from work to study chess.

If being a chess star was a passport to the good life, Soviet style, the machine had no pity on losers. Mark Taimanov, champion of the USSR, grandmaster, inventor of the clever Taimanov Variation of the Sicilian Defense and a gifted concert pianist to boot, had to run a humiliating gauntlet of punishment after losing an important international match. Rather than being waved through customs as usual on his return to Sheremetyevo airport, he was subjected to a thorough search and found to be carrying a copy of Solzhenitsyn's banned novel, *The First Circle.* As the customs official explained candidly, if he had won, "I would have been prepared to carry the complete works of Solzhenitsyn to the taxi for you." In Moscow, Taimanov was summoned before the Sports Committee for a harsh dressing down and Soviet-style "civic execution": kicked off the national team, he was stripped of his title of Merited Master of Sports, banned from publishing, forbidden foreign travel, and ordered to do no more piano performances.

America had been the world's strongest chess nation in the 1930s. The Russians ended that after World War II by crushing an American team in a radio match in September 1945. For the next three decades their only serious competition came from their East European satellite states, especially Yugoslavia. The idea that communist chess supremacy did actually demonstrate Western decadence took hold in certain quarters.

Enter an arrogant, paranoid Brooklyn brat named Bobby Fischer, perhaps the greatest genius in the history of the game. After winning the U.S. championship in 1957 at 14, Fischer showed up in Moscow the next year boldly demanding to play Botvinnik. But when the chief Soviet chess bureaucrat informed him that he would not be paid for the games, he abruptly declared "I'm fed up with these Russian pigs" and went home. When he did play top Russians later that year in Yugoslavia, he finished fifth, good enough to earn Fischer the grandmaster's title at 15.

At first he was respectful toward the Russians and was on relatively friendly terms with Boris Spassky. But as he observed the Soviet players in action he became convinced that they had rigged world chess against him by agreeing among themselves to throw games to each other during tournaments. He was largely right—even paranoids have enemies—but that didn't keep him from beating several Soviet grandmasters during the 1960s.

By 1970 the Soviet chess machine began to feel what Johnson calls "Fischer fear," with Botvinnik warning his comrades that the volatile American prodigy had become a threat to Soviet chess. Little did they know. Despite his mother Regina being a card-carrying member of the Communist Party U.S.A., Fischer had gradually become an ardent anticommunist ready to fight the Cold War. "It's really the free world against the lying, cheating, hypocritical Russians," he declared. The scene was set for the most famous chess match in history, Fischer vs. Spassky in Reykjavik in the summer of 1972. Johnson calls it "the Cold War's supreme work of art."

In the tense run-up to the contest, both President Richard Nixon and Secretary of State Henry Kissinger contacted Fischer with messages of support, saying in effect, Go over there and beat the Russians. As the two-month match got under way, world newspapers played it on their front pages, London pubs replaced dartboards with chessboards, and New York bars tuned their television sets not to Mets games but to live broadcasts from Reykjavik. (Even I, certified chess duffer, clipped the daily accounts of the games and duplicated them on my board.) Fischer himself called it hand-to-hand combat. Their superb, gripping13th game, which Fischer won after eight hours of play, doomed Spassky and ended the supremacy of the Soviet chess machine.

In this tale of those murky years of looking glass conflict, a final irony stands out: the strength that chess gave the unyielding Soviet dissident Natan Sharansky, a first-rate player, to resist his interrogators and tormentors. "The chessboard had improved my defense against false threats and concealed tricks," he later wrote. "I gave them no openings."

**Update:** *The post-Cold War destinies of Bobby Fischer and Garry Kasparov are a study in contrasts. Fischer, his neurons overloaded, became increasingly delusional and bitterly anti-American in his exile in Iceland. Meanwhile, Garry Kasparov, the last Soviet champion, became fervently anticommunist and the most prominent leader of domestic opposition to Vladimir Putin's resurgent police state. Fortunately not all grandmasters are driven crazy by chess.*

# HEAVY LIFTING FOR BERLIN

When a far-fetched idea saved a great, suffering city.

Context: *General Lucius DuBignon Clay, West Point '18, descendent of Senator Henry (the Great Pacificator) Clay, commander in chief of U.S. forces in Europe and military governor of the American Zone in Germany, had won his point. The terse message from the Joint Chiefs of Staff on July 24, 1948, to his headquarters in Berlin decisively backed his controversial plan to deal with the Soviet blockade. "We have ordered our planes all over the world to fly to Europe," it said. "You have our full support. God bless Berlin."*

EXACTLY one month before, Soviet authorities had suddenly decreed a halt "for technical reasons" to all road, rail and water traffic into occupied Berlin's American, British and French sectors. Its 2.1 million population was cut off from the rest of the world. Faced with Josef Stalin's bald move to annex the city by forcing the Allies out, President Harry Truman's senior national security advisers, including Secretary of State George Marshall and Secretary of Defense James Forrestal, strongly counseled withdrawing Allied troops and leaving the city to the tender mercies of the Red Army.

Force the blockade on the ground? The Allies had only 290,000 troops in all of western Germany, compared with at least 20 Red Army divisions in East Germany, plus another million or so Soviet troops in the rest of Eastern Europe. Supply the city, an urban island 100 miles inside the Soviet Zone, with the needed 15,000 tons a day of food, fuel and other supplies by an immense, unprecedented—and highly risky—airlift? All advisors except Clay dismissed the idea as farfetched. As America's most influential columnist, Walter Lippmann, pointed out, "To supply the Allied sectors of Berlin is obviously only a spectacular and temporary answer to the ground blockade... in the long run, especially in the fog and rain of a Berlin winter, the cost in lives of the pilots and crews... would be exorbitant."

But at a White House crisis meeting June 28, Undersecretary of State Robert Lovett was outlining options for exiting Berlin when Truman cut him off with an abrupt, "We stay in Berlin. Period." Fine, but how to overcome the logistical nightmares?

That is the subject of Richard Reeves's engrossing book, *Daring Young Men: The Heroism and Triumph of the Berlin Airlift, June 1948–May 1949*, about one of the Cold War's hottest episodes. Reeves, author of presidential biographies of Kennedy, Nixon and Reagan, among other works, tells the story of those who flew, guided, repaired and loaded the planes that were, for 324 days, the lifeline of a great, embattled city. These daring young men from places like Union City, New Jersey, Corpus Christi, Texas, and Mount Sterling, Kentucky, were another instance of the ordinary Americans of Tom Brokaw's "Greatest Generation" accomplishing extraordinary things.

It was up to Clay, a 50-year-old chain-smoking workaholic, to create the airlift, officially known as Operation Vittles. He began with virtually nothing. Needed immediately if not sooner were more planes, crews, loaders and mechanics, as well as more airports and better runways. For help he first called General Curtis LeMay. Ironically it was LeMay, the legendary commander of United States Air Forces Europe (USAFE), who had developed the bombing tactics and formation flying that enabled his mighty 8th Air Force to turn much of Germany into rubble. When Clay asked if he had any planes that could carry coal, LeMay chewed his trademark cigar a moment, then yelled incredulously into the phone, "We must have a bad connection. Sounds as if you're asking whether we have planes for carrying coal." When Clay confirmed, he got his answer: "General, the Air Force can deliver anything, anytime, anywhere."

But LeMay's typical bravado couldn't magically supply the necessary hundreds of planes and the pilots to fly them. The airlift began shakily with whatever old, twin-engine C-47s (known wryly as Gooney Birds) could be scrounged up. The larger, four-engine C-54 could carry three times as much, but of the Air Force's 400 Skymasters, only two were in Germany; the rest were mostly at Pacific bases like Guam, over 11,000 miles from Europe. The Joint Chiefs' decision on June 24 sent them, their pilots and ground crews scrambling to Germany.

The Air Force sent telegrams all over America to call up reservists "for 30 days temporary duty." Many were just beginning normal postwar lives. One was Noah Thompson, who had flown 21 bombing missions over Germany and had recently passed his airline pilot's exam for a new career. When the TDY notice came he kissed his wife Betty and their new son, Glenn, goodbye. Twenty-four hours after arriving at Rhein-Main air base near Frankfurt, he was flying 10 tons of coal to Berlin. There was also Arlie Nixon, chief DC-4 pilot at TWA, who was suddenly 1st Lt. Nixon again, making $180 a month instead of $550. As one amazed RAF officer commented, "You'd be talking to some fellow and find out he had been a lawyer in Manhattan a couple of weeks before."

Others still on active duty got the call wherever they were. Lt. Harry Yoder, a former B-24 pilot, was on leave visiting his parents in Pennsylvania when the local police chief knocked on the door at 2:30 a.m.: "I have a cable here from the Air Force..." Lt. Richard A. Campbell got to Wiesbaden from his base in Japan via stopovers in Guam, Hawaii, California, Oklahoma, Massachusetts, Newfoundland and the Azores. He dropped off his bag at base ops and made five round trips to Berlin's Tempelhof airport before getting back to pick it up and settling in.

Even with planes taking off and landing every three minutes, flight crews and air traffic controllers stretched to the breaking point, less than half of the city's needs were supplied during the Airlift's first few weeks. Then LeMay brought in Major General William Tunner, deputy commander for operations of the Air Force's new Military Air Transport Service, to handle logistics. Arrogant, cantankerous, and coldly efficient, Tunner had run The Hump airlift of matériel over the Himalayas from India to China during the war. "Willie the

Whip" proceeded to increase daily loads by rationalizing ground operations, reducing turnaround time by 30 minutes per plane. He unified American and British resources, created competitions between squadrons and bases, and, most controversially, hired German mechanics to maintain the planes. Deliveries rose dramatically—at one feverish point, planes were taking off or landing in Berlin every 30 seconds.

Veteran, battle-hardened pilots were hard put to cope with Airlift conditions. Flying into Tempelhof's short runway meant following a glide path that put the plane's landing gear within feet of a nearby six-storey apartment building, diving steeply to touchdown on full flaps, then standing on the brakes while skidding over the strip's perforated steel planking toward the mud at the end. Weather was horrendous. In November thick fog blanketed Northern Europe and lasted weeks; flying was zero-zero visibility, tractors pulled planes to parking areas because pilots couldn't see runway lights.

Crews often flew with windows and doors open to avoid explosive buildup of coal or flour dust. The dust got into eyes anyway and flight surgeons had to clean it out. With crews lucky to get a few hours' sleep, both pilot and co-pilot occasionally dozed off and woke up when the plane suddenly changed altitude. Punchy air traffic controllers headed for mess halls muttering flight instructions to themselves.

Then there was the Soviet harassment. Yak and Mig-15 fighters tried to force down Airlift planes by buzzing them within a few feet—one pilot counted 22 Yaks on his tail. Other tactics: East German radio stations flooded the airwaves with loud polka music to make navigation difficult; the Red Army fired random anti-aircraft shells and beamed powerful searchlights to blind pilots (flying on instruments anyway, many just taped newspapers inside windshields). USAFE officially counted 773 incidents, with 96 involving close flying, 54 flak, 14 air-to-air fire, 59 flares, 103 searchlights, 11 barrage balloons. Many others went unreported to avoid paperwork.

Fatigue, worn-out aircraft and the weather inevitably caused crashes on takeoff or landing, once into a Berlin apartment building. Thirty-two American and 39 British personnel died during the Airlift. (The French did not participate in the Airlift because such military aircraft as they had were being used to combat communist rebellions in Indochina.) A German boy living near a runway wrote wonderingly of a C-54 crash, "The two pilots were killed... Only three years ago they were fighting against my country, and now they were dying for us. The Americans were such strange people...what made them do the things they did?"

Not only things like dying for their former enemies, but like becoming the Candy Bomber. That peculiar exercise began when Lt. Gail Halversen was stretching his legs around the perimeter fence after landing at Tempelhof. He came across a group of German school children and tossed them a couple of sticks of chewing gum. Seeing their excitement over the exotic treat, he promised to drop gum and candy next time he passed over them and to waggle his wings so they would know which plane was his. Before long, the Tempelhof ops office began receiving dozens of letters addressed to Uncle Wackelflugel

(Wiggly Wings) and Schokoladen Flieger (Chocolate Flyer). Soon other pilots joined in, donating their candy rations. In all, more than 23 tons were dropped on miniature parachutes the pilots made in their spare time.

As the months wore on, the Airlift became ever more efficient, the North Atlantic Treaty creating the NATO mutual defense alliance was signed in April, and West Germany moved closer to political reality. Stalin realized he had lost his gamble to get Berlin without a war. The lights running around the New York Times Building on May 5, 1949, said it all: "BERLIN BLOCKADE WILL END MAY 12." The West had won the Cold War's first eyeball to eyeball confrontation.

It was undeniably a heroic undertaking. But was it the best way to handle the crisis? It does not detract from the merit of those courageous, dedicated airmen to question whether the West should not have called Stalin's bluff and broken the blockade instead of circumventing it. After all, who had The Bomb?

At that same June meeting where Truman decided to make a stand in Berlin, he also ordered no less than 60 B-29 Superfortresses to bases in Britain—carrying the same type of Fatman atomic bombs dropped on Japan—under a secret plan code-named Charioteer. And as it happens, an eager Curtis Lemay, never one to back off from a fight, had already prepared a contingency plan in case of a Soviet blockade, insisting that USAFE's fighters and bombers could destroy every Soviet airfield and plane on the ground in a few hours. That was vetoed by the war-weary British and French.

Update: *Had we chosen to take off the gloves, we had the punch to put Uncle Joe on the ropes. As LeMay put it, "They had no atomic capability. Hell, they didn't have much of any capability." After the airlift ended in 1949, Berlin remained the flashpoint between East and West, with the Soviets constructing the infamous Wall in 1961. Only after it came down in 1989 could the city realize its potential of becoming the de facto capital of Eastern Europe.*

# A MORE IMPERFECT UNION

The French and Dutch try to stop "Europe's" *fuite en avant.*

**Context:** *The so-called European Union is anything but democratic. Indeed, Prime Minister Viktor Orban of Hungary has accused it of interference in his country's domestic affairs worthy of Eastern Europe's old Soviet overlords. And when the EU ruling oligarchy got around to actually asking Europe's citizens whether they wanted more rules and regulations, more open borders, and an artificial currency, they got an unpleasant surprise.*

IN BRUSSELS, self-styled capital of Europe, one of the oldest clichés is that "The European Union is like riding a bicycle. Stop moving and you fall."

The formula sounds boldly progressive. In fact it reveals an ugly truth about "Europe" the artificial creation, as opposed to the real, historical Europe: its seeming movement is really a frightened *fuite en avant.* Stop its incessant geographical and regulatory expansion and the EU loses much of its reason for being—and many of its well-paid, unaccountable Eurocrats in monumental buildings metastasizing all over the Belgian capital risk losing their jobs. Now the sham momentum of fleeing forward is stalling and the European bike is wobbling, victim of a rare exercise in direct democracy. The consequences are incalculable but not serious.

For decades the EEO (Euro Elite Oligarchy) ran things as they liked, with only the most cursory nod toward consulting the peasants. It didn't matter that they never said where they were leading Europe. The French Socialist Jacques Delors came as close as any Eurocrat to defining the EU's ultimate objective when as president of the European Commission he said, "We don't know where we're going, but we're on our way." Such a blind process could hardly be served by asking the varied peoples of Europe their opinion of the Common Market/European Community/European Union or whatever it's called next week. Especially when most of them couldn't care less about it: 46 percent of Europeans can't tell you how many member states belong, 62 percent don't know that Britain is a member, while many are convinced that Turkey already is.

So they weren't asked if they wanted Brussels to invade their daily lives with niggling rules and regulations, usually decided behind their backs, on how their traffic lights should flash, or the exact number of bacteria in a slice of camembert. Or to expand from six to 15 to 27 ill-assorted, contentious members and counting. Or open their borders to allow illegal immigrants and organized crime to circulate freely. Or to replace their venerable, beloved national currencies with the misbegotten euro, with its neutered images of virtual architecture carefully designed—a subtle lobotomizing of cultural memory—to avoid resembling any of Europe's tangible heritage. When the EEO finally got around this year to consulting public opinion, the citizen rabble took a closer look at what was going on and didn't much like what they saw.

One of the more exquisite ironies of French and Dutch voters' resounding rejection of the proposed EU constitutional treaty in May and June, 2005, was that one of its stated purposes was to bring the faceless, soulless organization closer to the people of Europe. In this summer of their discontent, Europeans were reacting negatively to the central thrust of the EU rather than to the constitution itself, which few have read. The document, laboriously entitled "Treaty Establishing a Constitution for Europe," is an incomprehensible thicket of legalistic Eurospeak (polls show only 10 percent of Europeans are familiar with its contents) comprising two preambles, four main parts, 20 chapters, 19 titles, 15 sections, 17 sub-sections, 36 annexed protocols, and a two-part final act—just what you would expect from a polyglot international committee of functionaries.

It addresses the peasants with all due condescension. Whereas the seven-article American constitution, only about one-tenth as long, begins with the ringing, lapidary "We the people of the United States," the EU document intones, "His Majesty the King of the Belgians" and goes on to say that other majesties, highnesses and heads of state "have agreed on the following dispositions." (And back into your hovels, commoners.) If constitutions imply a nation-state and the collective will of a self-governing people, this is no constitution in any meaningful sense, the EU being neither a government nor a nation and the Europeans not anything like a coherent people.

It is, rather, another example of the Potemkin slight-of-hand and flim-flammery the EU habitually uses to puff itself up. Example of the emperor's new clothes: it creates an appointed "president" but without popular election, sans executive powers, and, of course, no armed forces of which to be commander-in-chief.

When President Jacques Chirac decided last year to put the treaty to a French referendum—most EU member states are rubber-stamping it in their complaisant parliaments—he was reacting to Tony Blair's announcement of one for the United Kingdom in 2006. Besides, polls then showed it would pass easily. To promote it, he and his strange bedfellows, the French Socialist Party, played the anti-American card as hard as they dared, stressing that a yes vote was to be *forte face aux États-Unis*, strong against the United States.

With his place in political history riding on the result, Frère Jacques spent over half a billion dollars of French public treasure in his campaign for a *oui* vote. He also tried to buy support among civil servants, farmers, vintners and others with still more pay, subsidies and benefits, while the EU Commission cooperatively delayed any new moves that could antagonize the French. He invited the German Socialist prime minister Gerhard Schröder over to France three times to give pro-treaty speeches. He spread scare stories about what would happen if they voted *non*: they would be "the black sheep of Europe," France would "cease to exist politically." He took to TV several times to plead, cajole, and threaten. In the end, the French, in an unwonted access of revolt against the powers that be, voted overwhelmingly to make Chirac look like a Jacquesass. The rejection was a huge personal defeat for him, one which will forever taint his political legacy.

For the usually docile French to have resisted the propaganda onslaught of their government, the major parties and the mainstream media showed a truly monumental case of up-to-here with the EU's euphemistically termed "democratic deficit." As a goatherd on Noirmoutier Island off the Atlantic coast, where I am often, told me as he offered a portion of his ewes' mellow product, "Everybody I know is voting no. We're fed up with the way things are going, with being ignored. This is the only way we can get the message across to those guys in Paris and Brussels."

When Holland, another of the six original founding members and traditionally an ardent EU supporter, followed suit with a thumbs down, the constitution was effectively finished, along with the Eurocrats' superstate ambitions. In any case, if French and Dutch voters had not given it the coup de grace, the Euroskeptical Danes and Brits would have.

There is little to lament, either by Europeans or the rest of the world. The frequent claim that the EU is necessary for peace in Europe is patently fraudulent: It was the American nuclear umbrella and U.S.-led NATO that let the Europeans get on with closer economic cooperation and pleasantries like high pensions, free spa cures, and six-week vacations. Europe's real post-war success stories, like the Ariane rocket launcher and Airbus airliners, have had nothing to do with the EU, being the result of sovereign nations freely entering into joint projects.

Europe is probably in for a prolonged period of stagnation and neurotic introspection, so what else is new? Of course, if the Eurocrats have not learned by now that political union can only be based on a common history, culture and sense of community, they could just put the whole shebang on the path to slow disintegration. Anybody want to buy some euros?

Update: *The EU continues to stumble on, with Europeans increasingly skeptical of it. The main achievement of the Schengen Agreement, which abolished borders and passport controls between member states, has been to facilitate organized international crime. Its artificial common currency, the euro, is in danger of disintegrating under the pressure of the 2008–10 financial crisis. Its future remains doubtful, with many political leaders and commentators calling openly for its abolition.*

# FUNNY MONEY

This is what happens when sorcerer's apprentices play politics
with national currencies.

Context: *Brussels-based Eurocrats decreed the end of Europe's
historical currencies. At a stroke, Europeans lost their familiar
financial references points. No wonder they hate the euro.*

IMAGINE, if you can, that the Federal Government abolishes
the dollar. Just does it because our betters have determined, in
their wisdom, that it's what we need. This will boost the
economy, they say, create jobs, make us healthy, wealthy and
wise, yada yada yada. But not to worry, it will be replaced by a
brand new currency called the amer. One amer will be worth
6.56 dollars. All you have to do to understand how much you are
really earning or spending is multiply by 6.56. No problem!

In a scrambled months-long operation, our suddenly
obsolete bills and coins are withdrawn from circulation and
replaced by the new ones. Obliterated are the iconic likes of
Washington and Jefferson, Hamilton and Lincoln, along with
old-fashioned national symbols and embarrassing mottos like "In
God We Trust." In fact, the new currency refers to nothing that
has ever existed in the U.S.A. It is graced with figurative bridges,
imaginary buildings, schematic maps—neutered virtual images

carefully designed to avoid any reference to American heritage. "To prevent dangerous nationalism and promote peace," we are told.

Familiar reference points gone, everyone carries a calculator to comprehend and compare the prices of goods and services on the fly. Many bewildered older folk simply hold out their wallets and pocketbooks at the supermarket check-out and trust the right sum will be taken. In converting to the amer, merchants round off their prices—always up, of course—and take advantage of the confusion to keep on raising them; strangely, official government statistics somehow show no rise in inflation.

Political fiction? Not in "Europe," also called the European Union, where the citizens of 17 countries have gone through exactly that ordeal. The unelected Eurocrats in Brussels, the same who have trouble operating the $6,400 expresso machines in their offices, decreed the end of beloved historical currencies like the franc, guilder, peseta, escudo, drachma, and that prized symbol of Germany's postwar comeback, the Deutsche Mark. Overnight disappeared the monetary relics of centuries of European history. In their place was a warped, deracinating political tool dubbed the euro. In the 4,000-year history of money this was the first and only example of an artificial currency, created unbidden by the populace, sans a nation-state behind it.

Like it or not, today the euro is a fact of life. Officially launched as a theoretical accounting unit for 11 EU nations in 1999 (six others have adopted the euro since; actual banknotes and coins were circulated in 2002), it has become, by default, the second most important international reserve currency after the U.S. dollar. The eurozone covers a population comprising fully one-fifth of the global economy. Nearly 20 percent more euros circulate worldwide than dollars.

Marking the tenth anniversary of its creation is David Marsh's *The Euro: The Politics of the New Global Currency*. A London-based investment banker, columnist and author of several books on European finance and politics, Marsh is well placed to give us a blow-by-blow account of how it came to be. It's a revealing tale of intrigue, rivalries, and arm-twisting among European central bankers and politicos, prime ministers and presidents.

Prime mover behind the Economic and Monetary Union (EMU) of the 1990s that produced the euro was France. Beginning 30 years earlier, French policy makers saw a European currency bloc as the way to parry dollar domination. It would also, they reasoned, help shackle an industrializing post-war Germany visibly heading for reunification and fast leaving France in the dust economically.

More generally, European central bankers feared the surfeit of offshore dollars around the globe imperiled the monetary arrangements of Bretton Woods. America's policy of benign neglect gave the impression that the U.S. was exporting its economic problems to the rest of the world. That idea was reinforced by the brusque style of Richard Nixon's Treasury Secretary, John Connally. In one memorable exchange, Connally bluntly put it to Europe's finance chiefs, "The dollar may be our currency, but it's your problem." (Or as he formulated it less publicly, "Foreigners are out to screw us. Our job is to screw them first.") That spurred the European search to become less dependent on the dollar.

By the 1980s, France's wily president, François Mitterrand, and his advisers decided the best way to corral Germany into cooperation was to play on its strategic insecurity. They would parlay France's nuclear *force de frappe* into a deal that would negate the powerful D-Mark. When the Germans proposed a Franco-German Defense Council for joint decision-making, for instance, France countered with a Franco-German Economic and Finance Council in tandem with that. Mitterrand sent a top adviser, Jacques Attali, to bargain with Bonn. When German officials raised the nuclear issue, Attali surprised them by asking to discuss instead *Germany's* atomic bomb. "You know we don't have the bomb," they protested. "I mean," Attali cooly replied, "the D-Mark."

The Mark and the Bundesbank were the pride of renascent Germany. It took more than French defense guarantees to get Chancellor Helmut Kohl to part with them. After much haggling, other deal-sweeteners were found to calm German angst. The new European Central Bank (ECB) would be patterned on the Bundesbank, he was assured. It would have the same rigorous monetary guidelines and same overriding priority of fighting that old German bugaboo, inflation. Not only that, but the ECB could even be based in Frankfurt.

The clincher was German reunification. Kohl was bound and determined that it would happen on his watch. But he knew an enlarged Germany, again carrying the threat of what Churchill had earlier called "the mighty strength of the Teutonic race," scared the rest of Europe. France and its allies like Italy and the Benelux countries let him know they would pose no obstacles to his pet project if he would spring for EMU and its concomitant, the euro. With that carrot dangling before him, Kohl went ahead and signed the controversial Maastricht Treaty on February 7, 1992. Result: EMU, the euro—and the end of the Bundesbank and the D-Mark.

There would be much more heated horse-trading over details. Jacques Chirac and Kohl almost came to blows during one argument over the ECB's mandate. But the deal was done and Germany was irrevocably bound to the euro—even though the German public loathed it. As Wim Duisenberg, the Dutch first president of the new ECB, put it without realizing the ominous implications of what he was saying, "[The euro] is the first currency that has not only severed its link to gold, but also its link to the nation-state."

Perhaps because the euro was founded on little more than political wishful thinking, France and Germany were unable to convince all EU member states of its virtues. The pragmatic British, along with the Danes and Swedes, officially opted out. (When French and Dutch voters roundly rejected a new EU constitution in 2005, followed by the Irish, virulent dislike of the euro and the inflation it caused played a large part; this was the only way they could express their feelings about being railroaded into it.) Under the leadership of Margaret Thatcher, the Brits in particular were having none of it. This resulted in the irony that London, still Europe's largest financial center by far, is not in Euroland.

As the clear-sighted Thatcher noted in the 1980s, "A Franco-German bloc with its own agenda [has] re-emerged to set the direction of the Community." To the House of Commons she stated succinctly her position on Britain's joining the single currency: "No, no, no." In case he still didn't understand the lady, the German ambassador to London, Hermann von Richthofen, got an earful at a Buckingham Palace state dinner: "So you want me to go to Her Majesty the Queen," she asked mockingly, "and explain to her that, in a few years, her picture will no longer be on our banknotes?" She won the monetary Battle of Britain. Independence from the euro still suits most Brits just fine. "We have the convenience of using a single currency when traveling across the Continent," a commentator recently wrote cheerfully in *The Daily Telegraph*, "with none of the costs of belonging to the wretched thing."

Today the global financial and economic crisis is stress-testing the euro as never before in its brief existence. Increasingly divergent rates of inflation, debt, and unemployment among its 17 users are painfully pressuring its Achilles heel, the one-size-fits-all monetary policy. Informed speculation is rife that one or more of Euroland's debt-laden members like Italy, Greece, Portugal, Ireland or Spain could default, with a catastrophic domino effect throughout the area. Such an event would bear out the skepticism of economists like Nobel Prize-winner Milton Friedman and Harvard's Martin Feldstein, both of whom early questioned the validity of a currency based on politics instead of economic reality.

**Update:** *As this book went to press, the euro zone was in greater danger than ever of fragmenting. Greece and the much larger Spain were on the verge of being forced out due to their unmanageable debt, which was itself caused by the euro. But the bet here, against all odds, is that the artificial currency will continue to exist whatever happens. Here's why: To qualify for Euroland, EU states, particularly the Greeks, met "convergence criteria" by notoriously manipulating statistics, cooking the books, and other creative accounting. And you may be sure that having invested this much political capital in it, the EU and national politicos will fudge the figures, bend the rules, and do whatever else necessary behind closed doors to ensure the euro's survival. That, after all, is how "Europe" works.*

# THE SLOW MELTING OF EUROFUDGE

Twin crises and rising populism threaten the European Union.

**Context:** *Robert Schuman, Jean Monnet and other visionaries set in motion the machinery for European unification in the early 1950s with the six-member European Coal and Steel Community. Their modest goal was to make another European war impossible by creating a common market for coal and steel. But bureaucrats eventually took over and did what bureaucrats do best: increasing and multiplying their purview and power. Today's reality is a bloated, faltering, 27-member European Union that no longer knows where it is going, or why.*

SKIES ARE DARK with chickens coming home to roost as the European Union faces its worst existential crisis since its founding. But EU officialdom has other creatures than chickens on its mind, namely, hamsters. Not just any hamster, but none other than the Great Hamster of Alsace. After thorough investigation and due deliberation, the Union's highest court, the European Court of Justice in Luxembourg, has solemnly threatened France with $24.6 million in fines if it does not better ensure the wee, timorous beastie's favorite diet of grass and alfalfa.

Thus goes "Europe"—the quotation marks distinguish the artificial creation from the real thing—today. The Eurocrats'

20th-century dream was to force Europe's vastly diverse nations, each with its own proud history, culture, language, and currency, into a single politico-economic mold—an early example of cookie cutter globalization. Today's 21st-century reality is something else: a surreal multinational botch run by a Brussels-based oligarchy. Busily fiddling while Rome burns, it spouts Eurospeak and produces a Eurofudge of questionable statistics, fake achievements (it claims to have singlehandedly brought peace to the Continent), and intrusive, pettifogging regulations.

The Eurocrats' two most radical measures for forging "Europe" were the 1985 Schengen accord abolishing borders between the 17 EU member states that adopted it, and the 1992 Maastricht treaty creating a monetary union with the euro single currency. With passport-free travel and the euro, the official propaganda went, Europeans would celebrate their newfound brotherhood, merrily mingling freely. Everybody would feel more "European." Initially these were the EU's most popular innovations, seemingly greasing the wheels of integration and making life easier. The irony is that today's twin European crises are precisely the result of 1) a borderless area open to uncontrolled population movements and, 2) a rigid, unworkable monetary union.

Now Europeans are rebelling from Madrid's Puerto del Sol, where tens of thousands of Spanish *indignados* chanted their refusal to pay for the Eurocrats' errors, to Athens's Syntagma Square, where outraged Greek *aganaktismenoi* rioted in clouds of tear gas against punishing austerity measures imposed to save the endangered euro. Anger is also boiling in Ireland and Portugal, where economies have gone bust due to soaring consumer prices and disastrous credit bubbles created by the artificially low interest rates of an easy-money euro.

The revolt caught the Eurocracy by surprise. It shouldn't have. After all, none of this was ever put to a Europe-wide popular vote. This oversight is delicately described in Eurospeak as "the democratic deficit." But on the few occasions when Europeans have had the chance to express their opinion in national referendums, they have shown contempt born of clear-sighted common sense. The Danes voted against the Maastricht treaty, the French and Dutch both tried to shoot down the new EU constitution. The Eurocracy's reaction was to order them to vote again (and again, and again, if necessary) until they got it right. When a majority of British and French citizens dared tell pollsters life had actually gotten worse under the EU, the oligarchy dismissed them as "nostalgic and insecure."

Post-war Europe's leaders were blinded by their vaulting ambition to create an ever bigger "Europe" as fast as possible before anyone noticed its flaws. Otherwise they would have realized the folly of a politically motivated monetary union, with fixed, one-size-fits-all interest rates and no possibility of individual member-states devaluing in times of economic crisis. It should have been obvious that it was impossible to combine strong economies like Germany and France with weaker "periphery" countries like Greece and Portugal. American free-market economists like Milton Friedman early questioned the validity of the euro, a currency based on utopian dreams instead of economic reality. But they reckoned without the European practice of arranging facts to obtain the desired result. Thus countries applying to join the eurozone were allowed to qualify by using off-budget accounting, getting special waivers, and other typical Eurofudge.

In the case of Greece, epicenter of the current euro crisis, the fudge was particularly thick. To start with, Greece flagrantly failed to meet the required fiscal criteria for membership when the eurozone was set up in 1999. Not to worry. In 2001, Brussels turned a blind eye to Athens' phony budget numbers and admitted Greece. Monetary union marched triumphantly on. With that, Greece was eligible to borrow at much better interest rates than it could have with the lowly drachma as its national currency. Thanks to abundant cheap money the Greek economy, rife with chronic corruption, cronyism and tax evasion, suddenly boomed. The Greeks knew they were living high on credit. They also knew that, when the crunch came, the hard-working Germans would bail them out to save the euro, for which they reluctantly had sacrificed their cherished Deutsche Mark.

When Greece's inevitable debt crisis hit, the solution was more Eurofudge: in breach of the Maastricht treaty, which forbids financial aid to a member state that gets into fiscal trouble, Brussels put together a $158 billion bailout. When that wasn't enough, it kicked the can farther down the road with a $17.4 billion loan to keep the government running through summer. And *that* loan was just to tide Greece over until the EU, after a series of embarrassingly futile summit meetings, could deliver still another billion-dollar rescue package. In return for continuing life support, the Greek parliament went through the motions of passing an emergency austerity package of spending cuts to public services, tax increases, and the sale of state-owned assets like the ports of Piraeus and Salonika. (And if you believe those deeply unpopular measures will ever be applied, thereby increasing unemployment and prolonging the recession, I have a tower in Paris I'd like to sell you.)

With Greek bonds downgraded to junk status by rating agencies, few believed the country could avoid default. (The agencies, like Moody's and Standard & Poor's, were American and therefore biased against Europe, sniffed the Eurocrats, bravely attacking the messenger who brings bad news.) Default by one member could put the entire eurozone in danger of domino-like contagion—Portugal's bonds are already junk grade, and there are doubts about Spain and Italy—and catastrophic financial failure, a Lehman Brothers disaster on a Europe-wide scale. As the economist Robert Samuelson says, "It has come to this. After a year of rescuing Greece from default, Europe is staring into the abyss. There is no easy escape."

Had it not been in such a hurry to achieve its fait accompli, the Eurocracy also might have foreseen the inevitable problems caused by its other *grand projet,* a passport-free Union. After their initial enthusiasm for leaving passports at home when heading for Mediterranean beaches, Europeans began to realize that free movement within the 25-nation Schengen area meant just that: once accepted in any member country after a cursory procedure, a new arrival from anywhere on the planet can roam freely and eventually settle in next door. He may not speak the language, he may not have a job, but he is eligible for free medical care and other generous social benefits paid for by local taxes.

This is now running head-on into the instinct for self-preservation and enduring nationalism of ordinary Europeans. Especially now that public opinion is being increasingly influenced by right-wing parties from France to Finland, Austria to Italy. One telling sign can be found in the usually liberal Netherlands. From the creation of "Europe" half a century ago, the Dutch have been stalwart promoters of greater integration.

No more. Now Dutch leaders are warning Eurocrats to heed the growing populist anger. "The most stupid thing is to neglect this and tell these people they are behind the curve, that they don't understand what's going on in the world," says Ben Knapen, the Dutch EU affairs minister. Pushed by the right-wing, anti-EU Freedom Party, the Dutch government is considering expelling EU migrants who have been unemployed for more than three months, and cutting benefits for those who fail a Dutch language test. As one Dutch parliamentarian puts it baldly, "We don't want jobless Poles, Romanian beggars and people from North Africa or Turkey."

In Denmark, the populist Danish People's Party, a coalition partner in the government, recently forced the reopening of Denmark's long-closed border checkpoints and customs houses. This direct challenge to the Schengen treaty— and the trend it represents—creates painful angst among EU faithful and draws frowns from the Eurocracy. "Stopping free movement endangers solidarity among Europeans and jeopardizes the European project," lectures José Manuel Barroso, a Portuguese former Maoist and now, most appropriately, president of the unelected, unaccountable, Politburo-like European Commission in Brussels. "Nationalists in every country will get the same idea," warns a foreign ministry official in Berlin. "They will model themselves on Denmark." How true. Denmark's new policy on border checks was hardly announced when France's National Front, led by the charismatic Marine Le Pen, began putting up posters with the slogan, "Denmark patrols its borders. Why not us?"

The campaign resonates in a country like France, struggling to accommodate tens of thousands of refugees fleeing the chaos of the Arab Spring. At last count some 40,000 Tunisians and Libyans had reached the Italian island of Lampedusa just 70 miles off the African coast. Silvio Berlusconi threw up his hands and freely distributed "temporary" residence permits to all comers, opening the door to the rest of Europe. The French-speaking Tunisians have made a beeline for France, where many have friends or family. When Nicolas Sarkozy asked Brussels to put the Schengen open borders rules on hold so France could stanch the flow, the Eurocracy reacted with the usual fudge: "temporary" border controls could be set up, it agreed with a wink, neatly undermining one of its own favorite measures.

Eurofudge is melting under the heat of a threatened euro, failing immigration policy, and rising populist parties. You can, after all, fudge some of the facts all of the time, but not all of the facts all the time. Poland, the biggest and most important in geopolitical terms of the EU's new Eastern European members, senses this. Rather than rushing to join the euro zone as expected, it is warily demanding better fiscal rules and crisis management before giving up its zloty and groszy for the dubious charms of the single currency.

The question is whether this is only a temporary crisis or whether the crumbling foundations of "Europe" signal the beginning of the end of the European Dream. Even the Eurocracy itself is beginning to have its doubts. A recent survey of European Commission staff in Brussels revealed that 43 percent thought European integration had "evolved negatively" over the past 10 years, while a convincing 63 percent said "the European model has entered into a lasting crisis."

What is certain is that, with Nicolas Sarkozy and Angela Merkel more interested in their own political problems and upcoming elections, no major European leader today is energetically promoting integration the way French and German heads of state did from the 1960s to the 1990s. As *The Financial Times* suggests, "We may be witnessing a generational change in European political dynamics. Traditional left-right divisions have narrowed… It may spell a new, unprecedented challenge to the European project."

Right now "Europe" is bobbing and weaving and playing for time. José Manuel Barroso, a president with no real power over anything, implores EU heads of state to resist what he calls the "populist temptation" created by rising regionalism, nationalism, and anti-globalism. But, while suffering what looks like the slow-motion collapse of the European Union in its present form, the real challenge to Eurocrats may be to salvage the things they do best. Like saving hamsters.

Update: *A surprising new challenge to the EU came from none other than French President Nicolas Sarkozy, always a loyal EU supporter, in the spring of 2012. Desperately seeking to siphon off right-wing votes in his campaign for re-election, he threatened to pull France out of the Schengen zone of passport-free travel unless Brussels placed more stringent quotas on immigration within a year. He also vowed to erect unilateral trade barriers unless the EU adopts a "Buy European Act" providing more protection from foreign competition in public procurement contracts. Suddenly even France was putting the heat on Eurofudge.*

# PARTY ANIMALS

The Chinese Communist Party maintains its implacable rule
over one-fifth of humanity.

**Context:** *It has outlasted and outsmarted its critics, fooling the
Western pundits who have predicted its imminent demise. As a
political machine, the Party is a phenomenon of awesome dimensions.*

THE QUESTION IS, how do they do it? They starved some 35
million Chinese in the late 1950s during Mao's disastrous Great
Leap Forward. They threw the country into social, economic and
political chaos in the Great Proletarian Cultural Revolution
terror purges of the 1960s and '70s. They massacred
prodemocracy student demonstrators in Tiananmen Square in
June 1989.

Today their arbitrary arrests and denial of free speech
and association continue. With the implosion of the Soviet
Union, total rejection of communism throughout Eastern
Europe, and the theoretical end of history, the era was supposed
to be over when a closed cabal of corrupt, self-serving goons
could dominate a country so vast and diverse. Much less create,
in only three decades, the world's second-largest economy and a
geopolitical rival to the U.S.

Richard McGregor sheds light on this conundrum in *The Party: The Secret World of China's Communist Rulers.* A *Financial Times* correspondent who reported from China for 20 years, McGregor gives us a detailed depiction of the hidden moving parts of the world's most powerful political machine.

The CCP's grip on power is based on a simple formula from Lenin's original playbook: complete control of personnel, propaganda and the People's Liberation Army. However China's smiling face may look to the crowds of foreigners flocking to the 2008 Beijing Olympics and the Shanghai World Expo 2010, the very names of the bodies exercising that power, the Politburo, Central Committee, Praesidium, etc., all reveal that China's system runs on Soviet hardware.

Principal tool of control is the Party's Central Organization Department. A direct descendent of Lenin's 1919 Orgburo, it faithfully replicates the Soviet *nomenklatura* system of reserving prize jobs for the happy few among Party faithful. Little known abroad and even within China itself, it operates out of a huge unmarked building near Tiananmen Square, its phone number unlisted. Its secret deliberations decide who will hold what positions not only in government, but also in business, the judiciary, media and academia. It's as if a single department in Washington arbitrarily appointed the entire U.S. cabinet, state governors and mayors of all major cities, Supreme Court justices, the chief executives of GE, Exxon-Mobile, Wal-Mart and dozens of other companies, plus editors of newspapers and heads of TV networks, along with the presidents of Yale and Harvard and chiefs of think tanks like Brookings and the Heritage Foundation.

Such a secret, systematic spoils system can only lead to colossal corruption. Party officials rule their local fiefdoms like virtual market places where government jobs are bought and sold under an unofficial "pay for play" system. One official in Suihua paid over $100,000 to the local Organization Department to become a party secretary. Another paid "only" $44,000 to be party secretary in a smaller locale, but parlayed that in two years into nearly $740,000 in graft, a gratifying return on investment of some 1,700 percent.

Addressing the Party's token anti-corruption commission in 2006, General Secretary Hu Jintao went through the motions of warning, "This time-bomb buried under society could... lead to a series of explosions which could cause chaos through society and paralyze the administration." But as he knows better than any, the Party system allows top officials to supervise themselves. Thus bribes now routinely run into millions of dollars to procure even low-level jobs. CCP corruption amounts to a transaction tax that distributes ill-gotten gains among the ruling class, becoming the glue that keeps the system together.

The system is communist to the core, but the rigid ideology that purportedly underpins it—and led to the collapse of Soviet communism—has been carefully airbrushed out. After the Tiananmen Square massacre, Deng Xiaoping, who had launched China's early market reforms in 1978, laid down the flexible new Party Line: "On economic matters, relaxed controls;

for political matters, tight controls." Party leaders quickly learned to talk out of both sides of their mouths, preaching Marxism in public statements while prodding businesses to keep getting bigger and richer.

The sleight of hand often works with foreigners: during a visit to Beijing some years back, Rupert Murdoch declared he hadn't met a single communist in China. Actually he could have found no less than 78 million card-carrying Party members, many multimillionaires. As for the Party's ideology, Chen Yuan, Party member, senior banker, and son of a Long March veteran, puts it succinctly: "We are the Communist Party, and we decide what communism means."

Above all, they try to avoid looking like communists. Leaders keep their Mao suits in the closet except for big party occasions. When Hu Jintao travels abroad on state visits, he wears a Western business suit and is officially described not as general secretary of the CCP, but as president of China. This lowers his ideological profile—communist, *moi?*—and gives the superficial impression he was democratically elected instead of picked by the Politburo behind closed doors. As a professor at Beijing University explains, "The Party is like God. He is everywhere. You just can't see Him."

To be sure, Chinese citizens still feel the Party's presence everywhere, but it is less heavy-handed. Although its thugs will strong-arm any person or group perceived as challenging its primacy, today it prefers persuasion, co-opting and seduction rather than coercion. The most striking recent example of this more relaxed attitude is *Tombstone*, a 2008 book by the Xinhua News Agency journalist Yang Jisheng.

After years of clandestine research, Yang details for more than a thousand pages the horrors and suffering of Mao's Great Leap Forward, a strictly taboo subject for the Party. Though no mainland bookstore or publisher would touch such a scorching condemnation of Chinese communist brutality, the book is available in Hong Kong. And, mirabile dictu, Yang has not been arrested or even harassed. The Party prefers to try to obscure it by banning mention of it in the media. "The authorities are not as stupid as they used to be," Yang says. "If this had happened in the past, I would be a dead man and my family would have been destroyed."

The Party's relations with business are ambiguous. Although the government has laid off nearly 50 million workers in state enterprises in its economic reorganization, this should not be confused with free-market privatization—the Party retains ultimate control of state businesses. The Chinese corporate animal is a bizarre beast, both commercial and communist.

For one thing, the state still owns either 100 percent or a majority of key sectors from oil, petrochemicals, mining and banks, to telecoms, steel, electricity and aviation. For another, all heads of large businesses are Party members and jump to it when Beijing gives an order—as when it told bankers to flood the market with credit, often against their better judgment, to deal with the current financial crisis. On the desks of about 50 of the most important sits a "red machine," a special encrypted telephone linking them to top Party, government and business players. The ultimate Chinese status symbol, the phone will be answered, promptly, by a loyal Party member.

Newspaper editors and TV producers also get frequent calls, even if they don't have red machines on the desk. It will be from the Central Propaganda Department giving the angle on the day's news. Here again, the Party now uses a soft sell, relying on the media's "self-discipline." Chinese newsmen don't really need to be told how to play a story; they have a red line in their head.

Americans will soon be getting more of the Party's perspective on current affairs as an increasingly media-savvy Propaganda Department develops Chinese news media overseas. The Xinhua agency recently announced plans to open a prominent newsroom in New York's Times Square, with Reuters, News Corp and *The New York Times* as neighbors. It will provide a Chinese-slanted news feed to CNC World, the agency's new 24-hour channel. This is part of the Party's decision to spend billions of dollars to create a global media empire to offset what it considers biased coverage of China.

Thus the wave of 90th anniversary CCP hoopla in 2011. The Party had thousands of researchers work up a propaganda barrage of its official history since its creation in 1921. The world is about to hear more than it really wants to about how the Party "successfully united and led the Chinese people to achieve miracles," as Central Committee Vice President Xi Jinping has put it.

When will the Party be over? On that inevitable, probably bloody, day when Chinese citizens decide that it's not enough in life to get rich, if they don't have the right to live free under a democratically elected government. They may already be part way there, having manifestly lost their communist faith. As a professor at Tsinghua University in Beijing says, "Party leaders realize that they don't have a dominant ideology they can use to run the country any more. The sole ideology shared by the government and the people is money worship."

Update: *The Party continues to blow hot and cold on human rights and greater transparency. The summary firing in March 2012 of Bo Xilai as party chief of the region of Chongqing—a rising star who seemed destined for the Politburo—as part of a power struggle showed how murky and merciless Party infighting could be. On the other hand, Prime Minister Wen Jiabao surprised many by telling a press conference that without political reform, China could suffer "another Cultural Revolution." Meanwhile, the Party is struggling to cope with citizens' increasing use of microblogs, or* weibo, *that challenge state propaganda.*

# SARKO'S WAR

He missed the Arab Spring. Then Libya caught his eye.

**Context:** *Ronald Reagan might have called him the mad dog of the Middle East, but Libya's Muammar Gaddafi was given the red carpet treatment by Nicolas Sarkozy when he visited Paris in 2008. The friendship soured when Sarkozy saw the chance to look good by leading a humanitarian mission against him.*

YOU'VE GOT to hand it to France's little big man, he has a way of getting what he wants. Whether it be the presidency of his country, a trophy wife, or generally punching above France's weight in international affairs, President Nicolas Sarkozy pushes, inveigles, argues and seduces until others let him have his way, if only to be quit of him. Now he wanted to lead a George Bush-style coalition of the willing into war with an Arab dictator. In March 2011 he got that too.

It was the first good week Sarkozy had had on the world scene in a long time. For months he watched as the Arab Spring spread across North Africa and the Middle East with tacit American encouragement but no French involvement. When it began in Tunisia, right in France's ex-colonial backyard, Sarkozy wasn't paying attention. Worse, his administration was caught wrong-footed when his foreign minister, Michèle Alliot-Marie, embarrassingly offered France's know-how in riot control to Tunisia's corrupt President Zine El Abidine Ben Ali. Then Sarkozy was silent as the U.S. deftly pressured Egyptian President Hosni Mubarak to step down and allow social and political reform. As the democratic virus infected countries like Bahrain and Yemen, France's diplomacy was absent.

At home, too, Sarkozy was faltering. With the next presidential election just a year away, his numbers in the 20s made him the most unpopular president in the history of the Fifth Republic. Poll after poll showed him losing to Dominique Strauss-Kahn, the socialist leader whom he had exiled to Washington as head of the International Monetary Fund in 2007, thinking to get him off the French political scene. Worse, surprising surveys had him beaten in 2012 by Marine Le Pen, the articulate, charismatic new leader of the right-wing National Front.

Then Libya caught his eye. Here were romantic bands of ragtag rebels rising up against one of the world's more obnoxious dictators. Just across the Mediterranean. With the U.S. bogged down in Afghanistan and unlikely to make a big move into what would be its third conflict with a Muslim country in less than a decade. Who wouldn't want to side with him in a humanitarian crusade against the despot?

Perhaps on the advice of his wife Carla Bruni, his conduit to the intellectual and art world, Sarkozy sought counsel from Bernard-Henri Lévy. A dashing penseur-poseur-showman who likes to be photographed with his shirt largely unbuttoned, Lévy advised him to officially recognize the rebels' National

Transition Council as a first step. This he did on March 10, 2011, receiving its members with full honors at the Elysée Palace. The Libyan "revolution" could only be carried out by Libyans themselves, he said then. He added, significantly, that in any case there should be no NATO-led operation against Muammar Gaddafi.

Next he maneuvered the United Nations Security Council to a vote on the loaded question of whether to protect Libyan widows and orphans. With his energetic new foreign minister Alain Juppé doing behind-the-scenes arm-twisting and special pleading, the Council voted the deliberately vague Resolution 1973 "to protect civilians and civilian populated areas under threat of attack." No mention of regime change. Or of the fact that the "civilians" were armed rebels attempting to overthrow the Libyan government. Of the European members on the Council, only Germany refused to go along with Sarkozy's war, abstaining in the vote. (Chancellor Angela Merkel is the only European Union leader who habitually stands up to him and resists his pushy ways.)

However distasteful Gaddafi might be (Ronald Reagan memorably called him the "mad dog of the Middle East"), however much we would like to see him gone, the Supreme Guide of the Libyan Revolution has been recognized for some 40 years as the legitimate power in the country. Western leaders also tended to view him as an ally against Al Qaeda.

In 2008, Sarkozy grandly welcomed him and his 400-person entourage—including 30 gaudily uniformed female body guards—to Paris for a full-pomp, five-day, red-carpet state visit.

"Gaddafi is not perceived as a dictator in the Arab world," Sarkozy explained at the time, adding as further justification, "He is the longest-serving head of state in the region." To the considerable discomfiture of many Parisians, he allowed Gaddafi to pitch his Bedouin tent in the elegant gardens of an official guest residence near the Elysée Palace. The visit concluded with contracts with Gaddafi for some $4.25 billion worth of Airbus airliners, fighter jets, air defense systems, and nuclear technology to power a desalination plant.

That was then. Now Sarkozy organized his next ploy, an international summit in Paris to implement the UN resolution. The meeting was nothing but window dressing. Its main event was the lining up of world leaders around Sarkozy on the steps of the Elysée for a group photo. "France has decided to play its part in history," he summed up with all false modesty. "The Libyan people need our aid and support. It's our duty." British Prime Minister David Cameron mumbled something about having to enforce "the will of the United Nations." Secretary of State Hillary Clinton backed away as far as she decently could, insisting, "We did not lead this. We did not engage in unilateral actions in any way."

Hours after the photo op, French fighter jets were heading for Libya, getting the jump on the U.S. and other coalition members. Much of France went into a paroxysm of national pride as television screens showed French fighter pilots gearing up, donning helmets, fingering their service pistols and heading out to the hangars where their planes were waiting. As one commentator put it, buttons fairly popping off his shirt front, "The Americans were ahead of us in dealing with the revolution in Egypt, but this time we're taking the initiative. We're clearly the leaders against Libya." Much was made of French planes striking first, while British and Americans merely brought up the rear.

Notably absent was any mention of the North Atlantic Treaty Organization. Usually the official subcontractor to the UN for military and peacekeeping operations, NATO was deliberately bypassed by Sarkozy. "NATO can act as an enabler and coordinator if and when member states take action," Secretary General Anders Fogh Rasmussen offered plaintively, trying for a piece of the action. But Sarkozy calculated that letting NATO take charge would put him in the shade.

Instead, this operation was, in his mind, a triumvirate composed of France, Britain and the U.S.—in that order. As the Quai d'Orsay put it, for once eschewing diplomatic doubletalk, "We do not want NATO involved. We do not think it would be the right signal to send that NATO as such intervenes in an Arab nation." Neither the U.S. nor any other Western nation publicly objected. The Alliance, in search of a new mission ever since the Soviet Union and its Warsaw Pact disappeared two decades ago, thus became just that much more irrelevant.

As for Nicolas Sarkozy, he was playing a high-stakes game in the hope of restoring some luster to his fading presidency and getting his sputtering election campaign off the ground. "If it works out well, it will be a triumph for him," said a hopeful aide. "He was on the ropes, and suddenly he has the whole world following his lead."

Update: *The Libya campaign dragged on far longer than Sarkozy had expected, with much bickering among the allies over who did what—and especially who got the credit. Finally turning the operation over to NATO wasn't much help, with it showing obvious weakness at coordinating member countries' efforts. Still, Sarkozy frequently cited the campaign as an example of his statesmanship.*

# NATO RECONSIDERED

Is it still our indispensable alliance?

Context: *When the North Atlantic Treaty was signed in Washington on April 4, 1949, it answered the pressing need for a system of collective defense uniting several European countries and the United States against a Soviet Union with the obvious goal of dominating Western Europe. The Alliance was always marked by transatlantic tension and doubts about its real ability to counter an attack. That led Charles de Gaulle to develop France's own independent nuclear deterrent and ultimately withdraw from the integrated military structure in 1966. After the fall of the Berlin Wall in 1989 and the disappearance of the Warsaw Pact in 1991, NATO lost its basic raison d'être and began seeking other missions to justify its existence.*

WITH POLICYMAKERS on both sides of the Atlantic slashing public spending and searching for ways to reduce military budgets, the North Atlantic Treaty Organization began construction in December 2010 of a splendiferous new $1.38 billion headquarters on a 100-acre site in Brussels. Designed by Chicago architects Skidmore, Owings & Merrill, renowned for luxurious commercial buildings including the tallest in the world, the Burj Khalifa in Dubai, the futuristic new NATO offices will feature eight sweeping wings covering 2.7 million square feet. Glass-walled elevators overlooking cavernous atriums showering natural light. Ecologically correct grass growing on the roof. Seventeen conference rooms. A range of amenities from cafeterias, restaurants and banks, to shopping, sport, and leisure facilities. Pentagon staffers, eat your hearts out.

The architects wax rhapsodic, comparing its weird configuration to "fingers interlaced in a symbolic clasp of unity and mutual interdependence." As one SOM design director glowingly describes the sprawling steel and glass structure, "We wanted to break the norm of what is perceived as a government service, bunker-like building. We made it look very classy, giving the illusion that it was a world-class, floor-to-ceiling-type glass building, very inviting. We also paid attention to how these grand spaces look."

For an organization that's been a perfect illustration of Parkinson's Law (bureaucracies expand over time, regardless of workload) since it lost its original raison d'être when the Soviet Union collapsed, it seems a normal entitlement. "A modern NATO needs a modern building," NATO Secretary General Anders Fogh Rasmussen insisted at the groundbreaking ceremony on December 16, 2010. Maybe. But does it have to be this extravagant, this grand, this pricey? The timing couldn't be worse.

The timing couldn't be *better*. The provocative new structure comes just when the Obama administration is pushing to trim federal budgets by some $1.1 trillion over the next decade, along with reductions in Pentagon spending by $78 billion. Other major NATO members are also cutting defense spending, Britain by 8 percent, Germany by some $11.5 billion. The spectacular project at least has the virtue of symbolizing what has gone wrong with this self-aggrandizing, self-perpetuating body whose main mission often seems to be not collective defense of its members, but its own self-preservation.

"It is somewhat ironic that NATO breaks ground on its new headquarters at the same time the fundamental sinews binding the alliance together are coming apart," says Marko Papic, a senior analyst at Stratfor, a global intelligence analysis firm based in Austin. As for NATO's image in a time of austerity, the controversial building is a well-aimed shot in the foot. "It is certainly unfortunate," Stephen Flanagan, senior vice president at Washington's Center for Strategic and International Studies, told me. "We don't need the crystal palace that's on the drawing boards. It's an easy target for critics when everybody is having trouble maintaining current operations."

I began covering NATO as a young Paris-based newsmagazine correspondent in 1966, when French President Charles de Gaulle abruptly tore up the lease on its headquarters near Versailles. Belgium hastily offered to house the organization in Brussels, and I covered the opening ceremony the following year. Built in just 29 weeks—the lavish new offices have taken a decade of planning, construction will take another four years— the prefab headquarters was simple, but at least it looked lean, keen, and spartan-military. Not like a stately pleasure- dome for coddled fat cats. (Having recently revisited the present headquarters, I can attest that working conditions are equal to those in many federal buildings in Washington.)

Over the years I interviewed NATO secretary generals and SHAPE commanders, rode in helicopters with SACEUR General Alexander Haig on maneuvers in Germany, went hunting for Soviet submarines in the North Sea on a Norwegian frigate, flew in an AWACS surveillance plane as it monitored bogey air traffic on the other side of the Iron Curtain. I wrote articles calling attention to threats like Soviet SS-20 missiles pointed at the heart of Europe. Never was there any doubt about the necessity of collective defense. NATO filled an obvious need.

No more. Behind the façade of variegated non-defense activities, bigger and more complex command structures, and far-flung operations, is an organization in identity crisis. "NATO's mission has been unclear since the end of the Cold War, and there is a sense of it trying to validate itself as relevant to today's world," Richard Perle, assistant secretary of defense in the Reagan administration and former chairman of the NATO High Level Group, told me. "It's no longer the indispensable defense organization it used to be. It's become so much less important that, if it didn't already exist, you couldn't start it today. It's living on its legacy."

The North Atlantic Alliance was marked by mixed motives from the very beginning. As its first secretary general, Lord Ismay, put it bluntly, NATO's purpose was threefold: "To keep the Americans in, the Russians out, and the Germans down." It managed that, then ironically faced its biggest crisis when the Warsaw Pact disappeared in mid-1991. With that ended the specter of an onslaught of Red Army tanks across the North German Plain—and the Alliance's mission.

NATO went into limbo and into a funk. "It entered a profound existential crisis two decades ago," explains Dominique David, executive director of the French Institute of International Relations in Paris. "But it managed to survive for several reasons. First, big bureaucracies never go away. They always find other pretexts to stay in business. Then, the U.S. wanted to keep an eye on Europe and NATO was a convenient way. But the biggest boost came in the early 1990s when former Soviet satellites requested membership. It became both a military organization and an instrument for the political stabilization of Europe. That made it a strange, schizophrenic animal constantly looking for new threats to relegitimize itself."

For the last 20 years NATO has tried hard to look relevant to Western security. From the homogeneous 16 members of the Cold War period, it has ballooned to 28 disparate countries with widely divergent perceptions of their individual security threats. Thus its recent operations far beyond the original Euro-Atlantic area threaten its cohesion. Is its place off the Horn of Africa, for instance, where its anti-piracy operation overlaps with two other international task forces? Many think not. "For us, the most important aspect of NATO is European operations," a well-placed European defense official told me. "I'm not sure that fighting pirates in the Red Sea is its best role."

The Alliance's eager quest for a convincing new role has led to mission creep on a grand scale. A new strategic concept formulated in 1991 tried to define a new threat environment that lacked any real dangers to its members. So security was redefined as not only a military issue, but one with political, economic, social and environmental dimensions. Dialogue and cooperation were NATO's new weapons "to reduce the risk of conflict arising out of misunderstanding." Another strategic concept in 1999 expanded its purview to humanitarian operations. Still another issued at the Lisbon summit in November 2010 covered every conceivable threat from energy security to non-proliferation, cyber war, health risks and climate change. It also invited Russia to participate in ballistic missile defense.

Originally NATO concentrated on its core activity of defending the Euro-Atlantic area. Going "out of area" was verboten. That changed in the early 1990s when, as Dutch analyst Hugo Klijn of the Netherlands Institute of International Relations notes, "NATO followed the usual course of big, self-perpetuating bureaucracies: seeking new missions and linking to other big bureaucracies." What new missions? Ill-defined and far from its designated area. What other big bureaucracy? The mother of them all, the United Nations.

In December 1992 the North Atlantic Council, NATO's governing body, declared that the Alliance was "prepared to take further steps to assist the UN in implementing its decisions to maintain international peace and security." Suddenly it was in the global peacekeeping business as a subcontractor to the UN. Says François Heisbourg, special advisor at the Paris-based Foundation for Strategic Research and one of France's top defense analysts, "They said in the 1990s that

NATO had to go out of area or out of business, and that was true. It did go out of area and it stayed in business. But it lost its geographical focus and turned itself into an ad hoc coalition where countries agree, or not, to share risks and burdens together. That's the new NATO."

It's a NATO that considers it has a universal mandate, and whose name, "North Atlantic," now bears little relation to its activities. In years to come, this might turn out to be more than many members, including the U.S., bargained for. Could the Alliance operate anywhere now? When I asked a high NATO official, the answer was clear. "I cannot envision a future in which NATO is not called upon to generate power of whatever kind for crises anywhere in the world," he replied. "We airlifted disaster relief into Pakistan. If you can go into Pakistan, what's off limits?"

With NATO's new vocation as a global, pro-active, security, crisis management, peacekeeping and humanitarian organization, it now commits Americans to fighting and dying in any hotspot on the planet. As a Cato Institute study puts it, "The transformation of NATO from an alliance to defend the territory of its members to an ambitious crisis-management organization has profound and disturbing implications for the United States... [with] the potential to entangle [it] in an endless array of messy, irrelevant disputes."

In the best bureaucratic tradition, the Alliance grew geometrically, membership metastasizing from its core area to the Baltic States, Central Europe, and, heaven help us, the Balkan powder keg. Enlargement aggravated its already complicated, consensus-based, decision-making process. Difficult with 16 members, it becomes virtually impossible to make timely, coherent operational plans with 28, even with—or because of—averaging over 5,000 meetings every year. "NATO's enlargement [has] increased the complexity of an already complex NATO bureaucracy," states another study by the Dutch institute, "and one wonders how NATO is managing its increasing bureaucracy with its complex procedures. One of the most important questions… is how this bureaucracy can remain effective and efficient."

Some allies ask the same question. "There's a tendency at NATO to create numerous bureaucracies, and they're not terribly effective," a senior official at the French Defense Ministry told me. "With the British, we're determined to slim down its command structure, which has become enormous, and reform its financial management." The official, who spoke on condition of anonymity, said France is particularly unhappy with the way NATO spends money. "They have only a vague idea how much an operation is going to cost when they get into it, just presenting us with the bill once it's under way. That's no way to run an outfit that has to be cost effective, especially nowadays."

Even the diplomatic perks and prestige of international functionaries, plus the prospect of spiffy new offices, no longer attract the best and brightest to NATO, to hear Richard Perle tell it. "Here's an indication of where NATO stands today," he says. "When I was in government during the Cold War, NATO was the prized assignment. Everyone in the diplomatic service wanted to be ambassador to NATO, military people wanted assignments there. It was the center of something important. It no longer is. The new dangers threatening us are no longer things that can be solved by an alliance like NATO."

Prized or not, the civil-military bureaucracy has kept busy with things unrelated to defending member states. It has, inter alia, helped stabilize Bosnia, assisted peacekeeping in Darfur, combated ethnic cleansing in Yugoslavia (an operation the Cato Institute called "just shy of a full-blown policy fiasco"). And it became embroiled in Afghanistan.

The mixed motives at NATO's creation also marked its stepping into the Afghan quagmire. Was the International Security Assistance Force (ISAF) turned over to the Alliance because it was best qualified and equipped to handle the job? Or to make it appear a less American, more international effort? (Fully two-thirds of the ISAF troops are American; some countries have less than a token 10 personnel there.) Or as a costly, lethal way of modernizing NATO? As Karl W. Eikenberry, the U.S. ambassador to Afghanistan, testified to the House Armed Services Committee in February 2007, "The Afghanistan campaign could mark the beginning of sustained NATO efforts to overhaul Alliance operational practices in every domain: command and control, doctrine, force generation, intelligence, and logistics." It could also, he implied, make or break the Alliance.

Right now NATO is positioning itself for a lifetime job in Afghanistan. Earlier this year its then senior civilian representative there, Mark Sedwill, declared that a long-term partnership would be required even after hand-over in 2014 to Afghan forces. NATO would then be in the business of Afghan socio-economic development. "We will be there as long as we are needed," he promised.

Canadian General Rick Hillier, who commanded ISAF from February to August 2004, came away bitterly disillusioned (he went on to Canada's top military job as Chief of the Defense Staff). In his bestselling book in 2009, *A Soldier First: Bullets, Bureaucrats and the Politics of War*, he writes that "NATO itself was looking for something, anything, to do that would allow it to prove that it was still a worthwhile organization." When he took over his command, Hillier was appalled by "NATO's lack of cohesion, clarity and professionalism." There was, he writes scathingly, "no strategy, no clear articulation of what they wanted to achieve, no political guidance, and few forces. It was abysmal. NATO had started down a road that destroyed much of its credibility and in the end eroded support for the mission in every nation in the Alliance... Afghanistan has revealed that NATO has reached the stage where it is a corpse, decomposing."

Strong words from a soldier known in Canada for speaking his mind. Small wonder that Hillier had little patience with NATO's ponderous bureaucracy, with its "enormous numbers of high-ranking civilians and military—general officers were a dime a dozen... It was a wonder that any decisions got made at all." Today about 4,500 staff are at the Brussels headquarters. Along with thousands of others in its multifarious agencies and strategic and regional commands, they engage in a giddy flurry of activities. Many have only an imaginary relation to security. For example:

- The Academic Affairs Unit runs a fellowships program and organizes conferences, seminars and visits for academics and think tank researchers to "project the Alliance's point of view and strengthen information on its goals." In other words, a glorified PR operation with academic pretensions.

- The Science for Peace and Security Committee "contributes to NATO's mission by linking science to society," whatever that means. Concretely, it funds grants for research on soft, fashionable subjects like civil science and environment.

- The NATO Undersea Research Center in La Spezia, Italy, has a vast program including Marine Mammal Risk Mitigation (sic) that studies the effects of sonar on marine animals, "to counter the threat from quiet submarines."

- Then there's the NATO Multimedia Library with its over 18,000 books and subscriptions to 155 newspapers and magazines. And its annual Manfred Wörner Junior Essay competition with a $6,800 prize. And the NATO photo competition for young shutterbugs who learn that, for example, "Taking photographs of random strangers can be risky."

Really lucky individuals from member states get to go to the NATO School in Oberammergau, Germany. Located in the heart of the spectacular Bavarian Alps, the school is, as NATO puffs it, "a very special place... blessed with the beauty of the mountains." After a grueling day studying intelligence or joint operations, participants can relax at the NATO Recreation Center with skis and snowboards and then get a massage.

One of the clearest signs of the Alliance's identity crisis is its bloated PR operation—when its mission was obvious, it didn't need an advertising campaign—euphemistically known as the Public Diplomacy Division. Its multinational staff of 125 labors "To raise the Alliance's profile with audiences worldwide." Equipped with two television and 10 radio studios, it generates a torrent of programs, press releases, pamphlets, magazines, DVDs, and audio-visual presentations. It also organizes frequent international conferences, seminars and other media events boosting NATO. It runs the web-based natochannel.tv, where slick films show what it's like aboard a submarine or to go on patrol in Afghanistan. But mainly it carries every speech, statement, declaration and press conference by Secretary General Anders Fogh Rasmussen.

Variously described as dynamic, bossy and high-handed, Rasmussen, a former prime minister of Denmark, seems to think he is still leader of a country instead of a multinational organization where policy is made by consensus among members. "For him, ambassadors to NATO are just flunkies, he doesn't bother to consult them," one exasperated official of an Alliance member told me. Like a chief of state, he is given to churning out his own declarations on world crises that have little to do with Euro-Atlantic defense (Egypt, Libya, et al.), calling for the usual democracy, freedom of expression, less violence, etc., etc..

He travels widely promoting new roles for the Alliance—in effect, new markets. In February 2011 he was in Qatar and Israel selling NATO's services in the Middle East. "NATO's new strategic concept is relevant to the Middle East," he explained earnestly to an Israeli newspaper. "It gives NATO a clear role in taking on the security challenges that will dominate in the 21st century… I imagine anyone in the Middle East can see the relevance to your region." But the secretary general appears subject to homesickness. As I walked through the quiet, mostly empty headquarters hallways one recent Friday with my NATO minder, we passed the impressive glass doors to his office. "Is he in?" I asked. "Not likely," came the answer. "Every Friday afternoon he heads back home to Copenhagen."

Rasmussen does get some credit for responding to allies' prodding for reform, not that he really has any choice at this point. "We have committees for nearly everything," sighs a headquarters official. "Whenever a topic has to be examined, like armament systems, they create a committee. We had over 400 of them until we recently began eliminating some. Now there are 200 and we hope to get that down to 100." NATO's 14 agencies in seven countries, employing 6,000 people, with a separate budget of over $13.6 billion, are also due for slimming one of these days.

The military command structure, still basically unchanged since the Cold War, is due to be reduced from the present 13 headquarters scattered among member countries—which value them more for job creation than defense. That will be a long and difficult reform, Stephen Flanagan of CSIS explains. "Right now they're trying to decide which commands in which countries can be eliminated, but for some members that's the only part of NATO they have in their territory, so they resist cutting. The new strategic concept gave a better sense of where the alliance should be going. Now the question is, will they really do it?"

What's certain is that NATO will approach reform softly, softly. It is giving itself two to three years to implement changes, and few if any personnel layoffs are planned. As one official admits, "We hope to make savings, but the NATO budget is so complicated, it's hard to put a figure on how much we'll save."

Going global is clearly one of Rasmussen's top priorities. Two objectives, involvement in the Middle East and closer relations with Russia, worry many allies, especially when he acts like a loose cannon. He unveiled a Middle East peace plan of his own at a 2009 conference in Abu Dhabi, shocking ambassadors back at headquarters. "None of the NATO ambassadors or Missions had any advance warning of the statement," leaked documents say. "Many acted with incredulity to his statement."

He has been trying to cozy up to Russia, making him the first secretary general in NATO history who seems to believe the Russians can be trusted. Not everyone is comfortable with that.

"The new members in central Europe joined the Alliance for protection against a resurgent Russia and want NATO to return to its original mission of collective defense," says Marko Papic of Stratfor. "But Western members like Germany and France now consider Russia a partner, not a potential enemy. These incompatible threat perceptions make me wonder whether the Lisbon summit is not the beginning of the end for NATO."

Defense analyst Thomas Skypek, a Washington Fellow of the National Review Institute who believes America should do a hard-headed cost-benefit analysis of NATO membership, points to France's recent $2 billion sale of Mistral-class ships to Russia as an example of the lack of common threat perception. "What really is the Alliance's mission?" he asks. "Ask the 28 member states and you'll get 28 different answers." The Mistral is a force projection helicopter carrier that can land 450 assault troops. France went through with the deal despite Washington's protests. As for NATO's Baltic members, they worry where Russia might project that force.

The U.S. Mission to NATO has warned off Rasmussen from exceeding his mandate, according to confidential cables released by Wikileaks. "We strongly urge you not to get ahead of Allies' deliberations by announcing new NATO-Russia initiatives that have yet to be formally considered by the Alliance," said one. Another cable said that after a December meeting with President Medvedev and Prime Minister Putin, Rasmussen had exaggerated their interest in cooperating with NATO. (In response to my repeated requests, the U.S. Mission, the largest at NATO with 100-plus staff, declined to be interviewed for this article.)

Such differences within the Alliance about its proper mission are one indication that it has become a futile exercise in herding cats. Another sign is that several European members are already developing alternative, regional alliances while retaining the U.S.-supplied advantages of NATO. Baltic countries are talking with Nordics like Sweden and Finland about their mutual security. Poland, Slovakia, the Czech Republic and Hungary are building a European security architecture in the Visegrad group. The European Amphibious Initiative led by France held its first out-of-area exercise last year in Senegal. And France and Britain recently signed a historic new defense agreement to pool and share military resources.

Meanwhile, the U.S. continues to shoulder the bulk of the NATO burden. Ten years ago America accounted for about 50 percent of the Alliance's total defense spending. Today that figure is up to 75 percent. Spending by European members has dropped $61 billion over the last two years. The French defense official quoted above says frankly, "Many European members are investing as little as possible in military equipment. As long as they think they can count on the Americans to provide AWACS, transport aircraft, and so on, why bother to maintain an adequate defense force?" Richard Perle agrees. "Other NATO countries are getting a free ride, and have been for a very long time. But even more now, because they don't feel any sense of danger. During the Cold War you could push, say, the Germans to do more, because their security depended on NATO. Germany doesn't depend on NATO anymore."

Many on Capitol Hill are now looking closely at our relationship to NATO. Congressman Barney Frank, a ranking Democratic member of the House Financial Services Committee, argues that we should spend less on defending the wealthy nations of Europe. "NATO is a great drain on our treasury and serves no strategic purpose," he declares. Without going that far it's fair to ask that we re-evaluate our membership in the Alliance. As Senator Richard Lugar, ranking member of the Foreign Relations Committee, put it in an e-mail to me, "The Alliance must be judicious about its missions. NATO should not function as a 'universal peacekeeper.' But NATO remains extremely important to U.S. security." At Lugar's request, the Republican staff of the committee is currently reviewing NATO's mission, as well as its future role and financing.

To be sure, some instrument for mutual defense, like the Alliance's Article 5 —an attack against one is an attack against all—is useful. Furthering interoperability of equipment so allied forces can act together is also worthwhile. But with American interest in Europe waning while concern over Asia waxes, it's time to recognize that the rigid, fixed alliance of Cold War days is outdated and in urgent need of revamping.

"NATO is here to stay," Anders Fogh Rasmussen declared with bravado at the groundbreaking for the new headquarters. As if an expensive new building project could ensure its survival and counter the growing doubts about it. The

U.S. should send a clear message that a new, frugal, defense era is here, and start by questioning the suitability of that exorbitant new headquarters. For such a message, the timing is perfect.

**Update:** *NATO got itself a brand new mission in April 2011, when the Libya campaign was turned over to the Alliance. Within weeks it became apparent that NATO was not up to either mobilizing its member nations or keeping them on target. Only 17 members out of 28 participated in the campaign, and most of those reluctantly put up a mere token force. Alliance spokesmen were kept busy trying to answer questions about why a campaign whose objective was to protect innocent civilians was actually killing many of them due to bombing errors. None of which kept it from proceeding with construction of that extravagant new headquarters building.*

# EPILOGUE

I BEGAN by saying that France is probably not the country you think it is. Seen from afar, it still appears to resemble *la France éternelle,* a beautiful land of great art, high culture, fine food, and self-confident, tolerant people. It does still have these things to some extent. But if any coherent picture emerges from the mosaic formed by these pieces, I believe it is one of a once-proud country now plagued by self-doubt, social unease, and rigid, unresponsive institutions poorly adapted to deal with its current problems.

The French today appear to have lost their way. Due largely to their ingrained resistance to change and their leaders' lack of the political courage to tell them the truth about their situation—that these are not mere cyclical difficulties that will go away by themselves, but an existential threat—they are confused about their place in the world. To borrow a line from the 19th century British poet Matthew Arnold, they are "Wandering between two worlds, one dead / The other powerless to be born."

Too often they try to live on their past. But the world in which France was a political power and cultural force to be reckoned with is dead. Aborning is a world which values efficiency, not elegance; pragmatic results, not pirouetting style; realistic flexibility, not stubborn insistence on winning rhetorical points. It is also the sort of interconnected, multi-ethnic world we Americans are at home in, but that sparks resistance and resentment in the French. After all, they were long taught in school that they were a separate ethnic group, an actual race unto themselves. And a superior one at that.

Thus it is that, for the first time since I came to know France some decades ago, I feel that its circumstances are going to get worse, maybe catastrophically worse, before they get better. Portents of that abound. One is the European politico-economic maelstrom into which France has been swept due in large part to its progressive surrender of sovereignty over its own affairs to the unelected Eurocrats of the so-called European Union. Another is the backward-looking return to the meretricious chimera of socialism that emerged from the elections in 2012. Potentially most explosive are the smoldering immigration/racial problems.

Just as dangerous is the corrosive discouragement of its best and brightest young people. Many are simply dropping out or emigrating to lands that appreciate initiative and reward risk-taking. At the other end of the demographic spectrum, the bourgeoisie, that middle class that cements all nations, feels disoriented and threatened by trends they see as running out of control. They too are tempted to give up on France. Can any country long survive such destructive centrifugal forces without radical upheaval?

That consummate Frenchman, Charles de Gaulle, once wrote that the France he loved so well—seemingly more than he loved the French themselves—always had to be, somehow, exemplary. "France is not really herself unless in the front rank," he wrote in his memoirs. The country today does exemplify many of the dilemmas faced by the post-industrial Western world. If it can summon its inner resources, which are still great, perhaps France can serve as a 21st-century socio-economic laboratory. The solutions it finds could then make it as exemplary as it was in the 17th and 18th centuries, at the dawn of the modern world.

# ABOUT THE BOOK

In his third book on France, veteran international journalist Joseph Harriss cautions that it is probably not the country you expect. He explores persistent myths about that complex nation and analyzes its rapidly evolving situation today. What have 70 years of Socialism done to it? Are French culture and cuisine still the gold standard? He ranges from politics—why the French were so disgusted with Nicolas Sarkozy—to wrenching socio-economic change, from the outsized sway of women to the influence of les intellectuels. International affairs, including critical scrutiny of the European Union, UNESCO and NATO, are also covered. The result is a thought-provoking assessment of France today. Foreword by R. Emmett Tyrrell, Jr., Editor-in-Chief, *The American Spectator.*

# ABOUT THE AUTHOR

A career American foreign correspondent, Joseph Harriss studied French and international relations at the Sorbonne and the Institut d'Études Politiques before joining the Paris bureau of *Time.* Besides covering French affairs from politics and economics to couture and cuisine, he also reported from Algiers and Brussels. He later covered Western Europe as a roving correspondent for the European bureau of *Reader's Digest* in Paris. His articles and columns have appeared in many newspapers and magazines, such as *The Dallas Morning News* and *Smithsonian.* He is now the Paris correspondent of *The American Spectator.*

16503413R00195

Made in the USA
Charleston, SC
23 December 2012